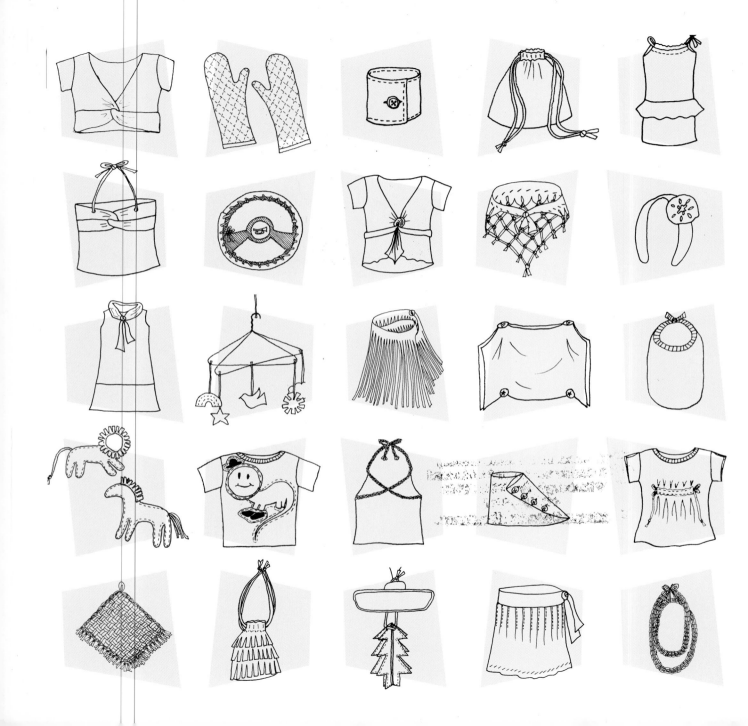

Generation T
beyond
fashion

120 new ways to transform a T-shirt

megan nicolay

WORKMAN PUBLISHING • NEW YORK

"It's all about the T-shirt."

—Jason Lee, as Jeff Bebe in *Almost Famous*

Copyright © 2009 by Megan Nicolay
Illustrations copyright © 2009 by Megan Nicolay

Cover and principal photography copyright © 2009 Rafael Fuchs

Additional photography by:
Jenna Bascom p. 26, 36, 40, 45, 46–47, 60, 94, 104, 106, 109, 117, 120, 130, 132, 135, 172, 176 (top), 184 (bottom), 188, 192, 206, 222, 240, 245, 247, 248–249, 254, 256, 262; **Jen Browning** p. 14; **Luke Bumgarner** p. 112, 224 (top), 228, 251; **Megan Nicolay** p. 1–3, 4 (top and bottom), 140, 142, 145, 156, 158, 178; **Sophia Su** p. 83, 98, 100, 102, 114, 125, 146, 148, 151, 152, 157, 166, 174, 176 (bottom), 187 (inset), 196, 210, 220, 226, 297, 300, 302

Color Section: **Jenna Bascom** p. 13 (inset); **Sophia Su** p. 11 (inset)

Special thanks to Urban Outfitters for additional wardrobe.

Library of Congress Cataloging-in-Publication Data
Nicolay, Megan.
  Generation T: beyond fashion: 120 new ways to transform a T-shirt / by Megan Nicolay.
    p. cm.
 ISBN 978-0-7611-5410-5 (alk. paper)
1. Clothing and dress—Remaking. 2. Clothing and dress—Alteration.
3. T-shirts. 4. Handicraft. I. Title.

TT550.N5423 2009
646.2—dc22   2008052217

Workman books are available at special discounts when purchased in bulk for premiums and sales promotions as well as for fund-raising or educational use. Special editions or book excerpts also can be created to specification. For details, contact the Special Sales Director at the address below.

Design by Janet Vicario and Jen Browning

Workman Publishing Company, Inc.
225 Varick Street
New York, NY 10014-4381
www.workman.com

Printed in the United States of America
First printing May 2009
10 9 8 7 6 5 4 3 2

acknowledgments

It all starts with the old, worn-down T-shirts. Many thanks to everyone who contributed to the mountain of jersey fabric I used as raw material to make the projects for this book: Nick Caruso, Andy Taray, and Christy Taray (www.wearecampfire.com); Becca Hanson (boxes!), Richard Heiss, Luke Janka, Loren Klein (walkietalkietees.com), Andra Miller, Cassie Murdoch, Ariana Nicolay, Sophie Nicolay, Katrina Shaffer (more boxes!), Sara Rowbottom, and Lissa Ziegler.

But I wouldn't have been able to complete all the projects in time for the photo shoot if not for my incredible Tee Timers who partied it up for the cause: Terri Landon Bacow, Jim Basili, Elia Herman, Sara High, Drew Koncz, Susan Lirakis, Cassie Murdoch, Andrea Fleck-Nisbet, Natalie Rinn, Helen Rosner, Anne Seiwerath, Manel Silva, Kim Small, Sarah Stacke, Mary Heath Swanson, and Lily Tilton, with supersize gold stars going to Ariana Nicolay who spent a week in the workshop for me, Luke Janka who spends his life in the workshop, and Chloe Godwin, Cori Epstein, Andra Miller, and Sara Rowbottom for all the nights and weekends!

Thanks to talented friends near and far for late-night brainstorming, project suggestions, inspiration, and research: Haley Pelton; Ashley Roth; Kristina Ramos Callan; Emily Janka Edson (and Dorothy); the bookseller in Milwaukee who inspired the Coast to Coasters project; Abby Pecoriello, whose projects inspired the Mohawk hat and the baby blanket; Enid Crow whose travel utensil carriers inspired Fork 'n' the Road, Diana Rupp who inspired the Diamond Mining scarf; and Otto von Busch who inspired me to make a grocery tote out of a T-shirt (and the rest of the Istanbul posse of Fall 2007 for your creative energy when I was just starting this manuscript!). Thanks to my friends Kim Buffington and Anissa Blackwell at Prym Consumer USA. And thanks, especially, to the incredible Rebecca Schiff, for filling in the spaces when I was running on empty.

To the Generation T models, thanks for making the designs look great: Kerry Barker, Matt Burns, Bonnie Calean, Yvonne Guillen, Danielle Hark, Li Jun Li, Tisola Logan, Brent Malcolm, Michael Miller, Sophie Nicolay, Zachariah Sky, and Chrissa Yee. What a team! Not to mention my pint-sized supermodels Charisma, Isabella Bleu, Leilani, London, Sofia, Sophia, and Stella. I'm so grateful to their parents, Natasha Caballero, Suzanne Davidman, Michaela and Jacob Getz, Yvonne Guillen, Ellen Korbonski, and Robin Rosenthal and Matt Hall, for allowing them to participate! And, lastly, to my pretty pooch models for being so fierce: Eloise (and mama Cassie Murdoch), Mabel, and Madison (and mama Mary Heath Swanson).

Thanks to photographer Rafael Fuchs and his team, Nikki Petitpierre, Rob Teten, and Nick Dannys for their joyful enthusiasm (despite the temperatures!) and beautiful images. Thanks to stylist Basia Zamorska and her assistant, Lindsey Brush, for a killer sense of fashion, calm, and rock and roll charm. And to hair and makeup artist Dina Kinion and her team for masterfully keeping up with all the faces with grace and humor!

Everyone at Team Workman: thank you for going through this process again with me and for continuing to be so passionate about what we do. To Anne Kerman, Danielle Hark, and Sophia Su for planning a magnificent photoshoot; to Janet Vicario and Jen Browning for pulling all the elements together in an artful way; to Irene Demchyshyn for keeping us on track; to Maisie Tivnan for a close and thoughtful read; to Julie Primavera and Barbara Peragine for stepping up at make-it-work time; to Selina Meere and Robby Brown for getting out the good word;

to Suzie Bolotin for her continued support of my split lives; to Peter Workman for making it happen; to Michele Ackerman, Pat Upton, Kristin Matthews, Kristina Peterson, Sara High, Jill Dulber, Andrea Fleck-Nisbet, Justin Nisbet, Nancy Mace, José Martin Vegas, Kylie Foxx McDonald, and Frank Grealy for help along the way; and to Ruth Sullivan, most of all, for her unrelenting attention to detail, cadence, and function—she is an amazing editor, colleague, and friend.

To my family, immediate and extended, for being so supportive of the many genres of creativity: Mom, Dad, Henrieke, Franz A., Sophie, Ariana, Charlene, Richard, Emily, Dave, and Dorothy. And to all of my friends who, over the past year, had to act as the third wheel on dates with me and my laptop during the writing process—thanks for being so open to unconventional relationships!

And lastly, thank you to my best friend and most patient supporter, Luke Janka, for mastering the sewing machine, for making sure I ate and slept on occasion, for all the high fives and hugs.

Contents

Chapter 3
House Party 96

Beyond the wardrobe, 16 T-shirt makeovers for your kitchen, living, dining, and dorm room—even the bathroom!

Chapter 4
Kid Rock 138

For the next Generation, here are 20 mini tees for your mini me's, including superhero capes, stuffed animals, and blankies.

Chapter 5
Pet Central   184

*From tee-riffic toys to style-leash accessories, six
surprising ways to personalize your pooch and pretty
up your kitty.*

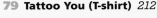

Chapter 6
Mr. T   198

*Cuff links, spats, ties, and tees—get ready, get set for
15 sweet projects you can make just for him.*

Chapter 7
Road Trippin'   224

*Head out on the highway with 14 top-down projects
to decorate your car and yourself.*

Chapter 8
Out on the Town   258

*A sassy mix of 20 fast and fabulous dare-to-bare tops,
brazen boas, and garters to put flirt in your skirt.*

By Hand or by Tee

Introduction

What's your T-shirt to you? A bulletproof vest that makes you feel indestructible? A luxurious wrap coat? A flirty little black dress? It's all those things and more. It can become the softest pillow, the warmest blanket, the coolest belt, or the sassiest bag. It can make you feel like a princess or a stage-diving rocker, or turn you into the toughest cowboy in the room.

I started my first book with the idea that the T-shirt, that humble garment, is a universal superhero in our global wardrobe. And *Generation T* readers around the world, a diverse community of jersey knit–wearers, have not disappointed.

I've hosted many Tee Parties in the past few years, workshops and gatherings where we transform T-shirts into exciting new garments. From T-shirt refashioning booths at summer music festivals to a weeklong workshop in Istanbul to one-on-one over-the-phone tutorials, the party has raged on. The Internet has allowed the members of Generation T to find one

The author with some T-shirt transformers in Istanbul.

another, and to keep the party going across time zones and oceans, state lines and zip codes. The largest Tee Party I hosted, in Tennessee, lasted three days and partygoers refashioned 355 T-shirts that were otherwise bound to remain in a giant storage bin for all time.

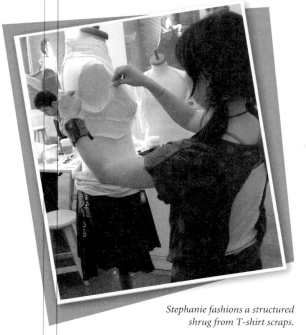

Stephanie fashions a structured shrug from T-shirt scraps.

The first *Generation T* book was structured around your wardrobe, its chapters broken down by tank tops, halters, skirts, and accessories. This book moves beyond your wardrobe to your whole world—whether you're out on the town, out on the open road, decorating the dorm room or apartment, dressing your pet, or simply navigating the adventure that is the everyday. DIY fashion is still important in this book (when is it not?), but many chapters go beyond fashion to multidimensional DIY projects, unexpected objects like a plant hanger made of braided T-shirt scraps, or a kitschy accessory for your car. When your T-shirt becomes an art piece, the sidewalk is your catwalk and your home is your gallery. Your audience may be the guy sitting next to you on the subway, the woman who sold you a smoothie this

morning, or your best buds over at your place for movie night. It's time to spread the T-shirt love!

You can make refashioned T-shirts. You can wear refashioned T-shirts. You can gift refashioned T-shirts. Host a friend's bachelorette party and craft unforgettable uniforms for your queen and her ladies-in-waiting. Arrive at the doorstep of your new neighbors' apartment with a handmade housewarming gift. Celebrate your birthday with something better than a birthday suit. Toast the graduate by reinterpreting the cap and gown in jersey knit. Picnics in a park on a patchwork tee blanket, baby showers where you make tiny tee projects, a walk with your decked-out dog, and team-bonding retreats where you work on projects together—this is T-shirt transformation for every occasion.

Every time you snip your scissors, you extend the life of a T-shirt—keeping one more tee out of a landfill. Think about it: We have bins for recycling paper, plastic, glass (some separated by color!), and metal, but nothing for those exhausted clothes. All refashioning is good for the environment, because you're both reusing and recycling, but some projects in *Beyond Fashion* go the extra "green" mile by using T-shirt scraps ("tee debris") as materials or allowing you to avoid plastic (like the T-shirt grocery bag). These are noted by the "Green Tee" stamp.

And so you know just how easy it is being green, each project is rated 1 through 5 according to difficulty. Any project that's a Level 1 or 2 is completely no sew and an easy starter project for a beginner. Project levels 3 through 5 introduce needle and thread. Don't let the 5s scare you, though; everything is doable if you have the patience.

If you're feeling shy with your scissors, go for strength in numbers, and organize a Tee Party with friends to learn and make projects together. A Tee Party can be simple. Have a couple of friends over on a weeknight. Ask them to bring some old T-shirts. You don't have to be super formal or festive, just committed to creating something together: a meal, a dessert extravaganza, a tradition, a look. Knitters have the right idea here with their Stitch 'n Bitch groups—there's something about everyone working on their own projects, talking about their lives, sharing ideas, and helping one another that just plain feels good. And T-shirt art is something that even those who wouldn't hazard to pick up the needles can get together and create. Everyone goes home with a new garment, accessory, or gift in hand. (Of course, if you're too excited to wait, you can also wear your T-transformation home!)

Don't forget to add a soundtrack to the occasion, so T-shirt snips may be interspersed with spontaneous dance parties— I know I'm not the only one who likes to "vogue" from time to time. Because music always puts me in the DIY mood, I've included a suggested playlist at the start of each chapter to inspire you. Turn up "Free Fallin'" or "Road to Nowhere" while you fashion a picnic blanket in the Road Trippin' chapter; pre-party it up to the tune of "Girls Just Wanna Have Fun" in Out on the Town. If the beats are thumping and the *tee* has been served, and your hands start twitching at the sight of a shiny pair of scissors, don't fight it. It's just the beginning. If you're like me, your desire to transform T-shirts will only get stronger.

And if the piles of T-shirts insulating my tiny apartment are any indication, refashioning has become a full-blown obsession. I'm still intrigued by the feeling I get when looking at an old T-shirt and recognizing its potential. I'm still curious about the processes of cutting, stitching, braiding, twisting (and new techniques that haven't been invented yet). And I still live for that magical moment when, presto chango, that once bland, boring, and boxy tee morphs into a sultry halter, a practical tote, or a rockin' set of placemats.

Thanks for reaffirming my belief in this garment and my love for refashioning. I wrote this book to give you more projects, more freedom to explore your own ideas, more of the satisfaction that comes from creation and re-creation. But don't take my word for it—do it yourself. Go ahead. Party on!

Rose gets "animal" with her refashioned tee.

Chapter 1

Getting Technical

Ace of Basics

The complete guide to getting started with the best no sew, embellishing, and sizing techniques "fit" to print.

In order to break the rules, you have to know the rules. In order to color (or cut!) outside the lines, there have to be lines. In order to practice abstract art, you have to first prove yourself in figure drawing. In T-shirt transforming, you have to build a strong foundation of techniques in order to improvise, embellish, and really put your personal touch on a project.

The language describing what we do ranges from the delicate and deliberate "T-shirt surgery" to the more dangerously subversive "hacking" to the meditative "transformation" to the rather harmless (with hints of glamour) "refashioning." I say toh-may-toh, you say toh-mah-toh. I like it all. Let's cut up some T-shirts.

Mary Heath cuts T-shirt strips for a dog lead (page 196); Cori cuts out a toddler dress (page 162).

No Sew? No Problem.

I love to sew both by hand and by machine. I enjoy the quiet meditation of making tiny ordered stitches or listening to the steady hum my trusty Janome machine makes as I feed fabric under the presser foot. I go so far as to decorate my sewing machine cover like a musician would his guitar case—with stickers of bands, teams, festivals, and political causes. My sewing machine is my "axe," my "git-box," my "six-string orchestra." That said, not everyone starts out there, and sometimes you need to begin with something simpler. If you're familiar with my first book, you know I'm also a huge advocate for "no sew"—that is, techniques that avoid stitchery, special seams, hems, needles, or thread of any kind. Here are some of the fundamental no sew (and no glue, please!) techniques for attaching no-fray (i.e., T-shirt) fabric.

Tying and Knotting

As any sailor or Boy Scout can tell you, there are different kinds of knots for different occasions. Your choice of knot depends on the effect you want to create and the nature of your project. Here's an overview of a few that I use all the time.

Overhand knots—the kind you tie at the end of the strands when you thread a needle—are the simplest. The application of the overhand knot for *Generation T* is creating a secure and tidy start or end point for one or more strands of T-shirt fabric. Simply cross the end (or ends) around the strand(s) to form a loop. Bring the end(s) through the loop, and pull taut at both ends.

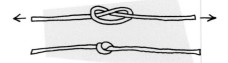

The overhand knot offers a firm hold and completes ends neatly (when two or more pieces are tied together in this way, the ends all point in the same direction). It's the first step when you're braiding strips or the last step when you're tying off a sack. When tied, the knot creates a "knob" in a cord, making a nice finish to drawstring ends (see Stuff It sleeping bag stuff sack, page 245) or when crafting a tail (see Mouse Padded, page 188, or Let's Get Animal, page 172). When tied *around* another strand or group of strands, the overhand knot is called a half-hitch (see Macramé, page 7).

Double knots (using two strands) are comprised of the classic granny knot (think of the first step in tying your shoes) multiplied by two. You wrap and weave the two ends around each other (right over left, and then right over left again) and pull tight.

A double knot has the advantage of being easier to maneuver (than an overhand

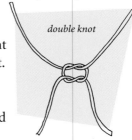

double knot

knot) when you're stuck with two really short pieces that need to be tied off. The ends of a double knot split off in opposite directions, offering a more spontaneous, haphazard finish. See the Knot So Fast tank top (page 266) for an example. Cutting fringe into the sides of fabric and double knotting them together is a no sew alternative to making a seam. A more secure and permanent relative of the double knot is a *square knot*, made up of two granny knots turned in opposite ways. For a square knot you wrap right over left, pull tight, and then left over right. The two knots look almost identical but a square knot is far stronger.

square knot

Cow hitch knots are useful for attaching

two pieces of fabric together, for adding decorative interest (in the form of fringe) along a hem edge, or for attaching a drawstring or strap to a tank or halter top without sewing. Thread both ends of a single strip through a hole near the edge of the fabric, creating a loop; thread the two ends through the loop and pull tight.

See the Mohawk Mo' Rock! hat (page 200) as an example of attaching fabric edges together to mimic a seam, or the Madame Butterfly halter top (page 54), which uses the cow hitch knot to attach the straps to the garment.

Slipped reef knots, resembling both

square and cow hitch knots, are sturdy ties where you take two loops and fasten them together in a strong and symmetrical way. Lay the end of one loop over the other and draw the ends of the "over" loop under and through the "under" loop. Pull tight. Notice how it resembles the square knot in its completed state.

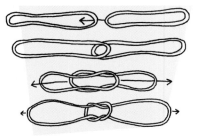

Use a slipped reef knot to attach two or more strips together end to end when a drawstring cord is too short. It may also be used when you are weaving (see Dream Weaver, page 106) and run out of length or want to change colors seamlessly. Snip narrow holes in each end of a strip or cord. Draw one snipped end through the hole in the second. Pull the unsnipped end of the second through the hole in the first. Pull the strips in opposite directions to tighten their hold.

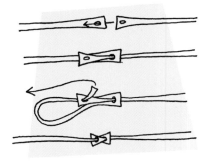

Macramé is a decorative textile art that is created without weaving or knitting but uses a series of knots to create a pattern. In A Lead of Their Own pet lead (page 196), a series of half-hitches wrapped around the remaining strands makes a thick rope. In Mad About Macramé belt (page 83), the half-hitches are applied across a series of strands, one at a time, to create a horizontal or diagonal line of knots. A Knot Above the Rest knotted capelet (page 30) makes use of alternating double knots to create netting. Various combinations of the knots above (half-hitches and square knots) make for elaborate patterns and durable projects.

Twisting, though it lacks the permanent commitment of a knot, provides decorative texture to a garment. It can precede a knot, succeed a knot, and so on—it often relies on a knot (if not a stitch or two) to keep it in place. It's a surprise element, a hiccup across the front, back, or side of a shirt where you make the fabric switch direction, as in With a Twist halter top (page 281) or High Tied wrap shirt (page 271). A length of fabric is simply rotated from one end and then secured.

Faux Sewing

Weaving strands of T-shirt in and out of holes poked into a T-shirt edge isn't exactly sewing. It's similar, but a whole lot easier, given the size and form of the materials you're using. In fact, with no skinny needle to thread or lose, and no thread to tangle, it's a welcome relief in the fabric refashioning world! Faux sewing techniques can replace a stitched seam in most projects—whether it's functional or decorative. Here are a few basic "stitches" to try that could convert a "sew" project to the status of no sew.

Running stitch is the simple over-under motion that is *the* backbone of standard sewing. In the no sew version, attach a safety pin at the end of a length of cord, knot it at the opposite end, and thread the cord over and under through an odd number of small pre-snipped or poked holes so both ends end up on the same surface side of the fabric.

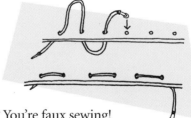

See? You're faux sewing! You can use this technique to attach two pieces of fabric together at a seam or run your "stitches" through a single layer (around a neckline, as shown, or across the bottom edge of a skirt) as decoration. Endlessly versatile, you can even use the running "stitch" to create a gathered drawstring effect without having to sew a casing (see the Tree Hugger plant skirt, page 130, for example). Not sew bad!

Whipstitch uses pre-poked holes and has similar uses as the faux running stitch. Attach a safety pin to one end of a cord and knot the opposite end, as you would for the no sew running stitch. The difference is that

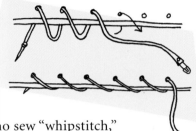

with a no sew "whipstitch," you wrap the cord *around* the edges of the fabric and you always come up through the fabric in the same direction. Instead of "sewing" with that familiar up and down motion, you maneuver the fabric cord in a circular motion around the edges of the T-shirt.

Again, you can choose to adhere two edges together in a no sew seam using this technique, or work with only one layer to decorate the edge of a neckband or sleeve, or to weigh down a skirt hem.

Looping involves doubling a cord over by threading it up and down through pre-poked holes, as you would for a no sew running stitch. But rather than pulling the cord down through an adjacent hole, pull it down through the *same* hole (move to the second hole only after an up *and* down action has

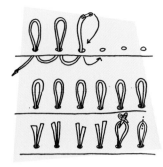

been performed through the first).

Loops may be left as loops (rug-hooking-style), or snipped through to make playful fringe, like on a shag rug—see Cruise Control, page 226).

Another form of looping involves cutting parallel slits in a piece of fabric to create bands of fabric that can be wrapped around and pulled through each other in succession (taking on a crochet-like effect). Pin or tie the last band at the end of the sequence of loops to secure the entire netting (otherwise, it will quickly unravel!). See how this technique can be applied to a T-shirt in Back in Action (page 260).

Lacing, Braiding, and Weaving

Lacing should conjure images of shoes (not the Velcro kind) or corsets or football pants. This technique can be used to connect two edges of fabric together. Poke an even number of holes along the edges of the two sides you want to join. Thread a T-shirt cord through the first hole along each of the two edges. Cross them and, threading them inside to outside, draw the end of

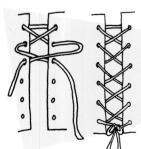

each cord through the respective second hole. Continue along the length of the fabric pieces and tie off the ends in a knot or bow.

For a starter project using this technique, try the Gimme Some Glovin' glovelets (page 264). When you're ready for something more challenging, the My Way or the Thigh Way leggings are fun (page 294). Once you're feeling comfortable, imagine and explore other ways you can use this technique, in lieu of sewing, on your T-shirt projects: For example, close up the sides of a tank top (shown) or cut a vertical slit at the center of the neckline and lace it up, leaving the ends dangling.

Braiding involves weaving three independent strands together. Braided strips from T-shirts provide sturdy cord that can be used as a bag handle or straps for a halter or tank top. They can vary in width, depending on the thickness of the original strands, from a fat Rapunzel braid to a scrawny rat-tail braid. Braids tend to be more about adornment than about joining one thing to another. When I first learned to braid, it was with the yarn on my doll's head or the hair on my sister's. It wasn't until I discovered embroidery floss around fourth grade that I realized braiding could apply to something other than hair. It rocked my world. I began to braid bracelets, anklets, headbands, belts. . . .

To get in on the action, start with three strands and knot them together at one end,

using an overhand knot. In your mind, label each strand from left to right as A, B, and C. Move A over B, so that A becomes the center strand. Then move C over A so that C becomes the center strand. Then move B over C so that B becomes the center strand. Move A over C so that A becomes the center strand again, and so on. Continue to alternate moving the side strands into the center. Easy!

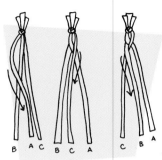

Check out the Caterpillar Thriller cat toy (page 186), for a simple variation on the braid. And despite how satisfying braids can be in their own right, try applying them to fabric surfaces with a little bit of stitching like in X Marks the Spot halter top (page 278) or the Braidy Character handbag (page 302).

Weaving, like braiding, employs that familiar over-under motion with two sets of strands. The two sets are arranged perpendicular to each other: One is called the warp (an even number of strands that run lengthwise), the other is called the weft (which interlaces with the warp strands). A weft strand is threaded alternately *over and under* the parallel strips of the warp threads (which are wrapped onto a loom) at a right angle. When you reach the end of the warp, you wind it around the last strand and return it back across the warp, this time going *under then over* in an alternating pattern.

Repeat, making as many rows as necessary to form a sheath of fabric across the base of your makeshift loom.

And though you can easily make a loom out of cardboard (see the Legalize Pot Holder, page 120) or a chair or an old CD rack (see the Dream Weaver welcome mat, page 106), you don't *need* a loom. Simply cut parallel slits into one side of a shirt, creating a warp, and weave a single, unattached strip through and around the bands, adding twists, ties, and whipstitches for flavor along the way. See the Love It or Weave It tank top (page 268) for another example.

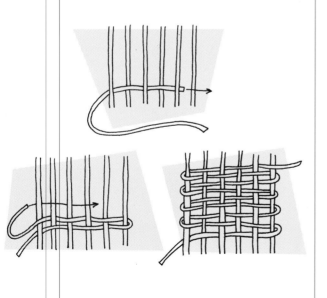

DIY Cheatsheet: sewing stitches

These are the hand stitches you'll need to complete the projects that are not **NO SEW**. You'll use the running stitch, the backstitch, or the whipstitch to sew simple side seams; a zigzag stitch or a whipstitch to sew hems or seams that require horizontal stretch; and cross-stitches for extra strength and decorative purposes.

Running Stitch This tiny, even stitch is used to complete seams. Here's how you do it:

1 Pick up a small amount of fabric (about ⅛") with the point of your needle. Working from right to left, weave the needle in and out of the fabric at about ⅛" intervals until there are several stitches gathered onto it.

2 Pull the needle through and repeat step 1. Your stitches should be small and even and look like a series of dashes. *Note:* A basting stitch (knotted only at one end) is a loose and temporary running stitch you use to make gathers.

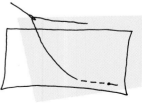

Backstitch (or Running Backstitch)

Though it looks like the running stitch, it is stronger and has better hold. Do it like so:

1 Pull your needle up through the fabric, from the back. Then poke it down about 1/16" to the right (or behind the point where the needle came out).

2 Pull the needle up through the fabric 1/8" to the left of the first stitch.

3 Poke the needle into the fabric right next to the beginning of the first stitch, making another 1/16" stitch.

4 Repeat steps 1 through 3, moving backward and then forward until you've reached your endpoint.

Whipstitch This strong overedge stitch is used to join two flat edges together. It offers room for horizontal give and needs very little seam allowance. Follow these instructions:

1 Starting about 1/8" from the fabric's edge, pull your needle from back to front through both layers of fabric.

2 Moving from right to left, continue pulling the needle from back to front, bringing the thread over the edge of the fabric, as shown. Pull thread snugly against the edge.

3 Repeat steps 1 and 2 (moving about 1/4" to the left along the edge with each stitch). Your stitches will look slanted.

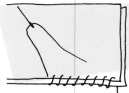

Zigzag Stitch Easier to do on a machine, the zigzag is a flexible stitch that offers some stretch so it's good for waistbands, neckbands, and tube tops. Here's how to do it:

1 Pull your needle up from the back of the fabric about 1/2" from the side edge. Moving from right to left, poke the needle down on a diagonal, 1/4" from the bottom edge.

2 Pull the needle back up just next to the spot where you went down in step 1.

3 Poke the needle down ½" from the edge on a diagonal perpendicular to the stitch you completed in step 1, as shown.

4 Pull the needle back up just next to the stitch in step 3 and repeat steps 2 through 4 until you reach the end.

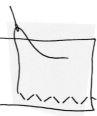

Cross-stitch The cross-stitch is used when you have a visible seam or want to add a little sumthin'-sumthin' to a project. It goes like this:

1 Starting ¼" from the edge of the fabric, pull your needle up through the fabric (A) and then poke it back down (B) on a diagonal along the edge you're sewing, about ½" to ¾" from your point of origin.

2 Pull the needle back up (C) at a point directly above B and ¼" to the left of A. Moving from right to left along your seam, continue making diagonal stitches, parallel to the first in step 1. (These are the beginning of your crisscrosses.)

3 When you reach the endpoint, pull your needle up through the fabric directly above the last stitch. Working left to right, go back over your previous path, making diagonal stitches that form Xs over the row you made in steps 1 and 2.

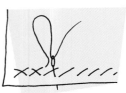

4 Continue moving from left to right until all your crisses are crossed (and you're back where you started).

Finishing a Stitch Make a single small backstitch on the wrong side of the sewing project, leaving a small loop. Send the needle and thread through the loop and pull it tight. Repeat the stitch a second time, on top of the first, and pull it tight again. Trim.

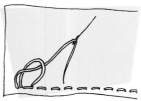

Sizing

I doubt this reminder is necessary, but just for good measure: DIY is empowering! You're in charge. And because you're the boss, you can direct how you want everything to be. In all seriousness, you get to 1) pick the material (in this case, the style, color, texture of the starting T-shirt), 2) choose the design or style you'd like (from the 120 projects in this book), and 3) try it on every step of the way so that it fits the way you want it to. A lot of this is about personal style. If the measurements in a particular project are slightly off, adjust as you go by trying your garment on, pinning, stitching, and trying on again. It's a process.

If you're uncomfortable with the style of neckline that's called for in a project—let's say it's a little more plunging than you'd like—you have two options: 1) Ignore the instructions and make the neckline more modest by cutting off less fabric (after all, you've mastered the techniques, so you have the skills to improvise a little) or 2) just go with it, make the garment as directed, and solve the problem at the end by layering a tank top of your own underneath the new garment. I like layering because it offers another opportunity to add interest to an outfit—especially if the T-shirt you've chosen to transform is rather plain. A colorful bandeau underneath that bland halter adds an energetic splash to your look.

If, after an impromptu "fitting," you peel off an unfinished skirt just knowing it's going to be too small to fit around your hips, try cutting an additional panel of T-shirt fabric (or two panels, one for each side) to make it wider. The shape of the panel will depend on the shape of your skirt (if it's a tube skirt, add a rectangular piece; if it's an A-line skirt, add a more trapezoidal piece). Cut through the skirt, turn it inside out, and pin the panel, right sides together, into the opening in the skirt.

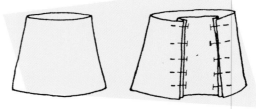

Try on this adapted version, and if it fits, go ahead and sew the panels in place. If not, trim a little off the panel and try again.

As you gain confidence in your DIY skills, you'll achieve the freedom to adapt as you go: If it looks like you can't spare that ½" of fabric for a seam allowance with a running stitch, modify the directions by using a whipstitch, which allows a smaller seam allowance of ³⁄₁₆". Because it takes up less fabric, you gain some width at a side seam or length at a horizontal seam.

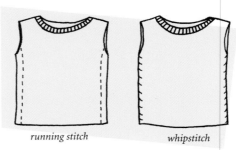

running stitch   *whipstitch*

Get Fit(ted)

I've mentioned that DIY allows you to get that perfect fit. With wearables in particular, it's not always about size per se, it's about *fit*. We're all different shapes and sizes, so why not embrace that? In each fashion project in this book, I've identified the ideal *fit* of the T-shirt that you should start with (fitted, regular fit, baggy—see images below). After all, a size L T-shirt will likely be baggy on one person but fitted on another.

With each "beyond fashion" project (accessories, housewares, and so on) where specific fabric measurements are concerned, I'll indicate an ideal *size* (XL, for instance, if you need to get 20" across the front of a T-shirt). If the project requires lots of material, the ingredients list will call for a baggier T-shirt. If size (or in some instances color) doesn't matter, there will be no specifications listed—meaning you're free to choose from the best color/pattern/logo/shape T-shirt you can get your hands on!

Fitted
A fitted T-shirt is tighter around the shoulders, bust, and hips (often due to a percentage of Lycra in the knit), and may have some tailoring for shape.

Regular
A regular fit T-shirt gives shape without being clingy; it's neither too tight nor too loose.

Baggy
A baggy T-shirt is oversize with lots of cinch-able fabric around the shoulders, sleeves, and waist.

Honey, I Shrunk the T-shirt

It's happened to all of us: Somehow that "preshrunk" T-shirt comes out two sizes too small after a cycle in the dryer. Or there's the opposite: You bought a larger size than necessary (maybe XXL was all they had at the merch booth at the concert) fully expecting that you could toss it in at high heat to shrink it down to size. Things don't always work out the way we plan. That's why the T-shirt powers made scissors. Here are two quick tips about resizing a tee while retaining the basic shape of the original T-shirt. The key is to work with the existing structure of the T-shirt. If you want to shorten the sleeves, for instance, cut off the ends *parallel* to the sleeve hem.

right   *wrong*

1 To expand a T-shirt, cut open the sides up to where the sleeve begins. Cut two rectangular panels from another T-shirt and taper the tip of one short end so it fits under the sleeve, as shown top right.

If you choose to expand the sleeve as well, cut through the sleeve seam and along the bottom. Make your rectangular pieces long enough to run up the side of the tee from the hem, turn the corner under your arm, and fold over at the bottom of the sleeve hem.

Pin the inserts into the T-shirt, right sides together, then sew a running stitch along the pinned edges. Remove the pins, turn your new T-shirt right side out, and try it on.

Note: For maternity T-shirt expansions, continue increasing the angle of the wedge shape of your panel down to the bottom seam. The insert should be triangular, not rectangular.

2 When a T-shirt is stretched out or just plain too big, get rid of some of that excess fabric by turning it inside out and marking a line up each side of the shirt. The line should be parallel to the existing edges of the T-shirt and continue around the armpit area and along the bottom of the sleeve. Cut through all layers along that line to remove the excess panels of fabric. Pin the open edges. Try it on and repeat, cutting off more fabric, if needed. Sew the edges back together with a running stitch or whipstitch.

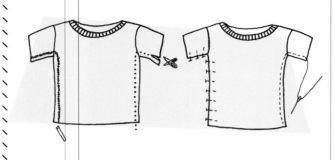

Embellish This

For some, having refitted or refashioned the garment they're wearing is statement enough. Others like to say something more (some people are just a little more long-winded than others when it comes to cutting and pasting). Luckily for the outspoken, you have options: You can add texture with stitching, layers with ribbon, a pattern with buttons, or a fairly literal statement or personalization, like "My name is Megan, and I approve this message" with iron-on letters. Abandon those straight lines with the simplest of decorative edging—a zigzag edge made with pinking sheers or a fringe cut with regular scissors. (Pinking shears are traditionally used to keep cotton weave fabric from fraying, and though you don't *need* them on no-fray knit jersey material, it offers a nice decorative effect.)

I'm not proposing that you go shopping for brand-new trinkets or fabrics to start layering onto your project—you don't need to. Try your local thrift store first. Or poke around grandmother's button box at home. Honor the intergenerational aspects of your personal history with a touch of lace from Grandma, bold mod fabric from Mom's hippie days, and a button from your childhood jumper. Or maybe it's all about you: Search for items that have childhood significance—charm bracelet trinkets, barrettes, award ribbons and medals, mood rings, worry dolls, even fabric from stretched-out hair scrunchies—all are potential raw materials for your embellishing effects. Sometimes even the recycling center (aka the dump) has some buried treasure—you might find an odd collection or material (bottle caps, postage stamps, old photos) to inspire you. Your project can be the scrapbook of your life. Your outfit can tell your story: Let it be a conversation among friends, a walk down memory lane.

Embellishing with Fabric Strips, Ribbon, and Lace

The barest dress can get a supersize reaction with just the right touch of ribbon edging, lacey cleavage, or cap sleeves. You can braid or twist T-shirt strips together to make trim or leave the strips in their raw form. Lay fabric over fabric, experimenting with the different ways you might arrange and attach it. Here are some ideas to start spilling those creative juices!

■ Coil the strips, pin them to a shirt or skirt, and stitch them down in patterns. (Remember to stitch through only one layer of T-shirt.)

■ Use an accordion fold on ribbons to fashion pleats for edging. Add this trim to the bottom of pants, the edge of a skirt, sleeves, or a neckline.

■ Use a zigzag fold on a ribbon and sew a running stitch to attach it to the front of a T-shirt Charlie Brown–style.

■ Braid thin cords (see page 9) and sew one to the raw edge of a neckline as trim.

■ Fold or curl ribbon into fabric buds or blossoms and attach to a shirt or skirt for a broochlike effect. Decorate the whole neckband for a cut-flower couture collar.

■ Trade out the drawstring of a halter top or the waistband sash of a skirt for different color accents. (You can make the design new by mixing and matching that one element!)

coiled strip　　drawstring　　zigzag fold　　braided cord trim

curled ribbon　　ribbon trim　　belt　　dollar sign design

ribcage design　　words　　equations　　ribbons on sleeves

■ Sketch shapes or characters with a chalk marker and then outline them with ribbons or T-shirt cords. Pin them in place, and stitch them down. Try musical notes for your personal anthem, money signs or other symbols, or various flora and fauna. Or illustrate your ribcage across the front of the shirt for an X-ray effect (stitch on the ribcage using lace—and don't forget to tuck a soft heart in there!).

■ If words are your thing, shape the ribbons or T-shirt strips into letters one at a time to decorate your own personal billboard. Make up your own graphics to advertise across your chest; make them in multiples to create your own "team" with matching uniforms.

■ Translate your name into Arabic script or Chinese characters and "write" it across the back of your T-shirt in ribbon. Get your friends together to pool your linguistic repertoire and translate "rock out" into three different languages.

■ Celebrate your scientific side with a cleverly balanced equation. Or maybe you're a math nerd: Remind everyone of the order of operations (PEMDAS) by writing them across your shirt.

■ Keep it elegant and simple by stitching ribbon around the end of each sleeve. Leave the ribbons long at the top of the sleeve and tie them in a bow.

Embellishing with Appliqué

Think of appliqué as a wearable collage. Or a new tattoo every day. If you can't commit to the ink, "tattoo" a design onto your T-shirt by stitching, ironing on, or gluing. You'll create a second skin that you don't have to worry about liking in twenty years when you're the head of the PTA. Appliqué, quite literally, is about applying a piece of fabric to another piece of fabric. The applied fabric can take many forms—scraps, embroidered patches, cotton silkscreen patches, iron-on letters, and decals. I like stitched appliqué because it lasts longer, and the thread keeps it light and moveable. I'm not a huge advocate of gluing on fabric (the result is too stiff), but there are several fabric glues available on the market. Stitching, because it takes a bit longer, makes you appreciate it more—plus the process generally has no fumes, and there's no waiting around for it to dry. I'd rather take the time *during* the process so I can have the immediate gratification of wearing it when I'm done (no waiting twenty-four hours, then washing, and so on, and so on). Attach your appliqué with a running stitch (see page 10), sewing as close to the edge of the appliqué as possible for a neat and ordered look. (A whipstitch will leave your appliqué a little rough around the edges.) Here are a few different ideas for appliqué embellishing.

■ Trace or sketch solid shapes onto scrap fabric, cut them out, arrange them on your tee, pin, and stitch them on. Try old-school throwbacks like cassette mix tapes, headphones, or a boom box.

■ Remember the dancing silhouette iPod ads? Make your own silhouette version and stitch around the edges to apply it to a brightly colored T-shirt or skirt.

■ Room for dessert? Cut out fabric scraps in the shapes of sugary treats and stitch them on. Then spell out captions using store-bought iron-on letters. Pair nicknames like "sweetie pie" with a pie shape, "baby cake" with a cupcake, "hey, sugar" with a sugar packet.

■ Cut out printed designs or shapes on an old T-shirt, arrange them across the front of a plain tee, and pin and stitch around the perimeter.

■ Pick a word, any word, or a phrase— "Vote!" or "It's Easy Being Green" or "Little Miss Sunshine" —that you'd like to shout from the proverbial mountaintop. Iron or stitch it on across the chest of your T-shirt or the hem of your skirt. Iron-on letters are easier because one pack generally has multiples of most letters and they'll adhere almost instantly with a hot iron, but the process of cutting out the letters and stitching them on carries its own charm.

■ Patches, also, can be sew or no sew, depending on the style and how you choose to apply them. Collect your old embroidered Girl Scout patches and iron or stitch them on (stitch close to the edges, for reinforcement). Stitch patches from your favorite bands across the back or sleeves. Or create your own thin fabric patches (a Sharpie marker and scrap swatches from a T-shirt sleeve can work!) and sew them on.

■ Using your computer printer and special iron-on paper available at most office supply stores, you can take any copyright-free or public domain image (photos, your own cartoon sketches, a child's artwork) and turn them into iron-ons for your T-shirt, skirt, or tote. Simply download an image, format it in a digital imaging program, print it, trim around the edges, and iron it on.

cassette tape   dancing silhouette

dessert   old T-shirt graphics

words   drawings

Embellishing with Thread

As secure as it is, stitching doesn't always have to be about function. In fact, it has an incredibly decorative and textured quality that isn't achievable with just paint or iron-ons. Plus thread comes in so many different colors that you know it was destined for far greater things than the folded depths of a seam.

Start with the basics in decorative stitchery by sewing around or along edges. You can make a chain of curlicues (you know, how you used to sign your name before you knew cursive), wavy lines, ocean waves, shark's teeth, scalloped edges, egg and dart patterns, or more structured art deco or art nouveau inspired borders. Page through quilting books 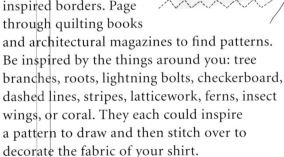 and architectural magazines to find patterns. Be inspired by the things around you: tree branches, roots, lightning bolts, checkerboard, dashed lines, stripes, latticework, ferns, insect wings, or coral. They each could inspire a pattern to draw and then stitch over to decorate the fabric of your shirt.

■ Free-form decorative stitching is fun to play around with. If you have a sewing machine, test out all the stitch options— have zigzag stitches and blanket stitches crisscrossing your garment in every which way (just make sure to go through only one layer of fabric at a time!).

■ Embroidering on jersey fabric can be tricky (since embroidery floss and other cotton and wool thread doesn't stretch like T-shirt fabric), but with the help of stabilizer "paper" (to prevent stretching while you stitch), there are a number of fun patterns you can stitch onto a top, skirt, or bell-bottom pants! How about roses or lassos for a cowgirl-inspired tee, sparrows or a sailor girl anchor for a more retro look? Use a standard running stitch, or expand your repertoire by teaching yourself some traditional embroidery stitches.

■ Experiment embroidering trompe l'oeil effects: headphones, track shoes, or ballet slippers "hanging" around your shoulders, or a pocket protector "sticking out" of your pocket. Then there's faux jewelry: a pendant, the gold "Carrie" necklace, a men's tie.

■ Embroider the more abstract: Draw concentric circles or other patterned designs with a chalk marker and stitch over your lines to hide them. Experiment with the placement of your embroidery designs, too. Stitch trees or vines stretching across your torso, stars in a solar system that wraps over your shoulder, a color spectrum that runs up the side of the shirt, or a maze that runs around your T-shirt.

■ Subvert logos: Draw and then stitch your own take on that classic preppy crocodile, or crossed oars, or anchors, whales, lobsters, or sew a cannonball with a fuse, or design your own crest.

■ Forget images altogether and stitch your favorite quotes, make cartoon exclamations (complete with stitched-on talk bubbles), or just plain sign your name to your art piece!

free-form stitches

shapes

trompe l'oeil

faux necklace

solar system

color spectrum

logos

stitched words

T-shirt Laundering

The only potentially restrictive element in fashion embellishing is its launderability. I know you regularly toss your T-shirt right into the washing machine fray, but it's important to take a moment and note the properties of the materials you've attached to your tee. They just might be a little more high-maintenance than you're used to.

Iron-on letters? Fine to throw in with the rest of the laundry. Beads or buttons? Also should be fine, as long as they're attached well (if you're unsure, play it safe and hand wash—you don't want to lose those antique beads to that monster in the spin cycle!). Hardware? Make sure it won't rust (or that if it does, you're okay with it staining your T-shirt a little—it could add character). Adding Grandma's delicate vintage lace to a sleeve? You should probably wash it by hand if you want it to last.

Whatever happens, don't let laundering get between you and your creativity! Just let your common sense prevail.

Embellishing with Beads and Buttons

Beads and buttons are tactile embellishments that don't cost a lot and add a little bling to the dull woven surface of a T-shirt or other garment (skirts, hats, bags!), especially when they catch the light. Just keep in mind that your garment can get very heavy the more you add.

■ String a length of beads and stitch each end (with a few whipstitches) to a T-shirt shoulder seam to mimic a necklace. Similarly, line up and stitch a row of buttons lower on the shirt to create the appearance of a drop waist belt.

■ String small seed beads together in long strands with a beading needle. Then arrange them across a surface to create popular (and easy-to-outline) objects: bugs (ladybugs, dragonflies, butterflies), flowers, peas in a pod, eyes, candy, fruit (cherries are a fave), cocktail glasses, googly eyes. Secure them in place on the fabric by stitching over the bead strand, in between the beads.

■ Cut out the neckband of a T-shirt halter top and replace it with a chain of buttons threaded together side by side.

■ Cluster buttons together in a broochlike flower or spread them across the shirt like a fireworks explosion. See Moth-Eaten Chic, page 202, for pattern arrangement ideas.

■ Add a button or three to each sleeve as a delicate cuff detail.

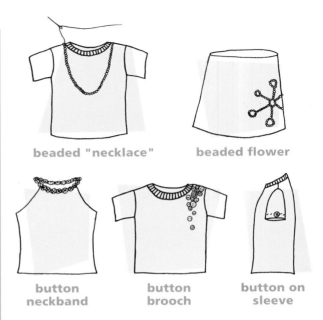

beaded "necklace"   beaded flower

button   button   button on
neckband   brooch   sleeve

Embellishing with "Junk"

The sky is the limit when creating your own couture design with found objects. The major thing to keep in mind is how you're going to wash your gussied-up tees. Beads on a garment can get snagged and damage the fabric of the tee, as well as the fabric of other items in the same load. So wash carefully (and don't use paper to beautify your T-shirt unless you plan on never washing it again). See page 21 for more. Other than that, go for it!

■ Raid the jewelry box: Pierce the edges of sleeves with studded earrings for a little bling on each side. Rescue an old earring that's lost its match to make a tassel that dangles elegantly from the center of the neckband or from the edge of one sleeve. Go for the naughtier version with two lost earrings situated as pasties! Remove the earring hook and use a few whipstitches at the top to secure it on the fabric.

■ Experiment with hardware: Washers and wing nuts and other supplies can be used as beads. Stitch them in rows around hems or gather them into designs. Make a faux chain-mail neck plate by lining the neckband with washers stitched side by side. Or scatter wing nuts across a skirt for a bit of sparkle. Just be sure to distribute the weight of the metal pieces evenly so the fabric doesn't stretch or sag.

■ Gather odds and ends from around the house instead of chucking them: old coins, safety pins, pen caps and other office supplies, CDs, and so

on. Pen caps sometimes have holes at the top, so they can be threaded like beads.

■ Safety pins are a standard in the T-shirt refashioning realm, and can be "dressed up" with beads or colorful wrapped thread.

■ Coins or old subway tokens, if they have holes punched in the middle, can also be strung or stitched on like buttons. Those without holes can be glued (or, if you're feeling adventurous, stitched on with a crazy weblike pattern over the top so they're barely visible but add some weight and intrigue).

■ Typewriter keys, if you can get your hands on some, can be great fun. Clip off the metal "arm" in back and either glue the key onto the fabric or glue a jewelry notion that includes a loop onto the back of the key so it can be stitched on.

Like I said: Sky equals limit.

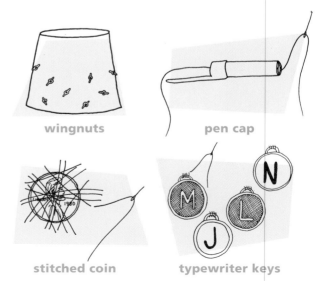

earring decoration   chain of washers   wingnuts   pen cap

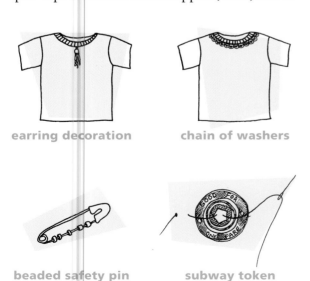

beaded safety pin   subway token   stitched coin   typewriter keys

Embellishing with Paint

Embrace the urban world of tagging: Create your own logo, then mark as many T-shirts as you have in your closet. When you're done speaking for yourself, spread the good tagged word to your friends: a T-shirt for your guy that reads "Off the Market," a T-shirt for your best bud that says "Friends 4 Life," or a tee for your tough-talkin' toddler that declares "Kickin' It Pre-school." Keep in mind that most printing and paint processes do require setting with heat before washing (an iron or a hair dryer usually does the trick). Read and follow the directions on the label of whatever fabric marker or paint you use (you can find a wide selection at your local craft store or online). And *always* insert a piece of cardboard between the layers of the fabric so the colors don't bleed through.

■ The poor DIYer's silkscreen: Buy or create a stencil out of paper or cardboard (or vellum, if you have it), tape down the edges, and spray paint over it or color in the image with markers. Regular spray paint is fine to use as long as it's applied lightly. A selection of thick Sharpies can do the trick as well. Hardware stores carry standard letter and number stencils; craft stores have more font variety.

■ Used like a stencil, masking tape can keep parts of a T-shirt's natural color while you paint it. Once the paint or ink is dry, carefully

stencil and spray paint

masking tape for stripes

plaid pattern

splatter paint

painted water lilies

graffiti-style tag

peel off the tape to reveal the pattern. Lay the tape in vertical stripes to make a referee shirt, horizontal stripes for inmate chic, or in a grid to make checks.

For a challenge, try plaid: Make stripes in one direction, let the paint dry, and remove the tape before applying new tape in the other direction. Or try piecing together bits of tape to spell a negative-image message when the tape is removed.

■ Splatter out a Jackson Pollack by dipping a paintbrush in your paint can and tapping or flicking it over your "canvas." Change out brushes for another color and repeat as many times as desired. No two will ever be the same!

■ If you appreciate a more tempered, less physically rigorous approach, attempt to paint your best "Water Lilies" repro across the front and/or back of your T-shirt.

■ Tag your T-shirt with a graffiti-style message. Design your own personal tag on paper and use markers, brush paint or spray paint to apply it to your T-shirt or other garment.

■ Use those same tools (markers or paints) to express yourself freestyle with any old message you choose—write in cursive, doodle, scribble, scrawl a self-portrait John Lennon–style. Whatever your method, speak your mind. Remember the first amendment? Exercise it!

Chapter 2

Everyday

A T-shirt Is a Terrible Thing to Waste

Make magic from the mundane with 29 top-to-bottom T-shirt transformations that will add oomph to your outfit and swagger to your stride.

I like to approach every day as a special occasion—why put together an outfit to celebrate only the first day of school or a new job? Why not the fifth day? Or the eighty-second? One of my best friends likes to dress up on any old occasion— she wore her tiara to all of her big med school exams, she hosts her friends for wine and cheese in a fabulous kimono, and she wears silk bustiers underneath her lab coat. And she's one of the happiest people I know. In many ways, what we wear can set our mood. Likewise, it projects it. If you can find inspiration in the day-to-day, you'll look and feel fabulous. What you wear can be your own personal affirmation; it can inspire bravery, hope, excitement, a flirtation . . . even on the most blah day.

Some like their dress to complement their mood; others like to counteract it. Whether you go for gothic black or sunny yellow when you're on top of the world is up to you. Personally, I like to dress up when I'm feeling under the weather. I find it especially uplifting to wear something fun when I have an annoying task to complete. Need to pay bills? Put on a superhero cape! Have a dentist's appointment? March over to the chair in knee-high boots! The projects in this chapter encourage you to rethink the mundane by refashioning clothing you've relegated to the only-at-home-by-myself-watching-TV category.

Speaking of TV, plopping down in front of the tube after a long hard day can be a needed relief, but as a nightly activity, it quickly gets boring. On an evening when you're not sure what to do with yourself, performing some quick T-shirt surgery or finally finishing a project you've been working on for weeks can end the day in an extremely satisfying way. It won't go down in history as "Wednesday" but rather as the "Day You Finally Made That Mod Dress" you've been coveting for so long.

The result of all this DIY T-shirt refashioning is that your everyday wardrobe will become more distinct, more hip, more you. I am convinced that most great dressers aren't just great shoppers—they put themselves into their clothing. They aren't afraid to ignore how a garment "should" be worn (my friend got sick of wearing a black skirt that had gotten too big on her, so one day she tied its drawstrings around her neck, and, voilà, she was wearing a sexy black dress).

Projects in this chapter—like Transformer (page 45), wherein your refashioned T-shirt is a magical chameleon (it can be a scarf, a halter, or a skirt), You Can Pleat Me (page 66), a swinging pleated skirt, and The Best of Two Tees (page 42), a flirty two-tee tank top—all let you experiment with fashion design, fabric construction, and fabric deconstruction, and the end results are not only wearable, but cute and cool. It's enough to brighten up anyone's day, to boot!

From spare T-shirts to bowling spares in style.

What's on Your Playlist:

"People Everyday"/ "Everyday People"
—*Arrested Development/Sly and the Family Stone*

"Everyday"
—*Bon Jovi*

"Lovely Day"
—*Bill Withers*

"Common People"
—*Pulp*

"Everyday Life"
—*Subhumans*

"Ordinary Average Guy"
—*Joe Walsh*

"It Happens Every Day"
—*Dar Williams*

"Manic Monday"
—*Bangles*

"Every Day I Have the Blues"
—*B.B. King*

"I Don't Like Mondays"
—*The Boomtown Rats*

1 **pinup girl** (halter)

NO SEW

This design morphed out of a halter top I helped a friend refashion at a music festival. With very few tools on hand, it was a challenge for this ETT (Emergency T-shirt Technician) to revive the tee after its tie-dye overdose. But the test results are in: This halter is comfortable (generous belly allowance), offers full coverage (without sacrificing the Marilyn appeal), and it's surprisingly glamorous for a five-minute surgery. For a more shapely fit and a taste of self-expression, gather it in with grandmother's rhinestone brooch, a political protest button, or a pin from the rock band that just rolled through town.

LEVEL 1

ingredients

- 1 T-shirt (regular fit)
- chalk marker
- scissors
- 1 punk pin (optional)

1 Lay the T-shirt flat and cut off the left sleeve, just inside the seam.

2 Mark and then cut through both layers from the bottom of the right sleeve to about 2" from the left edge of the neckband.

3 Try on the halter top, rotating the fabric to insert your head through the remaining armhole. If it fits, you're done! If it's still a little boxy, continue with step 4.

4 With the halter top still on, pinch fabric from both sides of the shirt just below the bustline. Gather the pinched fabric together at the base of the sternum with a punk pin. The back of the halter should fit comfortably against your skin while the front gives the belly some breathing room. *Note:* The front gathers make this top very practical as summer maternity wear!

variation

■ Instead of gathering the fabric in front, take the action to the back. After step 2, with the shirt still flat, cut vertically up the right side, opening up the back of the halter. Cut fringe into the open edges, and tie coordinating strips from each edge together to tighten the shirt in the back.

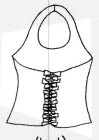

(back)

2 a knot above the rest

NO SEW

(knotted capelet)

This knotted, netted capelet is a saucy accessory that's unabashedly all about style. It's not going to keep you warm, but it boasts incredible versatility as a textured complement to your outfit. Wear it over your shoulders, wrapped around your hair, or slip it down to your waist and wear it rakishly over your hips.

LEVEL 2

1 Turn the T-shirt inside out and lay it flat. Cut off the sleeves just inside the seams and then cut straight across the shirt, through both layers, just below the neckband.

---
ingredients

■ **1 T-shirt (L or XL)**

■ **ruler**

■ **chalk marker**

■ **scissors**

2 Orient the tube so that the hem is at the top. Measure and mark 6" along the hem from one side. Extend the mark down, perpendicular to the hem. Cut along the marks, removing a rectangle of fabric.

3 Snip through the hem (on the side that you measured from in step 2), then lay the panel flat, wrong side up. With a ruler and chalk, mark an even number of approximately 1"-wide strips for fringe. Leaving a 1½" margin at the top (to keep the hem intact), cut the strips from the bottom of the panel up (it's okay if the strips are different lengths around the armhole).

4 Pair off each of the dangling strips and tie them in double knots.

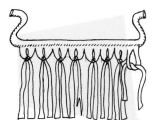

5 Then take one of the dangling strips from the first knot and tie it to one of the dangling strips of the second knot. Continue in this manner until a second row of knots has been made. Trim the unused strips from the first and the last knot.

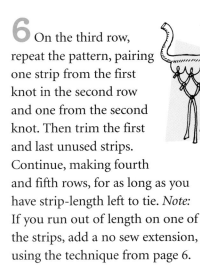

6 On the third row, repeat the pattern, pairing one strip from the first knot in the second row and one from the second knot. Then trim the first and last unused strips. Continue, making fourth and fifth rows, for as long as you have strip-length left to tie. *Note:* If you run out of length on one of the strips, add a no sew extension, using the technique from page 6.

7 Using the ends of the hem as a tie, wrap the capelet over your shoulders or over your skirt or jeans.

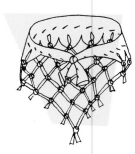

3 get it twisted
(tank top)

You know that weird satisfaction you get from wringing water out of a dishtowel? Or opening a bottle of wine with a corkscrew? Swiveling your hips at a party? There's something about twisting that makes people want to squeal with joy. I love this shirt, because it's flattering on almost everyone and surprisingly easy to make. The fun of twisting the straps into coils is exceeded only by seeing people's reaction to them. This is one of those shirts that causes strangers on the subway to tap you on the shoulder and ask, "How did you make that?"

LEVEL 3

ingredients

- 1 T-shirt (regular fit)
- scissors
- straight pins
- needle
- thread

1 Turn the T-shirt inside out and lay it flat. Cut off the sleeves just inside the seams and cut out the neckband.

2 Mark and cut the neck hole 3" deeper in the front. Widen the neck hole so the straps are about 4" wide.

3 Snip through the top of the straps at the shoulder seam.

4 Twist the front straps twice—twist the left strap clockwise and the right strap counterclockwise (so you're twisting each strap away from the neck, toward the sleeve) and pin them back at the top of the shoulder, right sides together. Sew a whipstitch along the pinned edge.

5 Remove the pins, turn the T-shirt right side out, and try it on!

In the Eye of the Tee-holder

Since the first person laid ink on a T-shirt, there hasn't been a more accessible canvas for self-expression. Today some of the best art and design is being printed on jersey knit. So why not hang them in a museum? The designers who founded tshirtmuseum.com had just that idea. Explore the "wings" of the museum for a nostalgic tour of some tee classics or submit images of the T-shirts in your closet to help build their collection.

4 snowflake fake (t-shirt)

NO SEW

When the holidays come around, many fashionistas run for cover—'tis the season for hideous snowman sweaters and light-up gingerbread man pins! But don't worry, when your Aunt Mabel's giving you a hard time about getting "in the spirit," here's a refreshing one-of-a-kind solution that even a humbugger like you can embrace. Celebrate the season with a hand-cut paper snowflake-style tee. You can even wear yours year-round to inspire a cool flurry in the dog days of summer.

LEVEL 1

ingredients

- **1 T-shirt (white is traditional, but you can have a colorful snowflake, too!)**
- **scissors**
- **clothespins or safety pins**

1 Lay the T-shirt flat on its side so that the back and the front are the new "sides," as shown.

2 Fold the bottom front hem up to the neckband and crease.

3 Pinch the neckband and hem together at the top right and fold them on a diagonal down to the bottom fold.

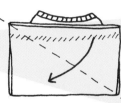

fold

4 The T-shirt is now folded in eighths (and should resemble the piece of white paper you folded for cutting snowflakes when you were in third grade). *Note:* You might want to practice some cuts on paper before you do step 5.

5 Smooth any wrinkles, then clothespin (or safety pin) all layers in place and begin cutting small, differently shaped notches (crescents, half-circles, triangles, zigzags) into the folded edges, as shown.

6 Unfold the shirt and layer it over a tee of a different color, or wear it over a plain undershirt for an elegant white-on-white look. (Every snowflake is unique, and so is every snowflake T-shirt!)

variations

■ Without folding the T-shirt, sketch a ghoulish skull onto the front or back. Cut along the lines through only one layer, and layer the tee for some wicked fun.

■ Sketch a spiderweb shape on the back of a T-shirt. Cut out, through only one layer, the geometric shapes in between the spiderweb lines.

(back)

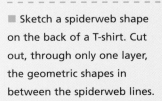

5 drawstring wings
(tank top)

Sometimes a mistake can turn out to be something really innovative—and comes out even better than what you had planned in the first place. Let me set the scene: While widening the neck hole of a T-shirt, you accidentally remove the entire top shoulder seam—how are you going to recover (and make this shirt stay on your shoulders)? Do you a) grab a handful of safety pins and remedy the seam as best you can, b) throw up your hands in despair and swear off scissors for the rest of your life, or c) follow the instructions below for some drawstring madness?

LEVEL 3

ingredients

- 1 T-shirt (regular fit)
- scissors
- needle
- thread
- straight pins

1 Turn the T-shirt inside out and lay it flat. Cut out the neckband just below the seam. Cut the sleeves off just inside the seam. Cut a strip off the bottom of the T-shirt just above the hem and use it to make two small drawstrings.

2 Make a cut across the top length of each shoulder on either side of the seam, removing the shoulder seam.

3 Fold down 1" of the front layer of fabric from the top of both shoulders. Pin it in place. Flip the shirt over and do the same on the back layer.

4 Sew a small whipstitch along the pinned areas in the front and the back, removing the pins as you go.

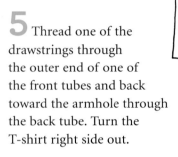

5 Thread one of the drawstrings through the outer end of one of the front tubes and back toward the armhole through the back tube. Turn the T-shirt right side out.

6 Tie the ends (to create a small gathered circle at the top of each shoulder) and snip any excess fabric.

7 Repeat steps 5 and 6 on the opposite shoulder.

variation

■ Use ribbons instead of drawstrings at the shoulders.

6 makes me wanna collar

(NO SEW)

(t-shirt)

Here's a rags-to-riches fairy tale of a project that's Elizabethan inspired, but that's not sixteenth-century stuffy. In fact, this no sew collar looks positively twenty-first-century chic under a structured jacket or coat. An old T-shirt recast for a modern-day princess.

LEVEL 1

ingredients

- **1 T-shirt (fitted)**
- **scissors**
- **chalk marker**

1 Turn the T-shirt inside out and lay it flat. Cut out the neckband just outside the seam.

2 Use your chalk to mark a ring around the entire neck hole, about ½" from the edge. Mark a second chalk ring about 3" from the first.

3 Find the center front of the neck hole and use your ruler and chalk to draw a straight vertical line from the edge of the first ring down to the second chalk ring. Mark a series of lines about 1" apart, but not completely parallel to the first line, connecting the inner ring to the outer ring.

4 Make a small snip at the end of one of the 3" chalk lines so you can fit a scissor blade through. Cut along the chalk line. Continue to cut along the chalk lines in the same manner around the entire neck hole.

5 Turn the tee right side out and wear!

Raising the bar on fashion.

variation

■ Cut completely through the slits on the neck hole side so that the strips fall as fringe around a wider neckline.

Generation T

7 if you pleats
(t-shirt)

Is a T-shirt ever work-appropriate? Well, it depends on your office, of course (doctors and lawyers, hold back), but in a more cutting-edge work environment, or on "casual Friday," you may be able to get away with this one. Making a refined, pleated neckline for your T-shirt will dress it up, and earrings and a skirt just might let you slip past the censors.

LEVEL 4

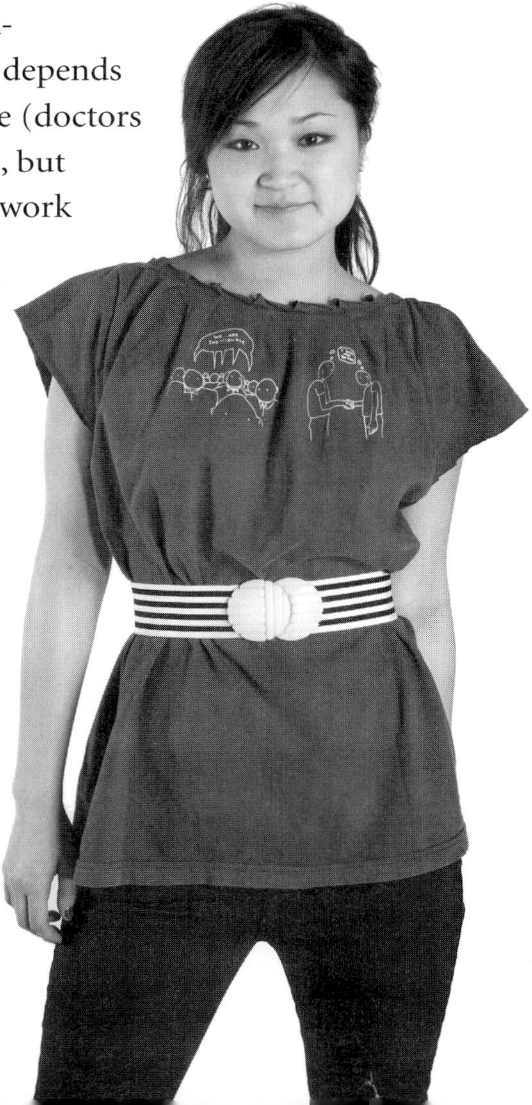

ingredients

- **1 T-shirt (baggy)**
- **scissors**
- **chalk marker**
- **ruler**
- **straight pins**
- **needle**
- **thread**

1 Lay the T-shirt flat and cut off 2" from the edge of each sleeve. Then mark and make a wide cutout about 3" to 3½" from the neckband (leaving about 2" of fabric between the neck hole and sleeve seam).

2 Make an even number of chalk marks approximately 1" apart around the entire edge of the neck hole, front and back.

3 Pinch one chalk mark over to the one adjacent to it and pin it flat.

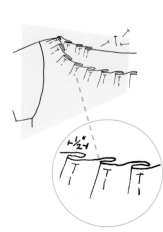

4 Moving around the edge of the neck hole in the same direction that you fold the pleats, pinch and pin the next chalk mark to the one after it. Continue until all chalk marks are paired.

5 Carefully try on the shirt to check that the neck hole is still wide enough for your head to pass through. Use a zigzag stitch to sew around the neck hole and over the pinned pleats about ½" to ¾" from the edge. Remove the pins and wear—belted or comfortably free-flowing.

8 the best of two tees

(tank top)

This tank top, with its neckerchief-style tie, celebrates the sexy librarian in all of us. Let the two colors represent your balance of fiction and nonfiction, poetry and drama, books and magazines. Tie up the neckerchief in a prim and proper bow or let the ends hang, dangling like participles. . . . Meet me over by the card catalog in ten.

LEVEL 3

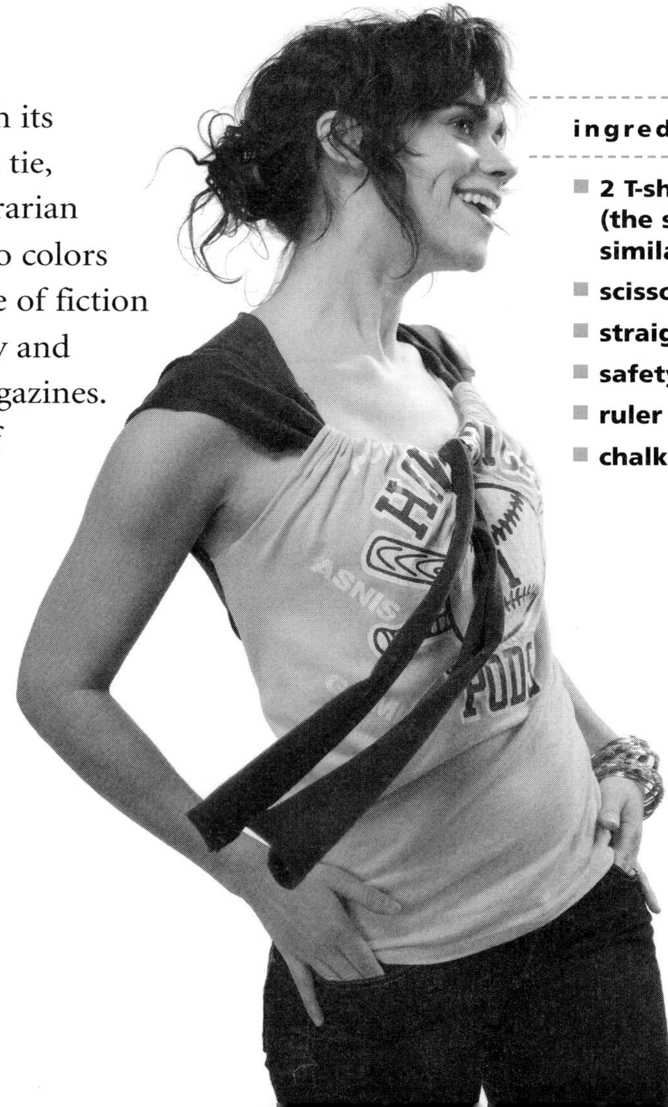

ingredients

- **2 T-shirts (the same or similar size)**
- **scissors**
- **straight pins**
- **safety pin**
- **ruler**
- **chalk marker**

1 Lay one T-shirt flat, back side up, and cut off the sleeves just inside the seams. Cut out the neckband, widening it about 2" at each side.

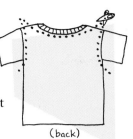

(back)

2 Cut through the sides to the armholes. Mark a vertical line even with the edge of the armhole and extending from shoulder to hem on both sides. Cut along those lines through just the top (back) layer.

(back)

3 Mark two vertical lines extending from the sides of the neck hole to the bottom hem. Cut along those lines, through just one layer, and discard excess fabric. Cut off the hem on the two resulting strips of fabric. Set aside. (This will be the back of the tank top.)

(back)

4 Lay the second T-shirt flat, front side up, and cut off the sleeves just inside the seams.

5 Cut vertically along the side from the hem to the armholes. Cut horizontally just below the neckband from the midpoint of one armhole to the midpoint of the other, through just the top layer of fabric. (This panel of fabric will be the front of the tank top.)

6 Turn over the panel so that the wrong side faces up. Cut a vertical slit that extends 4½" down from the center top edge.

7 Fold down the two top edges 2½" and pin. Use a running backstitch to create a seam 2" from the fold. Remove the pins.

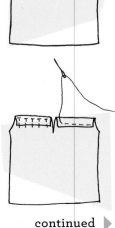

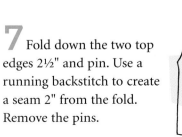

continued ▶

8 Place the front and back panels together, right sides facing. Line up the bottom hems, trim the bottom of the armholes so that they match, and pin together the two layers along the side edges.

9 Use a whipstitch to sew along the pinned sections. Remove the pins and turn the tank top right side out.

10 Attach a safety pin to one of the strips (from the back panel) and thread it through one side of the drawstring casing on the front panel and out through the center hole. Repeat with the second strip on the opposite side of the casing.

11 Pull the drawstrings, gathering the fabric over them, and tie them in a disheveled knot or an oversize bow. Try on the tank top and trim to adjust the strap width and length as desired.

❧ GREEN PARTY

Stop and Swap: Oh this old thing? A clothing swap is a great excuse to snag some of those fabulous pieces you know your friends no longer wear (but you've been coveting for years), and it's also a fun way to recycle. Instead of shopping for new gear and throwing out the old, invite friends to bring a bag of their tired duds, build a mountain of castoffs, and dig in! (*Note:* Some items, though unwearable, may provide fabric for your next DIY project.) Don't forget to designate an official chairperson in charge of taking any untraded goods to the nearest thrift store or donation center.

9 transformer
(scarf/shirt)

One garment. Infinite possibilities. A scarf, a tube top, a tank top, or skirt, Transformer is sexy no matter how you drape it. Wrap it any of the suggested ways (see next page), or invent your own stylish way to wear it. It ain't called DIY for nothin'.

LEVEL 3

ingredients

- **2 T-shirts of the same size (L or XL)**
- **scissors**
- **ruler**
- **chalk marker**
- **straight pins**
- **needle**
- **thread**

1 Lay both T-shirts flat and cut off the bottom hems, just above the seam.

2 Lay one T-shirt on top of the other, lining up the bottom edges. Mark and cut horizontally across the chest region of the shirts 17" to 20" up from the bottom to create two equal tubes.

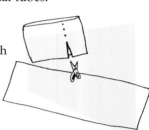

17"-20"

3 Cut vertically through each tube to create two wide rectangles.

variations for wrapping

Tie the ends tightly at the bust, leaving one 12" end dangling. Wrap the other end around your torso and tuck.

Wrap one end over your shoulder and twist it several times. Stretch it across the back, and around the front. Wrap it around your bust and continue down the torso, tucking the end.

4 With right sides facing, pin the rectangles together along one of the short edges. Use a running stitch to sew along the pinned edge. Remove the pins and unfold.

5 Wear it traditionally as a scarf or wrap it any of the four ways shown below—or invent your own!

variation

■ For a **NO SEW** version, cut 2" fringe into each short edge and knot them together.

Wrap one end around the back of your neck, covering both boobs. Fold the long end over itself and wrap it around the torso.

Wrap one end over your shoulder, across the back, and around to the front. Wrap it around your bust and continue down the torso, tucking the end.

Generation T

10 stop, crop, and roll
(cropped tank top)

NO SEW

Bucking that axiom of elementary school fire safety, this cropped tank top is anything but a dampener. In fact, you'll be sure to heat up the scene when you breeze onto the dance floor wearing this drapey number. Perfect for a summer day or a night out on the town, this top will surely have you capturing all of the attention. Caution: Wearing this top will cause the sparks to fly.

LEVEL 1

ingredients

- 1 T-shirt (baggy)
- ruler
- chalk marker
- scissors
- 4 punk pins

1 Lay the T-shirt flat and cut off the bottom hem just above the seam. Then mark and cut a rectangle, through both layers, as long and wide as the T-shirt allows.

2 Keep the two rectangles sandwiched together and rotate them horizontally. Attach two punk pins at the top, through both layers, about 8" from each of the side edges.

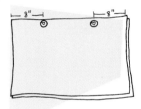

3 Try on the sheath, inserting your head between the layers and through the opening between the punk pins. Pinch the fabric layers at the bottom around your waist and pin at each side to secure the fabric at your sides. The "sleeves" will drape around your shoulders.

variations

■ Snip four small drawstrings from the hem piece. Poke holes through both layers where you put the punk pins and tie a small bow in each location instead.

■ For a more structured garment, you can sew from where you would place the punk pin to the adjacent corner.

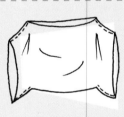

4 Keep all pins on when you remove the shirt. When you're ready to go out, layer it over a tank top for everyday wear or over a bikini top at the beach.

Generation T

11 superstar!
(halter top)

My sewing-phobic friend got really excited about making this halter, so much so that she was unfazed by the twelve inches of straight running stitch required. Okay, she was a little fazed, but pleasantly surprised at the process. It's super easy but transforms the T-shirt into a magnificent power halter that emphasizes the shoulders, arms, and back—and that's enough to give any beginner refashionista that DIY high.

LEVEL 3

ingredients

- **1 T-shirt (regular fit)**
- **chalk marker**
- **ruler**
- **scissors**
- **straight pins**
- **needle**
- **thread**

1 Turn the T-shirt inside out and lay it flat. Cut off the sleeves inside the seams and cut a 1" strip off the bottom (remove the hem stitching) to use later as a cord for the halter strap.

2 Cut a straight line across the top, through both layers, just below the neckband.

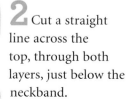

3 Mark the center front of the top edge and draw a diagonal line from that point to the bottom of each armhole. Cut along those lines through only the top layer.

4 Flip the shirt over. Mark and cut straight across, through only the back layer, from the bottom of one armhole to the bottom of the other. Remove the excess fabric.

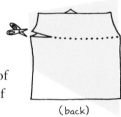

(back)

5 Poke or snip a small hole 1" from the top point on the front.

6 Fold the cord from step 1 in half and thread the loop through the hole. Thread the ends of the cord through the loop and pull tight in a cow hitch knot.

7 Try the shirt on (still inside out) and tie the two ends behind your neck. Pinch and pin any extra fabric in the back. Untie and carefully remove the halter. Adjust the pins and continue pinning along the edge to make sure it's straight.

(side)

8 Sew a running stitch along the pinned area. Remove the pins and cut the excess fabric ½" from the seam.

(side)

9 Turn the halter right side out, try it on, and tie the ends at the back of your neck.

(back)

variation

■ For a **NO SEW** version, use a fitted shirt, or lace or tie up the back to tighten. (See page 8 for the technique.)

(back)

Generation T

12 **wrap it up**
(kimono-inspired tank top)

The traditional Japanese kimono is T-shaped, and the fabric is sewn, dyed, and decorated by hand. If that's not DIY enough for you, enterprising folks often make their own new kimonos by recycling the fabric from old ones. Drawing on that inspiration, this East-meets-West wrap top is a match made in cotton. Tie yourself in, and get ready for a new kind of *tee* ceremony.

LEVEL 3

ingredients

- **2 T-shirts (regular fit)**
- **chalk marker**
- **ruler**
- **scissors**
- **straight pins**
- **needle**
- **thread**

1 Lay one T-shirt flat and cut off the bottom hem. Cut up each side of the shirt, and cut off the sleeves, just inside the seams.

2 Try on the tunic-shaped garment and trim more fabric off the shoulders if it's still too boxy.

3 Lay the second T-shirt flat and cut off the hem. Cut across the T-shirt, just below the sleeves, to make a tube.

4 Measure, mark, and cut the tube into four tubes of equal height, then cut through each loop to make four strips.

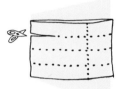

5 Pin the end of one strip to the left front edge of the tunic at about the waistline. Pin the end of a second strip to the right front edge, even with the first.

6 Pin the third strip to the left back edge, aligning it with the strip on the front of the tunic. Pin the last strip to the right back edge, even with the third strip. Sew a whipstitch along all the pinned edges. Remove the pins.

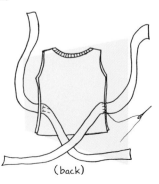

(back)

variation

■ For a **NO SEW** version, snip holes where you want to attach the ties and knot them to each edge in steps 5 and 6.

7 Mark and snip two vertical, parallel slits an even distance apart, at roughly the waistline, through only the back layer, as shown. The slit heights should be about half the width of your strips, and their placement should be about even with where you attached the strips.

(back)

8 Try on the top, threading the ends of the two front strips through the slits you made in step 7, from the wrong side of the fabric to the right side. Tie them in the back. Pull the two back strips to the front and tie them in a knot or bow. Trim the ends as desired.

13 madame butterfly
(halter top)

The T-shirt starts its life cycle as a humble caterpillar. After spending several months in a dark cozy cocoon (dresser drawer), it emerges, with the help of a young T-shirt-ologist (and some scissors, perhaps), more beautiful than ever as an adult halter top. Here's the top you can wear when you're ready to unfurl your wings and float like a butterfly.

LEVEL 3

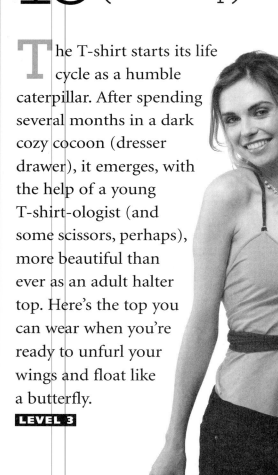

ingredients

- **2 T-shirts (L, in contrasting colors)**
- **scissors**
- **ruler**
- **chalk marker**
- **needle**
- **thread**
- **straight pins**

1 Lay one T-shirt flat and cut off the hem, just above the stitching. (Set aside the loop for the drawstring cords.) Mark and cut a diagonal from one bottom corner to the bottom of the opposite sleeve, as shown. Repeat on the second T-shirt.

2 Unfold the two triangles and place them together, right sides facing. Pin the triangles together along one of the short edges. Make a mark about 5" to 6" from the peak angle along that same edge.

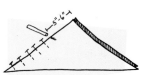

3 Use a whipstitch to sew along the pinned edge, from the base angle up to the mark you made in step 2. Remove the pins.

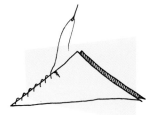

4 Cut the stitching from the two hems you cut off in step 1 and cut and stretch two long cords.

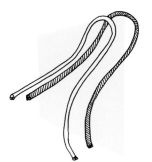

5 Poke or snip a small hole through both layers about 1" in from edge of the peak angle.

6 Unfold the triangle and rotate so the seam is centered vertically. Then fold in half one of the cords you made in step 4 and thread the loop through the hole in the opposite colored T-shirt. Thread the ends of the cord through the loop and pull tight in a cow hitch knot. Repeat on the other hole with the other cord. Mark about 11" up from the bottom point on the shirt and trim off the fabric below it, as shown.

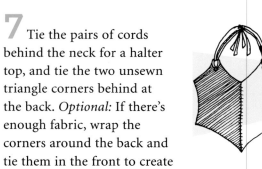

7 Tie the pairs of cords behind the neck for a halter top, and tie the two unsewn triangle corners behind at the back. *Optional:* If there's enough fabric, wrap the corners around the back and tie them in the front to create a waistline (see photo, left).

14 the dartful dodger
(tank top)

Texture, texture, texture. Simulate punk slashes by pinching the fabric of your tee, then stitching darts into this hip hybrid of a shirt. An odd marriage of prepster and punk for sure, but one that may very well launch a new subculture of cool. The quirky "pleats" make a boxy shirt more fitted, while showing off your unapologetic DIY aesthetic. Rock it!

LEVEL 3

ingredients

- **1 T-shirt (regular fit)**
- **scissors**
- **straight pins**
- **needle**
- **thread**

1 Lay the T-shirt flat and cut off the sleeves just outside the seam.

2 On the front, pinch ½" to 1" of the top layer of fabric and press it flat to one side. Pin it in place. (Be careful not to pin the dart to the back of the T-shirt.)

3 Repeat step 2 to create pleated patterns parallel and at angles to those you made in step 2.

4 Use a running stitch to sew along the edge of the dart ¼" to ½" from the fold, tapering at both ends. Make sure your stitches "catch" the three layers of fabric. *Tip:* Use contrasting thread to add color to the texture. Remove the pins.

It's a knockdown for this knockout!

15 **looney tunic**
(tank top tunic)

This all-season tunic is ready to perform no matter the temperature outside. In the spring, wear it with leggings. In the summer, layer it over your bathing suit for a trip to the beach. Come fall, let your skinny-leg jeans have a turn. And when the cold winds start blowing in winter, wear it as a bottom layer, protecting that gap between the bottom of your jacket and the top of your low-rise pants. Make this tank top out of a favorite T-shirt and you'll never have to pack it away for months at a time.

LEVEL 3

ingredients

- 1 T-shirt (baggy)
- seam ripper (optional)
- chalk marker
- scissors
- straight pins
- needle
- thread

1 Turn the T-shirt inside out, cut off the sleeves inside the seams, and cut out the neckband. Cut off the bottom hem or let out the hem with a seam ripper to allow for more length.

2 With the shirt still inside out, try it on and pinch and mark the fabric on either side, all the way down, to decide how many inches to take it in to make it more fitted. *Note:* You may have slightly different measurements to trim off along your torso and hips.

3 Mark with chalk where you want the bottom of the armholes, waist left and right, and hips left and right.

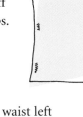

4 Take the shirt off, lay it flat, and use chalk to carefully and smoothly connect the marks you made in step 3.

5 Cut just outside the marked lines and then pin together the resulting edges.

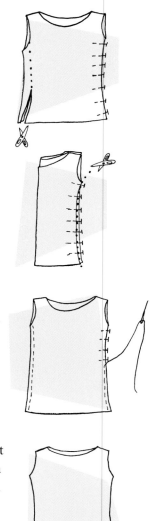

6 Fold the shirt in half vertically to trim the edges if needed to maintain the shirt's symmetry.

7 Unfold the shirt and sew a running stitch along the pinned edges. Remove the pins.

8 Turn it right side out and wear: Belt it high on your waist, low-slung on your hips, or not at all.

16 snug as a bug in a shrug

(twisted shrug)

Though the shrugging gesture usually indicates indifference, this garment is anything but ambivalent. With its twisted and gathered bust-enhancing front, this short-sleeved cropped shrug works wonders over a sundress or tank top as the quintessential summer layer.

LEVEL 4

ingredients

- **1 T-shirt (fitted)**
- **scissors**
- **ruler**
- **chalk marker**
- **straight pins**
- **needle**
- **thread**

1 Turn the T-shirt inside out, lay it flat. Cut out the neckband and cut off the bottom of the shirt, about 12" below the neck hole.

2 Mark and cut the neck hole lower in the front, so there is about 10" between it and the bottom raw edge. Then trim about 2" off of each sleeve.

3 Measure and mark a rectangle 5" up from the bottom and as wide as the shirt. Cut up the sides and across the marked line through only the top layer, leaving a flap in the back.

4 Make a vertical cut through the center of the front layer.

5 Cut a 5" loop from the bottom of the shirt (from step 1) and cut through it twice, vertically, to make two equal rectangles.

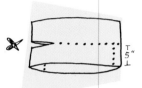

6 Pin the edge of one 5" rectangle to one of the 5" raw edges of the tee (from step 4), right sides facing. Repeat with the second rectangle on the opposite raw edge. Sew a whipstitch along the pinned edges. Remove the pins.

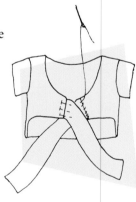

continued ▶

7 Try on the top. Cross the two dangling strips over your bust, twist them once around each other in the center, and pull them back to the sides. Pin the 5" ends to the sides of the back flap.

8 Carefully remove the shrug, keeping it inside out. Trim the ends, and make sure the pins on each end are right sides in. Pin closed the horizontal gaps on either side of the center twist. Sew a whipstitch along all pinned edges.

9 Remove the pins and turn right side out. Layer it over a tank top to keep out the chill or over a long-sleeved shirt to create texture.

variations

■ Wear it backward for a little edgy twist in the back.

- - - - - - - - - - - - - - - - - - - -

■ Stop partway through step 8, turn it right side out, and simply tie the ends in the back after you've twisted them in the front.

- - - - - - - - - - - - - - - - - - - -

■ Make a twist-front shirt or dress: Measure and stitch a tube from the bottom of another T-shirt around the bottom of your shrug, trimming the fabric as needed to fit beneath the twist.

- - - - - - - - - - - - - - - - - - - -

17 bubble, bubble, toil, and trouble

(skirt)

The bubble skirt is a hotly debated subject (should you or shouldn't you?) in the fashion world. But when made out of a soft jersey knit and topped with a wide waistband, you can hardly go wrong. With its playful '80s prom dress pouf, this structured skirt has a darling silhouette with a hint of humor. Whether you're strolling down the hall or sashaying down the sidewalk—make your world your runway.

LEVEL 5

ingredients

- **3 T-shirts (L or XL)**
- **ruler**
- **chalk marker**
- **straight pins**
- **needle**
- **thread**

1 Turn one T-shirt inside out, lay it flat, and cut off the bottom hem.

2 Cut a 14" tube from the bottom of the T-shirt. Divide your waist measurement by 2, and then subtract 1 to get x". Measure and mark x" from one side along the tube, and mark and cut off the excess fabric beyond the mark.

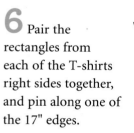

3 Pin and then sew a running stitch or a whipstitch along the open edge you just cut in step 2. Remove the pins (this is the inside layer of the skirt).

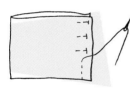

4 Lay the other two T-shirts flat and cut off the bottom hems just above the stitching. Cut a 3" tube from the bottom of one T-shirt, and then cut crosswise through one layer to make a strip (this will become the waistband).

5 Mark and cut matching rectangles 17" high and as wide as the fabric between the sleeves allows (use the smaller T-shirt as your guide) through both layers, from the bottoms of the two T-shirts.

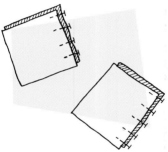

6 Pair the rectangles from each of the T-shirts right sides together, and pin along one of the 17" edges.

7 Unfold each panel and place one against the other, right sides facing, and pin again along *both* 17" edges. Sew a running stitch or whipstitch along all four pinned edges to create a large tube. Remove the pins.

8 Sew a basting stitch along the bottom edge of the large tube.

9 Gather the basting stitch evenly so that the circumference matches the circumference of the small tube (the inner layer) from step 3. Place the inner tube inside the gathered tube, right sides together. Pin the gathered edge to the matching edge of the inner tube and sew along the pinned edge with a zigzag or running stitch. Remove the pins.

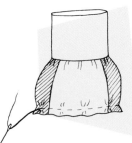

10 Unfold the layers so that both tubes are right side out. Sew a basting stitch along the open edge of the outer tube and gather it.

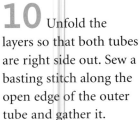

11 Fold the outer tube back over the inner tube so that the right side of the inner tube faces the wrong side of the outer tube, lining up the raw edge with the outer tube's gathered edge. Pin the edges together.

12 Take the 3" strip from step 4 and center it along the pinned top edge. Pin it in place, right side down (you should have three layers of fabric), letting the ends of the waistband dangle freely. Sew a zigzag or whipstitch along the pinned edge. Remove the pins.

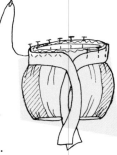

13 Fold up the waistband, slip on the skirt, and tie the ends in a bow in the back.

18 you can pleat me
(pleated skirt)

Part cheerleader, part student, you'll be the queen bee of the schoolyard in this pleated skirt. So, go ahead and stack the top of the human pyramid, or stack books at the library. Being a schoolgirl has never been so much fun.

LEVEL 5

ingredients

- **4 T-shirts (L or XL)**
- **scissors**
- **measuring tape**
- **chalk marker**
- **straight pins**
- **needle**
- **thread**

1 Lay three T-shirts flat, cut the bottoms off just below the sleeves (leaving the hems intact), and then cut vertically through the resulting tubes to get rectangles.

2 Line up the hems at the bottom and pin the three rectangles end to end along the short edges, right sides facing. Sew a running stitch or whipstitch along the pinned edges to create a large panel.

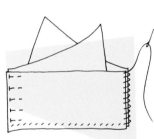

3 Remove the pins and lay the panel flat, right side up. Alternate making marks 1" and 2" apart along the top (unhemmed) edge. Multiply your waist measurement by 3 to get x and mark it from one side of the panel, ending at A.

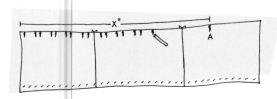

4 Pinch the 2"-apart marks together, creating a pleat, and pin them down. Pin the folds so they are about 7" long.

5 Continue pinning pleats, moving in the direction of your first fold, until you reach A. Measure the pinned panel against your waist to check it, add more pleats if needed, and trim off the excess fabric.

6 Sew a running stitch vertically along each pinned edge, close to the pleat fold. Remove the pins.

continued ▶

7 Fold the panel in half, right side in, so the hemmed edge is still at the bottom, and pin along the open side edge, careful to avoid the pleats. Sew a running stitch or whipstitch along the pinned edges. Remove the pins and turn right side out.

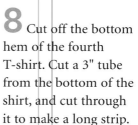

8 Cut off the bottom hem of the fourth T-shirt. Cut a 3" tube from the bottom of the shirt, and cut through it to make a long strip.

9 Center the strip at one of the side seams and press it against the top edge of the skirt, right sides together, lining up the edges. Pin it in place, leaving the excess strip pieces dangling at the side. Sew a whipstitch along the top of the pinned edges. Remove the pins. *Optional:* Iron the creases below the stitching on the skirt.

variation

■ Make the pleated skirt using just two T-shirts. Cut rectangles through all four layers of the tops of the shirts to make four alternating panels. Stitch them together, then cut the waistband from the bottom of one of the tees.

10 Fold the waistband up, slip the skirt on, and tie the ends.

S-tee-rike!

19 **gaucho marx**
(gaucho pants)

T-shirt pants are a hard look to pull off. It's true that jersey knit spawned sweatpants and yoga leggings, but there's a reason the fashion gods pair jeans with T-shirts. That said, if your bottom half craves T-shirt pants, gauchos are the way to go. They're as comfortable as a skirt (but allow you to sit cross-legged in the park), and they're perfectly breezy for dancing at an outdoor concert or summer music festival.

LEVEL 4

ingredients

- **3 T-shirts (L or XL)**
- **chalk marker**
- **ruler**
- **scissors**
- **straight pins**
- **needle**
- **thread**

1 Turn one T-shirt inside out and lay it flat. Starting just below the neckband, mark and cut through both layers a rectangle that is 15" wide and extends through the hem of the shirt. Repeat on the second T-shirt.

2 Lay the two paired rectangles on top of each other, lining up the top edges. Cut through all four layers just above the hem of the shortest rectangle so that all rectangles are the same size.

3 Separate the rectangle pairs. Take one pair and pin them together along one long edge, stopping 13" from the end. Sew a running stitch along the pinned edge, leaving a ¼" to ½" seam allowance. Repeat on the second rectangle pair. Remove the pins. (These are the legs.)

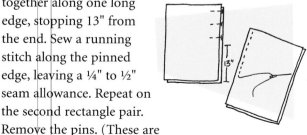

4 Take one leg and draw a gentle arc that starts ¼" below the end of the seam from step 3 (A) and ends about 2" in from the corner along the adjacent edge (B), as shown. Cut along the arc through both layers and repeat on the second leg.

5 Open up the panels and place them right sides together. Match the curved edges of one pant leg to the curved edges of the other pant leg, lining up the seams in the middle. Pin and sew a running stitch along the curved edges, leaving a ¼" to ½" seam allowance. Remove the pins and turn right side out.

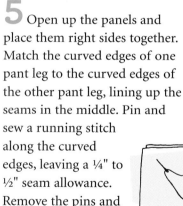

6 Cut two 2" tubes from the bottom of the third T-shirt just above the hem (or use scraps). Cut through one side of each tube to make two strips.

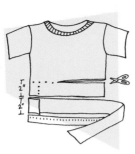

7 Center one strip at the center seam along the front top edge of the pants, right sides together. Pin in place. Repeat with the second strip along the back top edge. Sew a running stitch or a whipstitch along the pinned edges, fastening the two waistband pieces, respectively, to the front and back. Remove the pins and fold the waistband up.

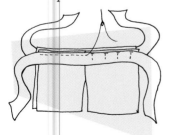

8 To wear the pants— brace yourself, this can be tricky!—place the front panel at your waist like an apron (the back panel will be hanging down in front). Wrap the ends of the waistband around you, and tie them in the back. Then pull the back panel through your legs to the rear, wrap the ends of the waistband around your waist to the front, and tie them in a bow! (The outside edges of the pant legs are open and wrap around your leg like a wrap skirt.)

variations

■ Rather than make each pant leg from a different T-shirt, mix up the T-shirt piece pairings in step 3 so the front panel of the pants becomes one color and the back panel becomes another.

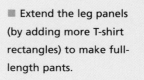

■ Extend the leg panels (by adding more T-shirt rectangles) to make full-length pants.

20 **fun in the sun**
(sundress)

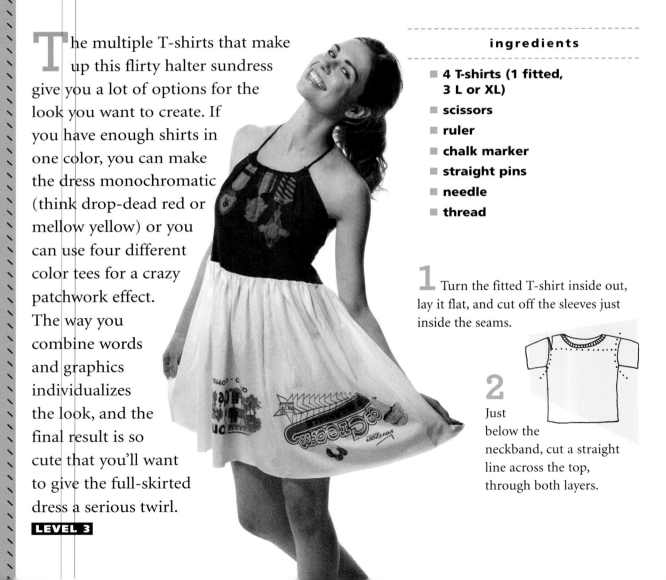

The multiple T-shirts that make up this flirty halter sundress give you a lot of options for the look you want to create. If you have enough shirts in one color, you can make the dress monochromatic (think drop-dead red or mellow yellow) or you can use four different color tees for a crazy patchwork effect. The way you combine words and graphics individualizes the look, and the final result is so cute that you'll want to give the full-skirted dress a serious twirl.

LEVEL 3

ingredients

- **4 T-shirts (1 fitted, 3 L or XL)**
- **scissors**
- **ruler**
- **chalk marker**
- **straight pins**
- **needle**
- **thread**

1 Turn the fitted T-shirt inside out, lay it flat, and cut off the sleeves just inside the seams.

2 Just below the neckband, cut a straight line across the top, through both layers.

3 On the back, mark and cut (through only the back layer) a gentle arc from the bottom of one armhole to the bottom of the other. Remove the excess fabric.

4 Flip the shirt back over and fold the top edge down 1" to 1½" against the front of the shirt. Pin in place.

5 Use a running stitch to sew along the pinned area, leaving a ¼" seam allowance. Remove the pins. This is your drawstring casing.

6 Cut the hem from the bottom of one of the T-shirts. Trim off the stitching. Snip through the loop to make one long cord. Attach a safety pin to one end of the drawstring and thread it through the casing, bunching the fabric over it. Loosely tie the drawstring ends together.

7 Flip the shirt so the back faces up. Measure and mark about 3" to 4" down from the lowest point of the top back edge. Cut off the bottom of the shirt at that mark. This is the bodice of the dress.

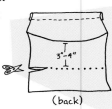

(back)

8 Lay the smallest of the remaining T-shirts flat and cut a rectangle as large as possible (between the sleeves, above the hem, and below the neckband) through both layers.

9 Using the rectangles you cut in step 8 as a pattern, cut two more rectangles (through both layers) from the remaining two T-shirts. (You will have six rectangles altogether.)

continued ▶

10 Arrange the panels in the order you'd like to see them around the skirt. Pin two adjacent rectangles, right sides together, along one of the long edges. Repeat on the other two pairs.

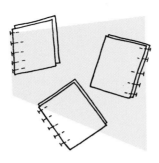

11 Pin the three pairs together along their remaining long edges (still right sides facing) to create a wide tube. Sew a running stitch along each pinned edge.

12 Remove the pins and sew a basting stitch along the top edge of the tube (the skirt). Gather the skirt evenly over the thread and turn it right side out.

13 Make six evenly spaced marks around the bottom of the bodice (from step 7). With the bodice still inside out, place it over the gathered edge of the skirt, lining up each chalk mark with a skirt panel seam (this ensures that the skirt gathers evenly) and pin them in place.

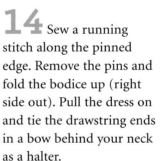

14 Sew a running stitch along the pinned edge. Remove the pins and fold the bodice up (right side out). Pull the dress on and tie the drawstring ends in a bow behind your neck as a halter.

21 tie, tie again
(halter dress)

A graduate version of Transformer (see page 45), Tie, Tie Again can be impressively wrapped multiple ways, too. Though it takes five T-shirts (and could set you back a few hours in the making), the payoff is huge. Experiment to find how many different ways you can wear it—just make sure everything you want covered is covered.

LEVEL 5

---

ingredients

- **5 T-shirts (L or XL)**
- **ruler**
- **scissors**
- **chalk marker**
- **straight pins**
- **needle**
- **thread**

---

1 Lay one T-shirt flat and cut 8" off the bottom, leaving the hem. Cut through the tube to create a rectangle.

continued ▶

2 Along the hem of the rectangle, mark your waist measurement (x"). Extend that line vertically and cut along the line to remove the excess fabric.

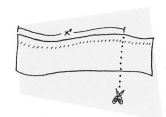

3 Fold the rectangle in half crosswise, right side in, and pin along the short edge. Sew along the pinned edge with a running stitch or whipstitch. Remove the pins.

4 Lay two T-shirts on top of each other. Mark and cut a 20" square through all four layers of fabric.

5 Divide your waist measurement by 6 to get y". (For example: A 30" waist, divided by 6, equals 5".) Mark y" along each edge of one corner.

6 Draw a straight line between the two marks you made in step 5, and cut along the line through all four layers, removing the corner.

7 Separate the four wedges and arrange them right side down in a square, as shown, alternating the panels of the two shirts.

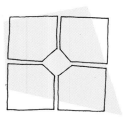

8 Pin two of the pieces together along their shared side, right sides together. Continue until all four edges are pinned, creating a square "ring" of fabric. Sew the four pinned edges together using a whipstitch. Remove the pins and turn right side out.

9 Place the ring of fabric (the skirt) inside the 8" tube (from step 3) with the right side of the skirt facing the right side of the tube (waistband). Pin the raw edges of the skirt and waistband together. Sew along the pinned edge using a zigzag stitch or whipstitch. Remove the pins.

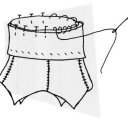

10 Lay the last two shirts flat. Cut through both layers on a horizontal line, from the bottom of one sleeve to the bottom of the other and just above the hem stitching.

11 Cut both tubes in half horizontally to make four smaller tubes. Separate the tubes and cut through each tube to make strips.

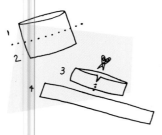

12 Place each pair of matching strips against each other, right sides facing, and pin along one of the short ends. Sew a whipstitch or running stitch along each of the pinned sections to create two very long strips.

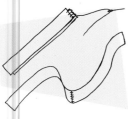

variation

■ Eliminate the waistband for a shorter dress or shirt.

13 Fold the 8" waistband (from step 9) up and pin an end of each strip at the center of the hem edge. Stitch along the pinned area. Remove the pins.

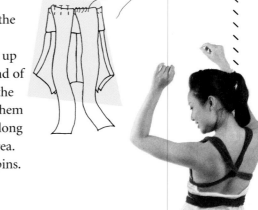

14 Pull the dress on, lay the strips across the bust. Tw the straps and lay them over each shoulder. Cross them in back, wrap them around to the front under the bust, then around the waist again, and knot in the front or the back (see color insert).

22 it ain't me, babe
(babydoll dress)

If, when you hear the words "babydoll dress," you picture a row of teenage girls in loose floral dresses in the '90s, think again. The babydoll dress has gotten leaner, meaner, and there's not a flower print in sight. Two T-shirts (one fitted, one larger and loose) come together with an edgy contrast of color and texture, taking the resulting dress firmly into this decade, and beyond.

LEVEL 3

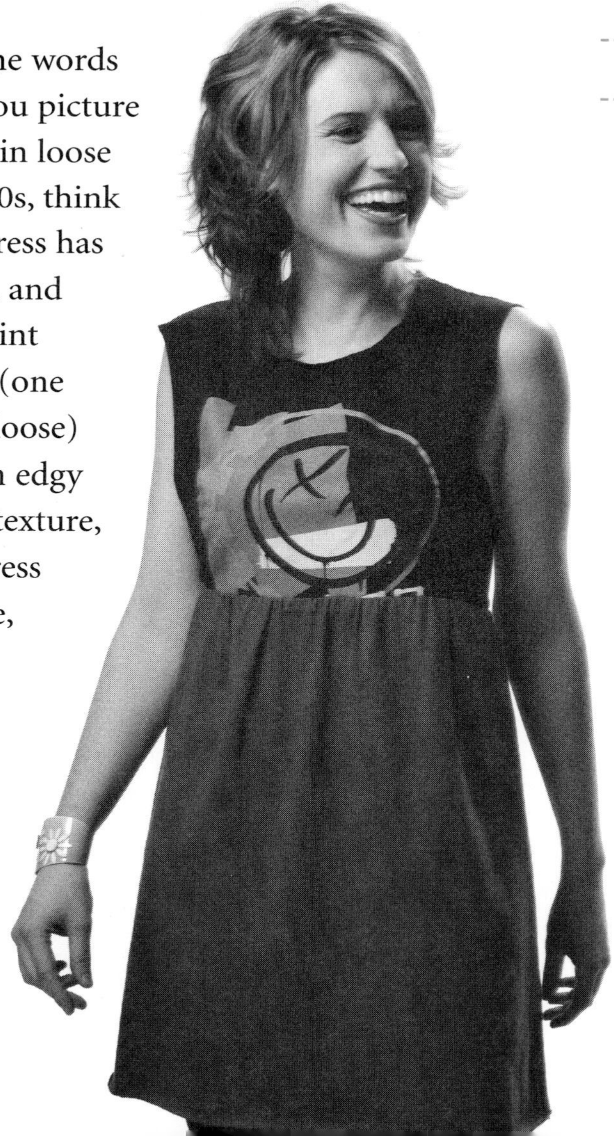

ingredients

- 2 T-shirts (1 fitted, 1 baggy)
- ruler
- scissors
- seam ripper
- straight pins
- needle
- thread

1 Lay the fitted tee flat and cut off the sleeves just inside the seams. Cut out the neckband and cut off the bottom of the T-shirt about 3" below the armholes.

2 Turn the XL T-shirt inside out, lay it flat, and cut off the bottom just below the sleeves. With a seam ripper, remove the stitching from the hem (to add more length).

3 Sew a basting stitch along the newly unhemmed edge of the tube and gather the fabric until the distance around the edge matches the distance around the base of the fitted T-shirt from step 1.

4 Place the top inside the gathered tube so that right sides are together. Pin the gathered edge of the tube against the bottom edge of the top. Even out the gathers and then sew a running stitch along the pinned area to secure them.

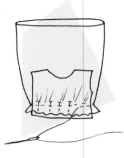

5 Remove the pins and the basting stitch (unless the latter is not noticeable), turn the dress right side out, and wear!

❧ GREEN PARTY

The average American throws away around 70 pounds of clothing and other fabrics each year, which amounts to more than 4 million tons of waste, three quarters of which is dumped into landfills. Think of all the cool projects and good causes those 70 pounds could go to before you decide to scrap 'em!

23 the mod squad
(cowl-neck dress)

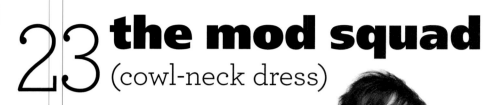

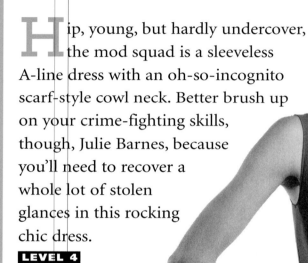

Hip, young, but hardly undercover, the mod squad is a sleeveless A-line dress with an oh-so-incognito scarf-style cowl neck. Better brush up on your crime-fighting skills, though, Julie Barnes, because you'll need to recover a whole lot of stolen glances in this rocking chic dress.

LEVEL 4

ingredients

- **2 T-shirts (XL)**
- **scissors**
- **chalk marker**
- **ruler**
- **straight pins**
- **needle**
- **thread**

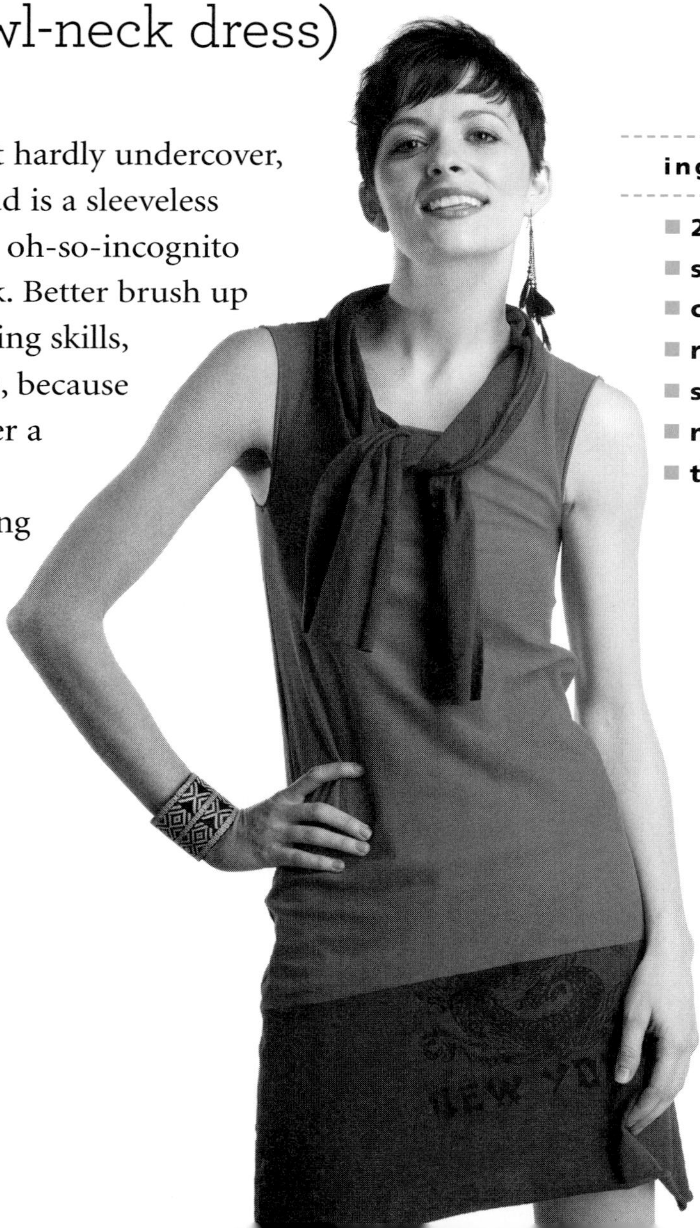

1 Turn the first T-shirt inside out and lay it flat. Cut off the bottom hem and the sleeves just inside the seams. Cut out the neckband.

2 Try on the shirt and mark the desired top and bottom of the armhole (most likely it will be farther in than the current armhole). Remove the shirt and trim off the excess fabric at the armholes, cutting concave arcs that are parallel to the original sleeve seam. Make a vertical cut from the bottom of each armhole to the bottom of the tee on both sides.

3 Lay the second T-shirt flat and cut off the top of the shirt just below the sleeves, leaving a tube. Mark and cut a line 8" to 10" from the top of the tube, setting aside the bottom tube. Cut through both sides of the larger tube to make two rectangles.

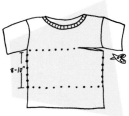

4 With right sides together, pin each rectangle to the bottom back and bottom front of the first shirt. Sew a running stitch along both pinned areas. Remove the pins and fold the panels down.

5 Turn the dress inside out. From the bottom of each armhole, draw a diagonal line to the corresponding bottom corner of the dress, as shown. Cut along these lines and remove the excess fabric.

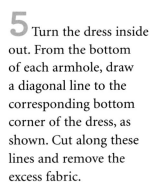

6 Pin along the open side edges from the armholes down to the bottom. Sew a running stitch or whipstitch along the pinned edges. Remove the pins and turn the dress right side out.

continued ▶

7 Cut crosswise through the bottom tube from step 3 to make a long strip.

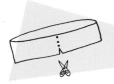

8 Arrange the strip so it's centered against the back of the neckline, right sides together. Pin the raw edge of the strip around the raw edge of the neck hole, leaving the front 4" to 6" unpinned. Let the ends of the strips hang loosely. Sew along the pinned edge.

Like to Layer?

In 2006, Mr. Mike McAllister, of Phoenix, Arizona, set the world record for number of T-shirts worn at one time: a whopping 155! The T-shirts were sized S through 10 XL and collectively added up to about 100 pounds of jersey. (See a video on YouTube!)

variations

■ If you're on the petite side (read: shorter than me!), one large T-shirt may be all you need. Follow steps 1, 2, 5, and 6, and you're good to go!

■ If you're on the tall side (like me!), but don't have the patience for the full dress, wear the shorter version (above) as a tunic shirt with leggings or jeans underneath.

■ Measure the neck hole and fit the strip from step 8 for a complete cowl neck on your shirt or dress.

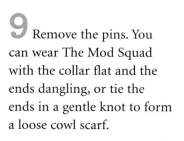

9 Remove the pins. You can wear The Mod Squad with the collar flat and the ends dangling, or tie the ends in a gentle knot to form a loose cowl scarf.

24 mad about macramé
(belt) NO SEW

This macramé belt is like a friendship bracelet for your waist, and making it will bring back other summer camp memories: Color wars, raiding the boys' cabin, camp unity songs, s'mores around the fire, and that time it rained for three days straight and the whole camp turned into a massive mudslide. Make a set of belts with your BFFs and trade each week so you have a constant stream of new accessories to show off.

LEVEL 2

ingredients

- **3 T-shirts (L, same or different colors)**
- **scissors**
- **safety pin**

1 Lay all three T-shirts flat and cut off the bottom hems. Then cut a 1"-wide coil off the bottom of each shirt, spiraling off as long a strip as possible. Stretch them out as cords.

2 Align three cords and loop them in half. Tie them all in an overhand knot about 1" from the top of the loop. Safety pin the knot to your pant leg or a pillow to keep it secure. Spread the six strips out in the order you'd like them to appear as stripes on your belt.

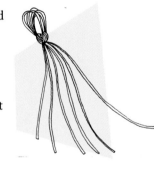

3 Wrap the first strip (A) around the second (B), and pull it through to make a single knot. Keep B taut as you tighten and slide the knot up to the top. Repeat.

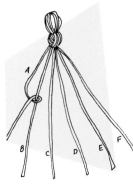

4 Tie A around the third strip (C) twice as you did in step 3. Continue with strips D, E, and F.

5 The strips are now realigned, left to right: B, C, D, E, F, A. And a series of knots appears in a row below the main knot. Wrap B around C, then around D, then E, and then F, then A.

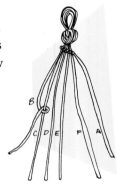

6 Wrap C around D, E, F, A, and B. Then wrap D around E, F, A, B, and C. Then wrap E around F, A, B, C, and D. Then wrap F around A, B, C, D, and E. You're now back at the original configuration.

variations

■ Finish the ends with a needle and thread and add belt clips from a sewing notions store.

■ Make shorter macramé versions for a headband, sweatband, wrist cuff, keychain, tote handles, dog collar—and anything else you can think of!

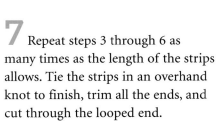

7 Repeat steps 3 through 6 as many times as the length of the strips allows. Tie the strips in an overhand knot to finish, trim all the ends, and cut through the looped end.

8 Wrap the belt around your waist or hips and tie. *Optional:* Rather than cutting through the looped end, wrap the belt around your waist or hips, cut the belt to fit, knot it, and insert the knot through the loop to secure it around your midsection.

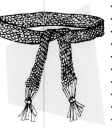

GREEN TEE

25 a head of the curve
(braided headband)

NO SEW

This accessory employs a simple technique, yet the result is remarkably versatile: Wear the headband up over your hair preppy-style through the hallways of academia, or wear it down over your forehead hippie-style in the drum circle out in the quad.

LEVEL 2

ingredients

- 1 T-shirt (or 3 T-shirt laces, ½" by 36")
- scissors
- safety pin

1 Cut three ½" by 36" strips from the bottom of a T-shirt, above the hem (or collect some scrap pieces of the same dimensions for color variation). Tie the three strips together in an overhand knot at one end and then tightly braid them. Pin the three ends together with a safety pin and trim the ends.

2 Starting at the nape of your neck with the knotted end and, going across the crown, wrap the braid twice around your head so it fits snugly.

3 Pinch the intersection of the two cords at the bottom and remove the headband from your head. Firmly wrap the safety-pinned end of the braid around the intersection about eight times, hiding the other knotted end.

4 Gently force the safety-pinned end of the braid through the "tube" created by the wrap you completed in step 3 and pull tight.

5 Tie an overhand knot at the end of the wrap and thread the safety pin end back halfway through the wrap.

6 Snip the end short and weave it under the layers of the wrap. *Optional:* If you have a needle and thread, you can secure the wrap with some stitches through all of the layers, but it's just fine without.

7 Slip the headband over your head, keeping your hair out of your face!

variation

■ For a simpler though less "finished" headband, simply wrap the braid twice around your head and tie the ends in a tight overhand knot.

26 **loop-tee-loop** (scarf)

Y ou may think that beyond the pattern on the fabric, a scarf is a scarf is a scarf. Au contraire! This refreshing design spins the scarf into a "hole" new shape. It's made in one continuous loop, so you never have to worry again about your scarf slipping open or getting left behind.

LEVEL 3

ingredients

- 1 T-shirt (L or XL)
- scissors
- ruler
- straight pins
- needle
- thread

1 Lay the T-shirt flat and cut off the hem above the seam. Cut across the T-shirt, through both layers, just under the sleeves to create a loop. Measure, mark, and cut across the loop horizontally to halve the loop, creating two equal loops.

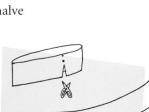

2 Cut through the loops to make two long panels.

3 Lay the panels against each other, right sides facing, and pin along both short sides. Sew a whipstitch along the pinned edges to create one large loop. Remove the pins.

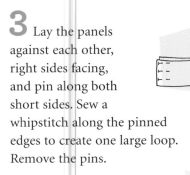

4 Loop the scarf around twice and adjust the layers to fit.

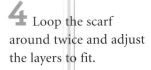

variation

■ Draw and cut a scalloped edge into one side of the loop.

GREEN PARTY

Refashioning old clothing is a great way to extend the life of an item, but here are a few quick tips for making both your new and revamped duds last:

- Slip into something more comfortable when you get home instead of hanging around in your "Sunday best." (Wear is the number one cause of fabric breakdown.)
- Wear your clothes a couple times before laundering, and when you do wash them, use cold water if possible.
- Line dry your clothes instead of heat-blasting them in an energy-guzzling dryer.

27 hoodnight moon
(hooded scarf)

This hooded scarf will bring out the kid in you. Wrap yourself up and hide from that blustery cold wind—or pretend that you're a mysterious spy in a foreign land. Better still, wear it in your real life while walking your dog in chilly Portland or Philly, hiding from the kids from your high school when you go back home to visit your parents, or taking a late-night trip to the deli to buy a pint of ice cream and the next morning's paper.

LEVEL 3

ingredients

- **2 T-shirts (L or XL)**
- **ruler**
- **chalk marker**
- **scissors**
- **straight pins**
- **needle**
- **thread**

1 Turn one of the T-shirts inside out and lay it flat on its side so that the front and back of the shirt are the new "sides," as shown. Measure about 14" along the bottom hem of the shirt and mark it. Measure about 12" up from the same corner and mark it.

2 Mark and then cut, through both layers of fabric, an exaggerated convex "J" shape from one mark to the other (this is the hood).

3 Pin and sew a whipstitch along the curved edge. Cut through the fold on the short straight edge and turn the hood right side out.

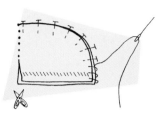

4 Lay the second T-shirt flat and cut off the hem. Cut across the T-shirt, through both layers, just under the sleeves. Cut across that loop horizontally to create two equal loops.

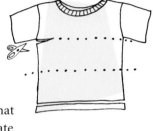

5 Cut through the loops to make two long panels.

6 Place the panels together, right sides facing, and pin along one short side. Sew the pinned edge with a whipstitch to create one long panel. Remove the pins.

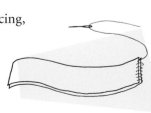

7 Rotate the hood (step 3) 45 degrees so the raw edge becomes the bottom of the hood (and the hem faces to one side). Place one of the long edges of the long panel (the scarf) against the bottom of the hood, right sides together, lining up the seams so that the hood is centered on the scarf. Pin along the shared raw edges and sew a whipstitch along the pinned section.

(side)

8 Remove the pins, fold down the scarf, and pull on the hood. Cross the scarf ends and toss them over your shoulders with ease—and slide on a pair of shades just to be mysterious.

variations

■ Follow steps 4 through 6 to make a simple scarf.

■ Make a pointier hood (by making the "J" shape you cut in step 2 more angular) and add a pom-pom or braided strip to the top!

28 diamond mining (scarf)

GREEN TEE

They say that diamonds are a girl's best friend. Mine some diamonds from the old T-shirts buried in the depths of your dresser drawers to make this scrappy, bohemian scarf. Mix and match colors, use pinking shears to make it look a little raggedy (that's a good thing!). Or go another route: Done all in white, this can look like an elegant boa.

LEVEL 3

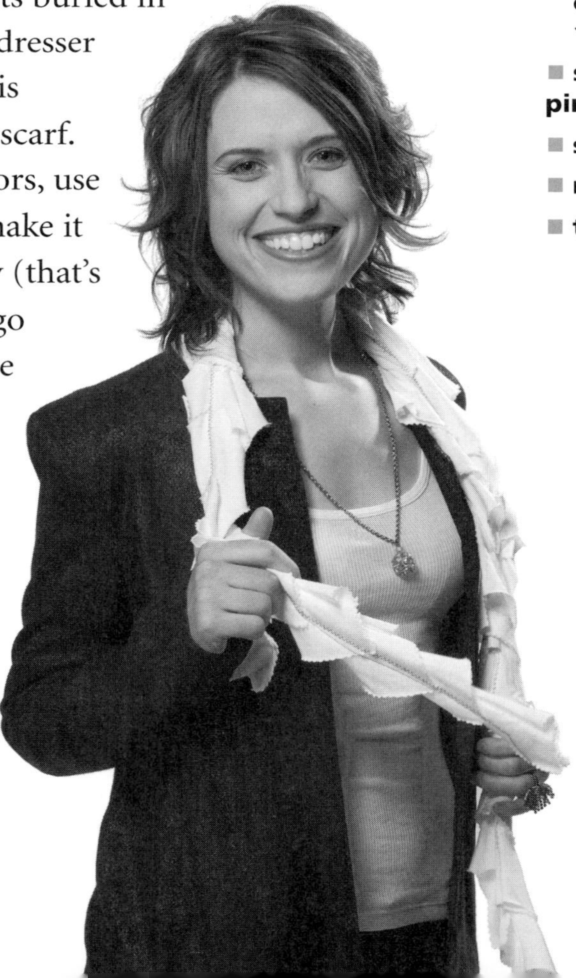

ingredients

- **T-shirt sleeves and other scraps (or 1 T-shirt, L)**
- **scissors (or pinking shears)**
- **straight pins**
- **needle**
- **thread**

1 Cut or gather between fifty-six and sixty-four 3" to 4" squares. *Optional:* Trim the edges with pinking shears for decoration.

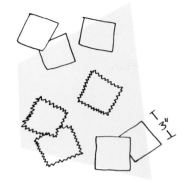

2 Layer all of the squares in pairs, right sides up. Overlap one pair about halfway with the second pair, as shown. Pin it in place.

3 Overlap a third pair halfway over the second. Pin it in place.

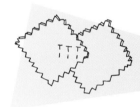

4 Continue arranging and pinning pairs, overlapping each one halfway over the former.

5 Starting at one end, sew a running or zigzag stitch down the center along the length of the pinned scarf.

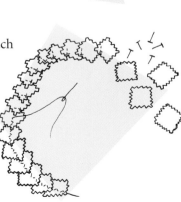

GREEN PARTY

Okay, so you know you shouldn't chuck your unwanted clothes in the trash, but what happens when you donate them to a thrift shop? The majority of items will be sold or redonated to specific charitable organizations, and those that can't be reused as garments are often recycled into industrial cleaning cloths or sold to salvage brokers.

6 Remove the pins and wear!

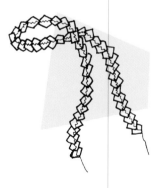

29 **fleur-de-tee**
(flower blossom appliqué) GREEN TEE

Plant flowers right on your skirt, shirt, headband, or bag. Gardening and refashioning come from similar impulses—a love for color and texture, a desire to watch something grow and evolve, and using your hands to make something beautiful. These scrunchy flower buds, which can be any color you want, attach and detach easily to add flair to an outfit. *And* they have the advantage of never wilting.

LEVEL 3

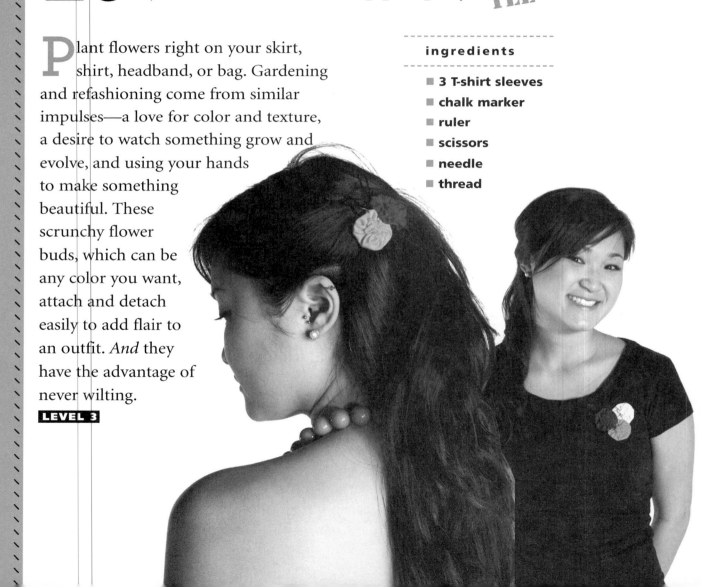

1 Trace and cut several small circles between 2" and 3" in diameter. (A 2" circle will make an approximately 1" rosette; a 3" circle will make an approximately 1½" rosette.)

2 Starting on the wrong side of the fabric, sew a basting stitch around the outside edge of one of the circles about ¼" in from the edge.

3 When you complete the circle, gather the fabric against the thread until the center bunches up tight (the fabric should gather into a pouch shape, right side out, with a puckered opening at one side).

4 Press the gathered opening flat into the center of the pouch, making a round flower shape. Sew several stitches through the center of the flower (through both layers) to secure the shape.

5 Stitch the back of the flower to a skirt hem, a shirt collar, a hat, a sleeve, a headband, a barrette, or a belt—or sew a safety pin to the back of the blossom so you can transport it from garment to garment.

6 Repeat on the remaining circles and "plant" a whole garden!

Chapter 3

House Party

Home Is Where the Art Is

Reaching beyond the wardrobe, here are 16 T-shirt makeovers for your kitchen, living, dining, and dorm room—even the bathroom!

Whether you're aware of it or not, you practice random acts of DIY around the house every day—you make a grilled cheese sandwich for lunch, you water the basil you're growing on your windowsill, you prop up your computer monitor with books. It's all DIY, it's just the medium that varies. Maybe you take your resourcefulness a step further, turning your old bed sheets into window curtains, cutting and pasting a card out of old wrapping paper for your friend's birthday, building a bookshelf out of planks and bricks left over from a local construction site. In fact, DIY has a long history in the home—from building to landscaping to renovating. It's only natural that decorating (and decorating with T-shirts!) be added to the mix.

DIY Kitchen: Cookies from scratch go well with coasters from scraps.

Take a page from our crafty scrapbooking friends, and think about how your T-shirts can be reformatted to tell a story in your home. Our clothes tend to define us at significant stages or fashionable phases in our lives, yet for the most part they're hidden once we "outgrow" the stuff. But those closet pieces needn't be forgotten memories—you can salvage your various sentimentally held "selves" along that T-shirt timeline *while* revitalizing your closet shelves.

Rescue those old, unworn shirts from storage, and bring them back to roost around your home, reincarnated as pillows and plant hangers, wine cozies and welcome mats. Decorate for apartment- and housewarmings, brunches and cocktail parties, holidays and birthdays, dorm room entertaining, and even watching your favorite sports team take the field. When you transform your T-shirts for your living space, you put your memories on display so you can share them (and make them last longer!). How else are you going to be able to tell people the story of your first 10K road race unless a guest notices the T-shirt you made your coaster set from?

So, whether you're pulling the pie out of the oven with a handmade pot holder, spiffing up your plants with retro braided hangers, or securing your laptop into its new padded jersey sleeve, you can make the everyday festive by applying some of these DIY fashion ideas to your home. (Hey, not only did you make the meal— you made the place settings, too!)

And you don't have to go it alone—in the spirit of barn raisings and potluck suppers, invite your friends to do it with you. Each guest can bring T-shirt scraps to contribute to a set of mismatched coasters for the host. Or arrange a "wine swap" party, where everyone brings a favorite selection and crafts a reusable cozy to trade along with their bottle. That said, you can also sit back and relax—simply invite your friends over to celebrate with you when you're done with the DIY.

What's on Your Playlist:

"Our House"
—*Madness*

"Come On-a My House"
—*Rosemary Clooney*

"Run's House"
—*Run-DMC*

"Little Boxes"
—*Pete Seeger*

"Safe European Home"
—*The Clash*

"I'm Going Back Home"
—*Nina Simone*

"House of the Rising Sun"
—*The Animals*

"Homeward Bound"
—*Simon & Garfunkel*

"I Ain't Got No Home"
—*Hank Williams*

"Take Me Home, Country Roads"—*John Denver*

"Sweet Home Alabama"
—*Lynyrd Skynyrd*

30 pillow talk
(knotted pillow)

NO SEW

I'll let you in on a little bedtime DIY secret: Knot-tying isn't just for Boy Scouts, kids. Knowing a basic knot or two—the easiest no-sew technique out there—will arm you for making this pillow, and so much more. Because before zippers, snaps, or buttons kept our pillows covered, how do you think people fastened things? They tied them.

LEVEL 1

ingredients

- **1 T-shirt (L or XL)**
- **scissors**
- **chalk marker**
- **ruler**
- **fabric scraps or poly-fill stuffing**

1 Lay the T-shirt flat and measure and mark the widest point between the sleeves. Measure and mark that same distance down toward the hem on both sides to make a square. Cut the square through both layers of the T-shirt.

2 Cut 2" squares from each corner through both layers.

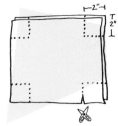

3 Cut fringe 2" long by ½" to ¾" wide through both layers into each edge around the perimeter.

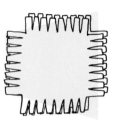

4 Use a double knot to tie each piece of fringe from the top layer of fabric to the corresponding piece beneath it.

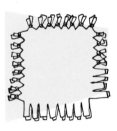

5 Work your way around the perimeter of the pillow until you have about three or four fringe pieces remaining. Fill the pillow through that hole with fabric scraps or stuffing, making sure to stuff the corners first.

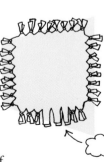

6 Tie the remaining fringe to close up the pillow.

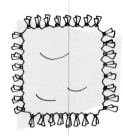

variations

■ Cut a circle (trace a large mixing bowl or other circular item) instead of a square and cut and knot 2"-long fringe around the perimeter.

■ Rather than cutting the corners or fringe in steps 2 and 3, place the two layers wrong sides together and stitch around the perimeter, leaving a 2" to 3" seam allowance and a 4" gap on one side. Turn the pillow right side out and fill the pillow with stuffing through the gap. Then stitch the gap closed. This will give your pillow winged edges.

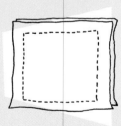

31 a time and a place mat

(place mat)

Whether you're eating alone or dining with family or friends, what says homemade better than an accessory for the meal? Why settle for boring, mass-marketed place mats when you can distinguish your tabletop and set yourself apart with individualized place mats celebrating your favorite sport, collectible, artist, vacation spot, or city? Click your heels together, clang your silverware . . . *there's no place mat like home.*

LEVEL 3

1 Measure and cut 12" by 16" rectangles through both layers of four T-shirts.

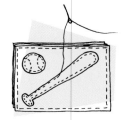

2 Place the rectangle you want as the bottom right side down. Place two plain rectangles on top of it, then place the rectangle you want as the top of the place mat right side up. Align all edges and pin. Use a running stitch to sew through all four layers around the perimeter, about ¼" from the edge.

3 Cut shapes, letters, or logos from other scrap T-shirts and arrange them onto the top of the place mat.

4 Create a scene or collage the items together. Pin them in place. Using a running stitch, sew ¼" in from the edges around the perimeters of the pinned items (being sure to go through all five layers). The more items you stitch on, the better the place mat will keep its shape through many washings. Remove the pins.

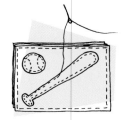

5 Repeat steps 2 through 4 to make the second place mat and continue to repeat to create a set of four, eight, or ten—depending on how many T-shirts you have to spare and how many guests you're expecting.

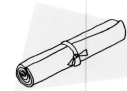

6 To store them for the next meal, roll up each one and tie it with a scrap strip of T-shirt.

variation

■ Without appliquéing anything to the place mat, use a running stitch to outline the existing designs onto the top layer of fabric as in Coast to Coasters (page 104) to create a reversible place mat.

32 **stocked up** (wine cozy)

It's often very chilly in wine cellars—as it should be! But when you pick out a bottle of bubbly or vino to bring to your friend's apartment warming (or graduation from med school, or birthday, or . . .) dress it up in a cute outfit and keep it cozy—it's a house *warming,* after all. (Not to mention, you're protecting it from clinking against anything else in your bag and springing a leak.)

LEVEL 4

---

ingredients

- **1 T-shirt**
- **ruler**
- **chalk marker**
- **scissors**
- **straight pins**
- **needle**
- **thread**
- **safety pin**

1 Turn the T-shirt inside out, lay it flat, and cut off the bottom hem. Trim off the stitching on the hem and cut through the loop to make a drawstring. Cut an additional 1" strip off the bottom of the T-shirt and set it aside.

2 Measure the circumference of the base of the wine bottle and add 1" for the seam to get x". Measure and mark an 11" by x" rectangle across the front of the shirt. Cut out the rectangle through only the front layer.

3 Fold the rectangle in half so that the 11" sides are aligned, right side in. Pin along the long open edge and sew a running stitch, leaving a ¼" to ½" seam allowance to make a tube.

4 Mark a circle with a circumference equal to that of the tube, or trace the bottom of the bottle and add ¼" for seams. Cut out the circle through just one layer.

5 Pin the circle, right side facing in, to the bottom inside edge of the tube. Leaving a ¼" seam allowance, use a running stitch to sew along the pinned edges around the bottom of the bag. Remove the pins.

6 Turn the bag right side out and mark a horizontal line 9" up from the bottom. Pin the 1" strip you cut in step 1 along that line, leaving a 1" space between the ends. Trim off the excess fabric.

7 Sew two parallel running stitch seams along the pinned area, each ¼" from the top and bottom edges of the strip, to create a drawstring casing. Remove the pins.

8 Attach a safety pin to one end of the drawstring you made in step 1 and thread it through the casing. Remove the safety pin and even out the drawstring ends.

9 Slide your favorite bottle into the bag, bottom first. Gather the ends around the neck of the bottle and tie them in a bow! After you've gifted it, encourage your friend to pass the cozy along the next time she brings wine to someone else's house.

variations

■ *The stockings were made from a T-shirt with care, with hopes that old tee could get some more wear . . .* Make a stocking-shaped cozy around the holidays (or just make a stocking—who needs to put wine in it? Hang it by the fire and perhaps Santa will fill 'er up).

■ You can also use this cover-up as a decorative cozy for a clear vase—so you don't have to look at the decomposing flower stems! Follow the same steps, paying attention to the dimensions of your new "model."

■ Simplify, simplify by stopping at step 5 and tying the strip around the neck (no casing needed).

Generation T

33 **coast to coasters**
(drink coasters)

Cheers! . . . Salud! . . . Prost! . . .
Bud'mo! . . . L'chaim! . . . Toasts
warm the heart and bring people
together in mirth and goodwill. Using a
shirt with either a flashy design or a fun
expression, make a set of six coasters to
support your drinks after the toast. The
more friends you have over, the more
fun you can have rearranging coasters
to make abstract images or absurdist
statements. (These
coasters serve double
duty, as a quick mop
for spilled drinks.)

LEVEL 3

---
ingredients *(makes six coasters)*

- **1 T-shirt (L or XL)**
- **scissors**
- **chalk marker**
- **ruler**
- **pins**
- **needle**
- **thread**

1 Choose a T-shirt with a bold graphic or pattern that would make a good matching set. Pin together the front and back layers to prevent shifting of the fabric.

2 Measure and mark six 3½" squares clustered together. (If you don't trust yourself with a ruler, make a 3½" square paper or cardboard pattern first and trace around it onto the top layer.) Cut through both layers around each square, keeping the two pieces sandwiched together.

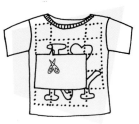

3 Mark nine more plain squares onto the rest of the shirt, cutting through both layers (to use as padding). You should have a total of 30 squares.

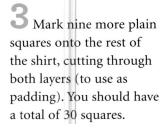

4 Layer five squares together, with the patterned piece on top and right side out. Pin them in place. Use a running stitch to sew around the perimeter of each square, leaving a ¼" seam allowance.

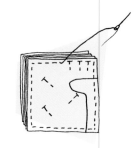

5 Use a running stitch to add decorative interest around letters or patterns on the fabric. Remove the pins.

6 Lay the coasters out for your next soiree (see how they fit together like a puzzle?). Or bundle them together (tie with a strip of T-shirt!) as an apartment-warming gift for a friend.

34 dream weaver
(welcome mat) **NO SEW**

I f you want your guests to wipe their feet, but feel that people your age don't actually *buy* welcome mats, weave your own. The process of making this project is really fun in its own right and can be the perfect bonding experience for new roommates who've just moved in together. Each of you can contribute a shirt, so the final result is the blending of your aesthetics and your pasts into something new.

LEVEL 2

ingredients

- 3–4 T-shirts
- scissors
- tape (optional)
- 1 ladder-back chair (with bottom rungs)
- pencil or pen

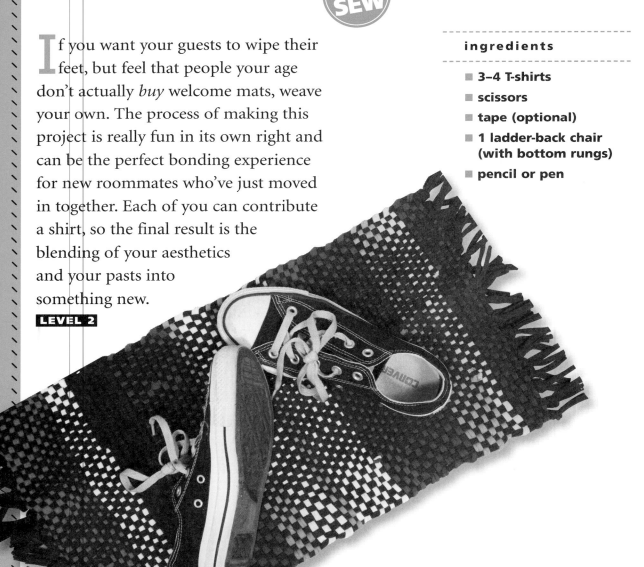

1 Lay one T-shirt flat and cut off the bottom hem. Then cut a 1"-wide coil off the bottom, spiraling off as long a strip as possible. Do the same on the remaining T-shirts. Stretch them out as cords.

2 Select two cords to be used as the warp. Tape or tie one end of one cord to the top ladder rung of the back of the chair (your loom). Wrap the other end down, around the bottom rung (below the seat), and back up to the top. Continue wrapping it down and up, creating a vertical webbing of T-shirt cord. Repeat with the second cord, making sure you end on an even number. Trim and tape the end to the bottom rung.

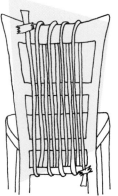

3 Attach (tie or tape) the end of a remaining cord to a pen or pencil (this will be your "shuttle"). Wind excess fabric around the implement for ease.

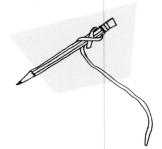

4 Start at one side, about 2" up from the bottom of the warp, thread the shuttle (and cord) over the first strip, under the second, over the third, and so on.

5 When you reach the end, gently wrap it around the last strip and send it back in the opposite direction, reversing the motion of the first row so it's under-over.

continued ▶

6 When you complete row 2, send the shuttle back in the same over-under pattern you created in the first row for row 3. Continue to weave the cord(s) up the back of the chair until you are within 2" of the top. Gently push down on the weft as you go, making sure to keep the weaving tight.

7 Weave the end about halfway through the last row and cut it.

8 Starting at the bottom, snip through the first two warp strings. Tie the ends together in a double knot. Snip through the third and fourth strings, tying those ends together in a double knot. Continue snipping and tying until the bottom of the weaving is detached from the chair.

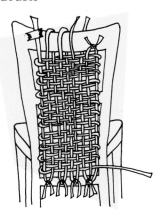

variation

■ It takes some dedication and patience, but you can string up a whole door as your warp to make a longer runner for your table or hallway.

9 Remove any remaining bits of tape. Repeat step 8 on the top of the chair, tying the ends one pair at a time. The last snip will remove the mat from the chair so you can place it appropriately at the front door (to your apartment, room, house . . .).

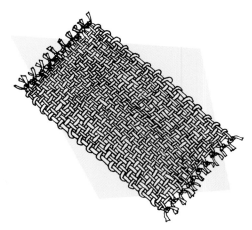

35 final countdown
(pocketed countdown calendar)

This is the perfect project for all those T-shirts with a breast pocket. Count down to your birthday, anniversary, Christmas or Hanukkah, or the due date of your baby (or dissertation defense) with a hanging calendar on which each pocket holds a small gift. Choosing pockets of various shapes, sizes, colors, and patterns make for a brighter, more festive display. You could even throw in an oversize sweatshirt or denim pocket for good measure. *Note:* Even though the recipe calls for pocketed T-shirts, you can just as easily cut a pocket shape from the sleeve of a favorite T-shirt and use that!

LEVEL 3

---

ingredients

- **1 T-shirt (L or XL)**
- **T-shirt pockets**
- **seam ripper**
- **scissors**
- **straight pins**
- **needle**
- **thread**
- **iron-on numbers**
- **iron**

---

1 Collect all of your pocketed T-shirts and use a seam ripper to separate each pocket from its shirt and remove its threads. Stack them and set them aside.

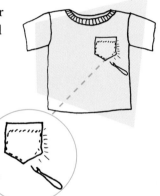

2 Spread the T-shirt flat and cut horizontally across the torso just below the arm to create a large loop. Cut off a 1" strip from the top of the loop and set aside.

3 Cut vertically through the loop and open up the fabric to create a rectangular banner with the T-shirt hem on top.

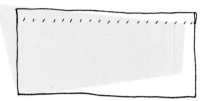

4 Lay the banner flat with the right side facing up. Arrange the pockets you collected in step 1 on top of it (five or ten pockets for a birthday, eight for Hanukkah, and so on). Pin them in place and use a running stitch to sew around the sides and bottom (i.e., along the edges where they were attached to your T-shirts). Remove the pins.

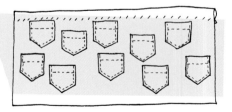

5 Arrange iron-on numbers on the outside of each pocket to indicate an order and press with a hot iron. *Optional:* Personalize the banner with the name of the guest of honor, a holiday theme, or a more generic "Countdown!" or "Party on!" with iron-on or cut-out and stitched letters.

6 Attach a safety pin to one end of the strip you made in step 2 and thread it through the casing—the hem of the T-shirt—to help hang the pocketed banner on the wall.

7 Before a special occasion, fill up each pocket with candies, gift cards (the bookstore, iTunes!), costume jewelry, handmade coupons (a free ice-cream cone, a complimentary back rub), and other sweet somethings. Now the countdown can begin!

variation

■ For a party, slip a different favor into each pocket. Each guest pulls a number (then matches it with a pocket on the banner) and retrieves a surprise party favor!

Generation T

36 running with scissors (table/desk runner)

The Dude's rug really tied the room together—but you don't even have space in your place for a rug! Your apartment's so small, the kitchen table doubles as your desk, and the bed sticks out of the closet. But that's okay. This simple decoration will bring a great amount of character to your snug abode. And, it's reversible, so that your "desk" can wear it one way while your "table" wears it the other.

LEVEL 3

ingredients

- 4 T-shirts (L or XL)
- chalk marker
- scissors
- straight pins
- needle
- thread

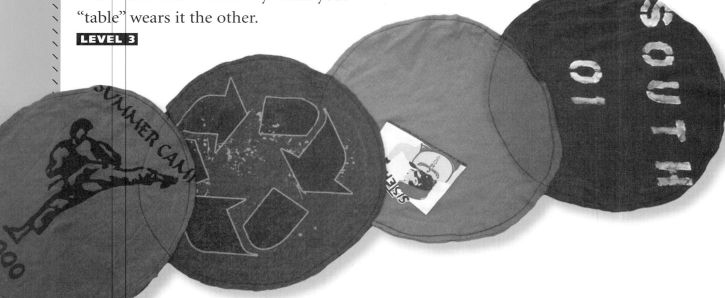

1 Lay the T-shirts flat and draw a 14"-diameter circle onto each of them. (Use a large mixing bowl as a pattern if needed.) Cut around the circles through both layers, keeping the fronts and backs paired together.

2 Sew a running stitch around the circumference of one pair of circles, leaving a ¼" seam allowance.

3 Insert the sewn disc between the layers of another pair of circles so that the layers overlap about a third of the way across the other. (This should look a little like a Venn diagram.) Pin it in place and sew a running stitch around the circumference of the second pair of circles, stitching through all four layers of circles when they overlap.

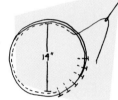

4 Overlap a third pair with the second. Pin and sew. Then add a fourth pair overlapping the third, and repeat. *Note:* Cut and add more discs for a longer runner.

5 Remove all pins and spread your championship runner over the center of a table or desk. Flip it over when it's dirty and you've earned yourself another few weeks before a visit to the Laundromat.

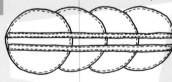

variations

■ Decorate the circles by stitching a pair of racing stripes down the middle. (Doesn't every runner need proper racing stripes?) Or better yet, sew on parallel strips of fabric down the center of the circles.

■ Make rectangular or diamond shapes to layer instead of circles.

37 major sleevage
(laptop sleeve)

If you're like me, you sometimes spend more hours with your friendly laptop than you do with your actual friends. Sure, the laptop's a little bland, but that doesn't mean it's a dull device. (Hey, it might even have voice-activated software—see, there, it talks to you . . . sort of.) Take one of your livelier tees and transform it into a padded laptop sleeve that'll make your desktop computer wish it could go on a field trip, too.

LEVEL 4

ingredients

- **2 T-shirts (XL)**
- **ruler**
- **chalk marker**
- **scissors**
- **straight pins**
- **needle**
- **thread**

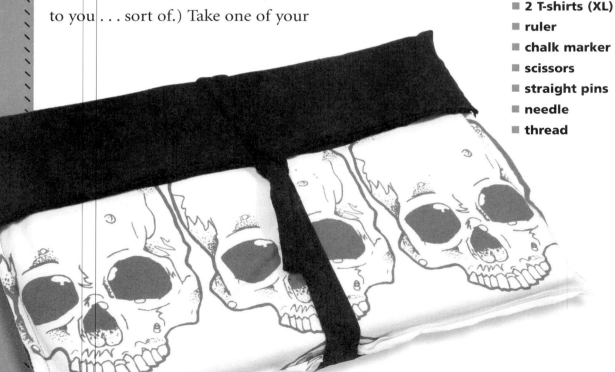

1 Measure the length and width of your laptop. Add 1½" to the length to get x" and 1" to the width for y".

2 Lay one T-shirt flat and mark two x" by y" rectangles across the front. Cut along the marks through both layers.

3 Mark a third x" by y" rectangle across the top of the second T-shirt. Below it, mark fourth and fifth rectangles that each measure 5" by x". Cut along all marks through both layers.

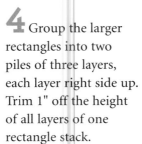

4 Group the larger rectangles into two piles of three layers, each layer right side up. Trim 1" off the height of all layers of one rectangle stack.

5 Pin along each of the top edges, right sides out, and sew a running stitch about ¼" from the edge. Remove the pins.

6 Press the two rectangle packets together, right sides facing out, lining up the open edges (the stitched edges will be staggered slightly), and pin around the three unsewn edges. Sew a running stitch along the pinned edges, leaving a ¼" seam allowance. Remove the pins and set aside the envelope you've created.

7 Take three of the smaller rectangles (you can save the fourth rectangle for another project) and place one on top of the other, right sides up. Pin along the bottom and the two side edges.

continued ▶

GREEN PARTY

If you're not feeling particularly creative but have a hankering to repurpose some old tees, cut unwanted items into cloth napkins and household rags! Americans throw away almost 3.5 million nonrecyclable tons of tissue, napkins, and paper towels a year—using recycled cloth packs a double whammy against your carbon footprint.

8 Cut a 2"-wide loop from the bottom of the second T-shirt. Cut through the loop to make a strip.

9 Center the end of the strip along the bottom pinned edge of the flap and insert it 2" between the top and second layers. Pin it in place and sew a running stitch along the entire pinned bottom edge and the two side edges, leaving a ¼" seam allowance. Remove the pins.

10 Place the unsewn top edge of the flap against the unsewn top back edge (the higher one) of the envelope. Pin and sew a running stitch along the shared top edge (through six layers), leaving a ¼" seam allowance.

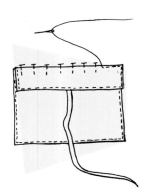

11 Remove the pins, slide your laptop inside, and wrap the strip once around before tucking it under itself to secure it.

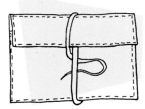

38 clean machine
(laundry sack)

In the back of your drawer or closet, you probably have a few tees that are stained, paint-splattered or bleached beyond repair. You could don them and try to start a new trend, but instead, take your tees and let them rejoin your wardrobe in a different format. By transforming them into this oversize laundry bag, you're letting those old, stained shirts hold and protect their unstained brothers and sisters. . . .

LEVEL 4

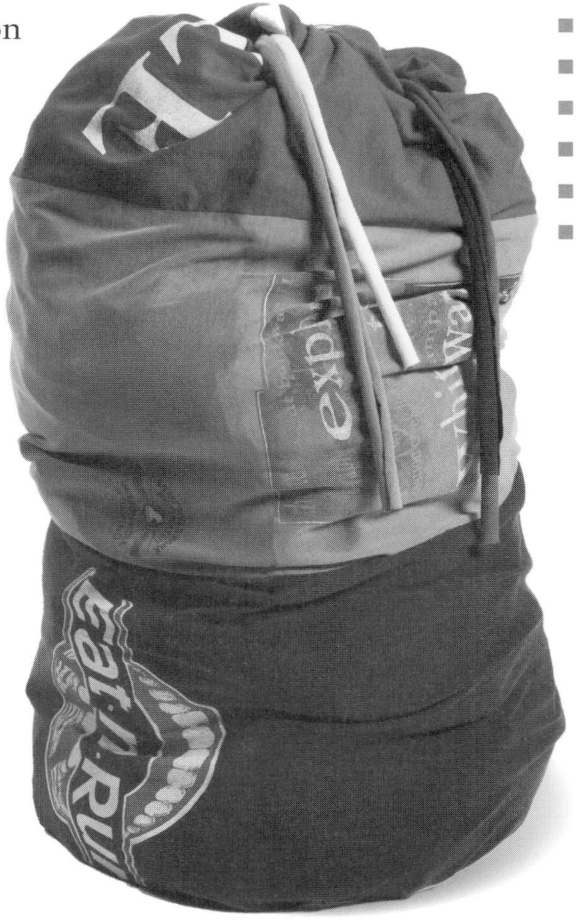

ingredients

- **4 T-shirts (L or XL)**
- **ruler**
- **chalk marker**
- **scissors**
- **straight pins**
- **needle**
- **thread**

beyond fashion

1 Turn one T-shirt inside out, lay it flat, and mark and cut a 14" by 24" rectangle through both layers.

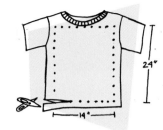

2 Keeping the rectangles layered (right sides together), pin along one short edge. Leaving a ½" seam allowance, sew a tight running stitch along the pinned edge.

3 Repeat steps 1 and 2 on two more T-shirts. Remove the pins and unfold the three extra-wide rectangles.

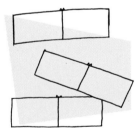

4 Place two of the rectangles right sides together and pin them along one of the long edges.

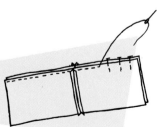

5 Attach the third rectangle along one of the long edges, as you did in step 4, and sew a running stitch along all pinned edges. Remove the pins.

6 Fold the large rectangle in half, right side in, so that the bands run horizontally, and pin along the open edge. Leaving a ½" seam allowance, sew a running stitch along the pinned edge. Remove the pins.

7 Measure, mark, and cut a circle with a 15" diameter from the front of the fourth T-shirt.

8 Pin the circle, right side facing in, to the inside edge of the tube. Leaving a ½" seam allowance, sew a running stitch along the pinned edges around the bottom of the sack. Remove the pins.

9 With the sack still inside out, fold down the top edge of the sack about 2" and pin. Sew two rows of parallel running stitches around the edge at ½" and ¾", as shown in illustration for step 8.

10 Cut out the underarm seam from four T-shirt sleeves and lay the pieces flat. Measure and cut a 2"-wide strip from the longest part of each of the sleeves.

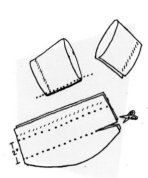

11 Turn the sack right side out. Evenly space the four strips vertically, right sides out, around the outside perimeter of the sack, so that each extends 1" below the casing stitching. Pin each strip in place.

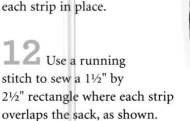

12 Use a running stitch to sew a 1½" by 2½" rectangle where each strip overlaps the sack, as shown.

13 After attaching all four strips, remove the pins, fill the bag with dirty laundry, and tie opposite strips to cinch the top.

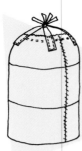

variations

■ Add a long strap (or two) from T-shirt scraps in case you have to drag (okay, carry) the bag farther than the coin-operated machine in the basement.

■ Sew an oversize pocket onto one side to carry detergent, quarters, or that extra sock that is just one too many to squeeze in at the top.

■ Mix and match the rectangles in steps 2 and 3 for a patchwork instead of banded look.

■ For a smaller version, use just two T-shirts to make two bands of fabric for the body of the bag (three T-shirts total when you add the bottom).

Generation T

GREEN TEE

39 legalize pot holders
(woven pot holders)

NO SEW

So you once spilled some gravy or dribbled some chocolate ice cream down the front of your favorite shirt, and now you won't be caught dead in it. It's too nice to throw away, and why relegate it to the pajama drawer? Let that shirt eat again! This time it's coming into contact with food on purpose—as adorable woven pot holders.

LEVEL 2

---
ingredients

- 8" by 8" scrap cardboard
- pen or pencil
- 13 to 15 scrap T-shirt strips (½" by 16") in bright, complementary colors)
- scissors

1 Cut out a ¾" square from each corner of the cardboard. Then mark and cut an even number of ¾"-long slits about ½" apart into each side.

2 Make sure that each of the T-shirt strips is 16" long, loop them, and tie the ends in an overhand knot.

3 Loop the knot-end around the first notch onto one side of the cardboard loom. Loop the loop-end around the first notch opposite it. Add the second loop next to the first, and the third next to the fourth, until the two sides are filled.

4 Attach the next loop to the first notch on one of the adjacent sides and thread it horizontally across the first set of loops, weaving it over and under the perpendicular loops. When you reach the opposite side, loop the end around the corresponding first notch. *Note:* When weaving, go over and under the entire loop (both strands).

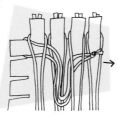

5 Attach the next loop to the second notch. This time you'll be weaving it *under* then *over* the perpendicular loops to the other side.

6 Continue to alternate the path of each subsequent loop until all notches are filled.

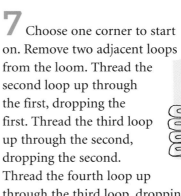

7 Choose one corner to start on. Remove two adjacent loops from the loom. Thread the second loop up through the first, dropping the first. Thread the third loop up through the second, dropping the second. Thread the fourth loop up through the third loop, dropping the third, and so on, around the entire perimeter. (Because of the placement of the knots, two sides will have fringe.)

8 Pull the last loop tight and knot it if necessary. Gently stretch the sides of the pot holder to even it out, and you're done!

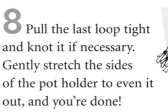

40 up in my grill
(grill mitt)

Sure, it's a mark of strength to work the grill with your bare hands and risk searing your flesh. But it's also hair-brained. Here's an alternative: Take the toughest T-shirts you own (one has your gym's logo, the other has a motorcycle or your favorite beverage or sports team), and transform them into quilted grill mitts. They'll keep your hands safe in a style that says, "Well done."

LEVEL 5

---

ingredients *(makes one mitt)*

- **2 T-shirts (100% cotton)**
- **pencil**
- **paper**
- **ruler**
- **straight pins**
- **½ yard batting**
- **scissors**
- **needle**
- **thread**

1 First, make a paper pattern by tracing around your hand (with your thumb at a 45-degree angle). Leave a 1" allowance, as shown. At the base of the palm, widen the tracing to 2" and extend it 7" down. Cut around the tracing.

2 Lay one T-shirt flat and fold it in half, bringing the bottom hem up to the neckband in the back. Lay the pattern on an angle on the front of the T-shirt and pin it through all four layers. Cut around the pattern. Repeat on the second T-shirt, *reversing the pattern* so that the thumb points in a different direction.

3 Fold a portion of the batting in half and pin the pattern onto it through both layers. Cut around the pattern and remove it.

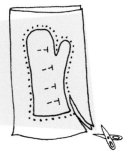

4 Sandwich a layer of batting between the layers of the T-shirt (there should be two layers of T-shirt, one layer of batting, two layers of T-shirt) to create one half of the mitt. Pin in place. Take that mitt half and sew a series of running stitches in crisscross diagonal lines, through all layers, to create a quilted look, as shown. Repeat on the other piece of the mitt.

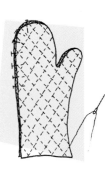

5 Lay the two pieces (sides) of the mitt right sides together (meaning the pieces with the logos are facing). Making sure to go through all layers, sew a tight whipstitch or a running stitch around the perimeter of the mitt, leaving the bottom edge open.

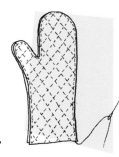

6 Carefully turn the mitt right side out (the thumb will be a little tricky—use a pencil to persuade it if necessary).

7 Measure the circumference of the bottom opening and add 1" to get x". Cut a 2" by x" strip of fabric from one of the T-shirt remnants. Line up one long edge around the opening and pin, right sides together. Sew a running stitch about ½" from the edge, being sure to "catch" all layers. Remove the pins.

8 Fold the edge down ½" and then wrap it tightly around the raw edge to the inside. Pin and carefully sew a whipstitch securing the edging in place. Remove the pins. *Optional:* Repeat steps 2–8 to make a second mitt.

9 The burgers are ready to be flipped and nothing's too hot to handle!

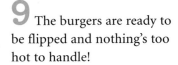

41 central cooking
(ruffled apron)

Cooking is a fun and good way to make sure you eat the food you like. It can also be a great way to stain or ruin some of your favorite clothes from splattering grease or sauce. This apron, requiring three tees to make, is an easy preventative measure. You can match up favorite colors, create abstract designs, or pair up two of your favorite bands for an apron that will have you flambéing in style. *Note:* If you want a pocket on your apron, use a pocketed shirt.

LEVEL 5

ingredients

- **3 T-shirts (M–XL)**
- **ruler**
- **chalk marker**
- **scissors**
- **straight pins**
- **needle**
- **thread**

1 Choose the T-shirt you want as the front of the apron and lay it flat. Cut off the bottom hem. Mark and cut, through both layers, a rectangle that extends about 14" to 16" below the neckband and as wide as the sleeves allow.

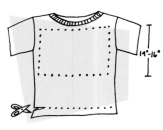

2 Mark and cut generous arcs from the two bottom corners of the rectangle, as shown. These two layers become the apron panel.

3 Lay the second T-shirt flat and cut off the bottom hem. Cut three 4"-wide loops from the bottom of the shirt.

4 Cut through the loops (to create long strips) and lay two of them on top of each other, right sides facing. Pin along one of the shorter edges and sew with a running stitch, leaving a ½" seam allowance.

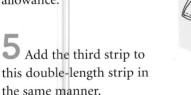

5 Add the third strip to this double-length strip in the same manner.

6 Once the three strips are attached (the resulting strip should be about 96" long), fold the strip in half lengthwise, wrong sides in, and pin. Use a basting stitch to loosely sew along the pinned edge.

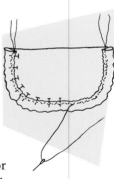

7 Gather the fabric evenly over the thread and pin it to the underside of the apron panel. It should run along the perimeter of three sides (not the straight edge at the top).

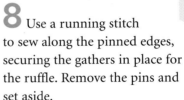

8 Use a running stitch to sew along the pinned edges, securing the gathers in place for the ruffle. Remove the pins and set aside.

continued ▶

9 Lay the third T-shirt flat and cut off the bottom hem. Then cut two 6"-wide loops from the bottom of the shirt.

10 Cut through both loops (to create two wide strips) and lay them on top of each other, right sides facing. Pin along one of the shorter edges and sew with a running stitch, leaving a ½" seam allowance.

11 Unfold and lay the long strip wrong side up. Fold down the edges of the long sides ½" and pin.

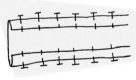

12 Fold the strip in half lengthwise and reposition the pins so that the folded edges are now pinned together.

variation

■ Add two (or more!) pockets onto the front of your apron to stash cooking tools or a dish towel.

13 Measure the straight edge of the apron panel and center and mark that length along the strip. Insert the top of the apron about 1" between the layers of the strip, aligning each corner at the marks. This will mean taking out the pins to insert the apron and repositioning them again. (Remember to keep the waistband edges tucked under.) Use a running stitch to sew along the entire length of the pinned edge, making sure to catch the apron panel between the edges of the waistband.

14 Tuck the raw edges of the waistband in at the ends and stitch them closed. Remove all the pins, tie it around your waist, and cook up something delicious!

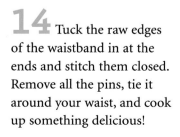

42 plastic surgery
(grocery tote)

GREEN TEE

Paper or plastic? How about neither! Both bags produce environmental waste and take months (or in the case of plastic, hundreds of years) to break down in landfills. Instead, choose cotton. Pick one of your most righteous shirts—one that reflects your athletic prowess, musical tastes, or political agenda, then turn it into a tote that's shaped just like a plastic supermarket bag (to help you with the emotional transition). Make a difference, "in style," as you load up on berries and broccoli at the local green market.

LEVEL 4

ingredients

- **1 T-shirt (L or XL)**
- **chalk marker**
- **scissors**
- **needle**
- **thread**

1 Lay the T-shirt flat. Cut off the sleeves just inside the seams, cut off the hem, and cut out the neckband. *Note:* You can use an already existing plastic bag as a pattern, but in case you already eliminated all plastic from the premises . . .

2 Mark about 7½" down the front of the shirt from each side of the neck hole. Then mark about 6½" down from the center of the neck hole.

3 Draw a wavy line connecting the sides of the neckband with each of the three marks(it should look like a rounded letter "W"). Cut along the line through both layers of fabric.

4 Mark 4" along the "shoulder" from each side of the neck hole. Draw a curved line from each mark, connecting it to the sleeve bottom. Cut along each line to remove excess fabric.

5 Mark 4" from each corner along the bottom on both sides (front and back).

It's easy being green!

6 Push the left corner of the T-shirt between the front and back layers of the shirt, toward the center, making a kind of pleat, until the marks on the front and back are aligned as shown. The result is a small accordion fold. Pin in place.

7 Repeat on the right side. Pin the front and back sides together along the entire bottom edge.

8 Sew two parallel rows of running stitches along the bottom edge at ¼" and ½" for a reinforced edge. Remove the pins.

9 Fold the 4"-wide handles in half lengthwise, wrong sides in, making them just 2" wide. Sew a running stitch along the shoulder seam, securing the fold and reinforcing the handles.

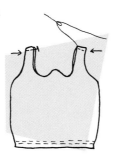

10 What are you waiting for? Go shopping already! *Optional:* Make two small arced cuts at the "peak" in the "W" to mimic the tabs on plastic bags.

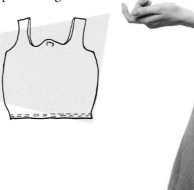

variations

■ If you have a spare T-shirt, insert another identical layer inside (attaching the layers at the seams) to make the tote "double-bagged" for reinforcement—those canned beans get heavy!

■ Make a more breathable produce sack by cutting alternating slits to create mesh.

43 tree hugger GREEN TEE
(plant/tree skirt)

Whether you have a Douglas fir, a cactus, or a Charlie Brown–size holiday tree, liven up the living room by making a sassy skirt for your plant—hey, you could even make a matching one for yourself! A T-shirt plant skirt is the kind of unexpected home décor that visitors will admire (and probably copy).

LEVEL 3

1 Lay the T-shirts flat and cut off the hems. Remove the stitching and cut through the strips to make long cords. Set aside. Then mark and cut a 16" to 20" square through both layers of each T-shirt.

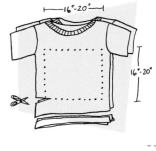

2 Layer the squares together and mark and cut a wide arc between two opposite corners, rounding off one of the corners to make a quarter-circle.

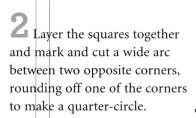

---

ingredients

- 2 T-shirts
- ruler
- chalk marker
- scissors
- measuring tape
- straight pins
- needle
- thread
- safety pin

3 Measure the diameter across the top of your flower pot or tree stand. Divide by 2 to get x". Mark x" along each edge of the uncut corners, as shown. Connect the marks and cut an arc parallel to the one in step 2.

4 Separate the four wedges and arrange them right side down in a large circle, alternating colors.

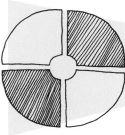

5 Pin the wedges along their shared edges, right sides together. Sew only three pinned edges together using a whipstitch.

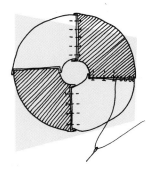

6 Remove pins and turn right side out. Mark and snip an even number of holes 1" from the inner edge and about 1" to 1½" apart.

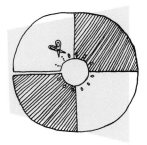

7 Pin the ends of the cords with a safety pin. Thread the pin down through one of the holes along the open edge, up through the next, and so on. Slip the skirt around the flower pot, above the lip, and tighten the cords and tie.

variation

■ Make a circle skirt for yourself! Determine your own radius ($r = c/2\pi$). You'll need to cut a larger arc out of the corner of the wedge in step 3 to fit your waist.

GREEN TEE

44 plant parenthood
(planter hanger) NO SEW

C hannel '70s kitsch with this groovy braided planter hanger. Recycle your oldest, and dare-I-say *ugliest* T-shirts (I have an ancient orange-brown tee that's just crying out to be turned into a planter hanger) to make a fun and functional home for the green leaves in your life. All you need is a shag rug and a couple of velour beanbag chairs to complete the room.

LEVEL 4

----
ingredients

- **2 T-shirts**
- **scissors**
- **chalk marker**
- **8 safety pins**

1 Lay the T-shirt flat and cut off the bottom hem. Then cut nine 1½" by 78" strips from a coil beginning at the bottom of the tee.

2 Stretch out the strips, then cluster them together and fold them in half. Tie a tight overhand knot about 3" down from the fold to create a loop.

3 Separate the eighteen cords into six groups of three. Braid each group into a 24"-long braid. Tie the ends of the six braids together in an overhand knot at the bottom.

4 Rest your planter between the six braids above the bottom knot. On one of the braids make two marks: one about 1" down from the lip of the planter and a second about two-thirds of the way down its side. Remove the planter.

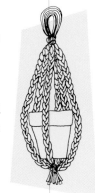

5 Cut two sets of three 1" by 26" strips from the remaining T-shirt. Attach a safety pin 6" from the end of each set, connecting the three strands. Attach a safety pin through the opposite ends.

GREEN PARTY

Did you know that the amount of energy needed to make one new 3-oz. cotton T-shirt is enough to power a standard lightbulb for four days? Additionally, about 3 pounds of chemicals are needed to grow enough cotton for that one little tee. So remember, if you buy nonorganic fibers, recycle, reuse, or repurpose them to make the most of all the energy spent on their creation.

6 Select one set and thread the safety-pinned ends *through* the vertical braid at the lower mark you made. Pull all three strips all the way through, stopping when the other safety pin is pressed against the vertical braid. (Let the 6" ends dangle.)

7 Braid the strips horizontally for a few inches until you reach the next vertical braid. Thread at least one strand *through* the vertical braid to join the others at the opposite side. Continue braiding a few inches (matching the length to the first segment), and then thread at least one strand *through* the next vertical braid.

8 Continue in this manner until you reach the first braid again. Thread the strands *through* the braid individually, then tie each active strand to a dangling strand from the other end. Remove all safety pins and trim the ends so they are even (still dangling).

9 Repeat steps 6 through 9 with the second set of strips, except start at the higher mark and at the vertical braid opposite the first. Insert your planter and hang it from the loop.

45 **royal flush** (toilet lid cover)

Y ou don't have to visit your Aunt Betty to indulge in '70s kitsch anymore. Now you can spruce up your own bathroom with a styling throne (so you can sit in comfort while you clip your nails or keep your roommate company while she dyes her hair in the tub). Go ahead—cover the toilet lid in avocado or burnt orange . . . and hum a tune about a family named Brady. . . .

LEVEL 4

ingredients

- **1 or 2 T-shirts (L or XL)**
- **piece of newsprint paper**
- **pencil**
- **chalk marker**
- **scissors**
- **straight pins**
- **needle**
- **thread**
- **safety pin**

1 Trace your toilet lid onto a piece of newsprint paper. Cut it out to use as a pattern.

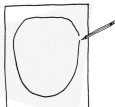

2 Lay the T-shirt flat and cut off the bottom hem. Remove the stitching from the hem and set aside (this is your drawstring). Pin the pattern to the front of the T-shirt. Measure and mark 2½" around the outer edge of the pattern with chalk. Remove the pattern.

3 Cut around the chalk line through only the front layer of the T-shirt. You should have a roughly oval shape.

4 Lay the oval flat, right side down. Fold the edge about 1" onto itself, gently puckering the fabric as necessary to fit, and pin.

5 Sew a running stitch along the pinned edge, about ¾" from the fold, creating a drawstring casing. Remove the pins and flip it over. *Optional:* Stop here and you have a cute toilet lid cover sans shag.

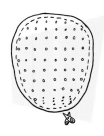

6 Starting 1½" in from the edges, mark and then snip horizontal and vertical rows of small holes about ¾" to 1" apart across the oval, stopping at the casing edge.

7 Cut 1"-wide strips across the back of the T-shirt (or from a second T-shirt to introduce another color).

(back)

🌱 GREEN PARTY

Recycling clothing isn't just for DIY diehards: Goonj, founded in 1998 to high acclaim from humanitarian and environmental groups worldwide, is a sustainable initiative to collect used clothing and textiles from all corners of India to then recycle into materials for clothing, sanitary products, and other basic amenities for people living in poverty-stricken communities across the country.

8 Attach a safety pin to one end of a long strip and thread it down through the first hole, leaving a 2" tail. Pull it up through the second hole. Then thread it back down through the second hole (the same hole you just pulled it through), leaving a 2" to 3" loop. Pull it up through the third hole, thread it back down through the same hole (leaving a loop). Then go up through the fourth hole, and so on.

9 Snip through the loops to create shag fringe.

10 Turn the cover over. Sew a running stitch between the rows, as shown, securing each strip on the underside.

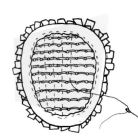

variation

■ Make a matching bath mat following the steps for the Cruise Control car floor mats (page 226).

11 Snip two small holes centered 1½" apart along the top back of the casing. Attach a safety pin to one end of the drawstring you cut in step 2 and thread it through one of the holes. Thread it around the perimeter of the casing and out through the second hole.

12 Lay the cover over the toilet lid, pull the drawstring ends to gather the fabric around the lid edge, and tie the ends in a bow to secure. Trim the ends if necessary.

Chapter 4

Kid Rock

Enrolling in Tee-School

Introducing the next generation to T-shirt fashion, here are 20 projects, including superhero capes, stuffed animals, blankies, and other mini tees for your mini me's.

Spread the DIY love in miniature! While many of the designs throughout the book can be made to fit smaller sizes, the designs that follow are specifically tailored with little ones in mind (whether they're here or on the way). In many ways, onesies are a baby's starter kit for a T-shirt-filled life ahead. T-shirts are like security blankets. In this chapter, some T-shirt scraps actually *are* security blankets (see page 178). Soft and loved, with bonding and parental scent added to the mix. How can you ever outgrow the softness?

Use the overflow of T-shirts in your dresser as an opportunity to make an unexpected gift for a friend who's expecting. Sure, new moms need diapers, bottles, and the newest SUS (sport utility stroller), but that's what gift registries and grandparents are for. Instead, make it personal—enough with the pink and blue, give her something as one-of-a-kind as she is!

Kid Rock is filled with meaningful gifts for baby, baby's mama, and don't forget big sis or big bro. Fashion a romper dress from a concert T-shirt for the new mom's kid; it'll remind Mom that she's still a rock star. Create a quilt made from T-shirt squares brought by each guest to the baby shower—you can actually tie the pieces together during the celebration.

And the projects don't end when the baby starts to walk and talk. Toddlers are such natural little fashionistas. The rules of costumes only on Halloween and dress-up only for dance recitals haven't set in yet, keeping kids open to every odd fashion possibility—a real advantage in the indie fashion world. Tutu to the grocery store? Dalmatian costume to playgroup? Yeah! Let them dress and accessorize themselves, so they learn that getting dressed in the morning can be its own little party. And you just might learn something from their "untrained" eyes, too. I have a friend who makes beaded jewelry and many of her best designs are inspired by trips to the bead store with her young nephew—he points out colors,

shapes, and sizes that he likes and they go home and craft together.

They may not appreciate it yet, but if you cultivate a crafting culture early, kids can grow up around it. If it's a rainy day and you're sick of playing dominoes and a little weary of watercolors, get out those shirts they've outgrown, some scissors, and go to town. Trust me, they'll enjoy the destructive element (they're the ones who always want to cut off Barbie's hair), and you can show them how to put things back together, too. Not a bad life lesson. The superhero cape in this chapter is a great activity for a child's next birthday party, a special "I'm a big sister" induction ceremony, or for a counselor to do with her bunk at camp.

Note: You most definitely do *not* have to be a mama to enjoy the projects in this chapter; I love making things for my niece. The list is always growing, but hats, blankets, barrettes (now that she has hair), fancy flip-flops (now that she's walking) are just starters. Every stage invites more project ideas. Plus, they grow out of things so fast, you can stay busy just keeping up!

What's on Your Playlist:

"Isn't She Lovely"
—Stevie Wonder

"Beautiful Boy"
—John Lennon

"We Are Family"
—Sister Sledge

"Son of a Preacher Man"
—Dusty Springfield

"Stay Up Late"
—Talking Heads

"Coal Miner's Daughter"
—Loretta Lynn

"Mommy's Little Monster"
—Social Distortion

"The Kids Are Alright"
—The Who

"Kids Don't Follow"
—The Replacements

"We're a Happy Family"
—Ramones

46 top knot
(baby hat)

This supersoft hat (with external seams that won't irritate the skin) will keep a newborn's tiny little head warm and cozy, after her—let's be honest—abrupt entry into this cold, cruel world. This hat is conveniently quick and easy to make either for your own kid or as a gift for a friend who's expecting, which is good since she'll be outgrowing it every week or so. Stay warm, little lady.

LEVEL 3

ingredients

- **1 T-shirt or large scrap**
- **measuring tape**
- **chalk marker**
- **scissors**
- **straight pins**
- **needle**
- **thread**

1 Cut off the bottom hem of the T-shirt. Measure the circumference of baby's head and divide by 2 (or get your hands on another hat that you know fits and measure it) to get x". Mark that measurement from one of the corners at a 45-degree angle from the bottom edge of the T-shirt.

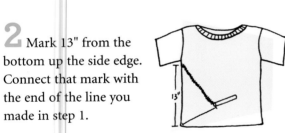

2 Mark 13" from the bottom up the side edge. Connect that mark with the end of the line you made in step 1.

3 Cut along the lines.

4 Pin along the open diagonal edge, right sides out. Sew a running stitch or whipstitch along the pinned edge for an external seam.

5 Remove the pins and tie the tip of the hat in an overhand knot, leaving about 2" at the top. The bottom edge will curl naturally.

variation

■ Supersize the hat to fit *you!*

Generation T

47 **wild thing**
(hooded towel/blanky)

Use your softest T-shirts to make this receiving blanket for your sister's first kid. At bath time, it becomes a hooded towel to keep baby warm and cozy. And as the little rugrat grows and starts tearing around the carpet, his blanky is the perfect costume when he's crowned ruler in the land of the Wild Things!

LEVEL 5

ingredients

- **2 T-shirts (L or XL, in complementary colors)**
- **ruler**
- **chalk marker**
- **scissors**
- **straight pins**
- **needle**
- **thread**

1 Cut a 24" by 15½" rectangle through both layers of each of the two T-shirts.

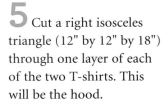

2 Lay two rectangles (the ones you want for the inside of the blanky) right sides together and pin along one of the long edges. Sew along the pinned edge using a running stitch, leaving a ½" seam allowance. Repeat on the remaining two rectangles (the outside).

3 Remove the pins and unfold the fabric panels for two 24" by 30" rectangles. Place the two panels against each other, right sides together, and pin around the perimeter. Use your scissors to round the four corners through both layers.

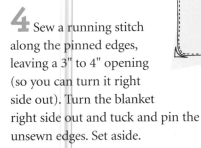

4 Sew a running stitch along the pinned edges, leaving a 3" to 4" opening (so you can turn it right side out). Turn the blanket right side out and tuck and pin the unsewn edges. Set aside.

5 Cut a right isosceles triangle (12" by 12" by 18") through one layer of each of the two T-shirts. This will be the hood.

6 Place the triangles against each other, right sides facing. Pin around the edges and cut through both layers to slightly round the right angle.

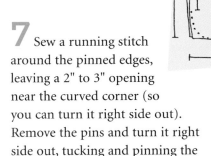

7 Sew a running stitch around the pinned edges, leaving a 2" to 3" opening (near the curved corner (so you can turn it right side out). Remove the pins and turn it right side out, tucking and pinning the unsewn edges.

8 Pin the triangle onto one of the corners of the blanket, making sure that the fabric facing up on the blanket matches the fabric facing down on the hood.

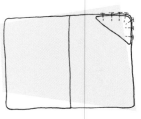

continued ▶

9 To make the ears, cut a sleeve from each of the two T-shirts. Cut two 2¾"-diameter circles through two layers of each.

10 Separate the circles and pair the contrasting colors together, right sides facing. Pin and use a running stitch to sew three-quarters around the perimeter of each.

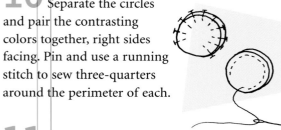

11 Take one circle and fold one side two-thirds of the way to the other side (for an ear shape). Pinch it and insert it between the pinned layers of the triangle hood piece and the rest of the blanket. Pin it in place and repeat with the second circle. The two ears should sit between 3" and 5" from the top corner, as shown.

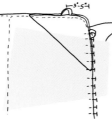

12 Sew along the entire perimeter of the blanket, ¼" from the edge, making sure to sew along the triangle's edge and to catch the ears in the seam as well. Remove the pins and sew a reinforcing running stitch along the seams of the main panel of the blanket.

variations

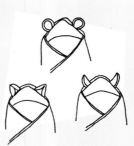

■ For different kinds of ears, try folding the discs different ways—can you make the ears of a bear, a perky mutt, a floppy hound, a mischievous kitten?

■ Though your kid's own smiling face is enough, you can make a monster face by appliquéing an eye or two onto the front of the hood. A set of orange hooded "dog" towels my brother and I roamed around in even had terry cloth tongues flapping over the edge of the hood.

■ To make the towel/blanket warmer or more absorbent, double the recipe, layering two more T-shirt panels to make it extra-thick.

13 Check again that all the pins have been removed and wrap up the little monster!

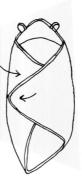

48 playing footsie
(baby booties)

Who needs blue suede shoes or ruby slippers? In these jersey booties, baby's feet will be both cool and hot! Just because Blahnik hasn't yet branched into the baby bootie business doesn't mean you shouldn't. Class up the tyke in your life by cutting into that fancy Supima cotton top (the one with a stain) for a great baby shower gift.

LEVEL 4

ingredients

- **1 T-shirt (or a collection of larger scraps)**
- **ruler**
- **chalk marker**
- **scissors**
- **straight pins**
- **needle**
- **thread**

1 Since it's often difficult to get an accurate tracing of a wriggling baby's foot, use the box, right, to determine the correct dimensions for your booties. Lay the T-shirt flat and, using the measurements for A (0 to 3 months) or B (3 to 6 months) at right, mark two sets of *both* rectangles.

2 Cut out all four rectangles through both layers. *Optional:* The smaller rectangles will be used for the soles of the booties, so if you make a larger pair for a munchkin on the move, mark those rectangles over a T-shirt with a logo to act as a nonslip footpad.

3 Stack the pairs of smaller rectangles and round the corners, making a pill or bean shape. Then split the four layers into two piles for the soles.

The following measurements will work for most 0- to 6-month-olds:

A: 0 to 3 months
Rectangle 1: 4" to 4½" by 2½"
Rectangle 2: 4" by 4¼"

B: 3 to 6 months
Rectangle 1: 5" to 5½" by 2¾"
Rectangle 2: 4¼" by 5"

4 Stack the pairs of larger rectangles and round two corners along *one* of the short edges, as shown. From the center of the opposite edge, draw a straight line about three fifths of the way across the rectangle. Cut along this line, then split the four layers into two piles for the tops of the shoes.

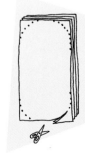

5 Take one top piece (two layers) and fold it in half lengthwise, long sides together and right sides out. Pin and sew a running stitch or whipstitch along the open short side, leaving a ³⁄₁₆" to ¼" seam allowance and making sure to sew through all four layers. Repeat on the other top piece. These are the heels.

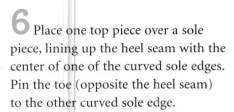

6 Place one top piece over a sole piece, lining up the heel seam with the center of one of the curved sole edges. Pin the toe (opposite the heel seam) to the other curved sole edge.

7 Pin around the rest of the sole, cajoling the top fabric into place, right sides out. Sew a running stitch or whipstitch around the pinned area.

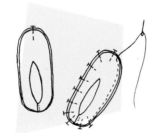

8 Sew a whipstitch around the perimeter of the opening for the foot, attaching the two layers together (*not* sewing it shut!).

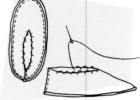

9 Repeat steps 6 through 8 with the remaining pieces to get a matching (or mismatched— your choice) pair!

variations

- If your booties were made from plain fabric and you'd like to dress them up a little, iron on baby's first initial or appliqué a shape onto the toe of each bootie.

- Poke a hole into each side of the foot opening for laces and use ribbon to tie a bow.

- For thicker booties, use four layers of fabric (instead of two) for each panel piece.

49 itty bitty mittie committee

(baby mittens)

These simple mittens are like soft boxing gloves for your little featherweight's tiny fists. A newborn's fingernails can be downright dangerous, so keep him cozy and warm *while* stopping him from scratching himself—and you!

LEVEL 4

ingredients

- **2 T-shirt sleeves (L) (or other equivalent scrap fabric)**
- **ruler**
- **chalk marker**
- **scissors**
- **straight pins**
- **needle**
- **thread**

1 Lay one sleeve flat and mark four 2½" by 2¼" rectangles, as shown. Cut out each rectangle.

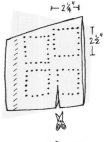

2 Layer all four rectangles together and round two corners along one of the short ends with scissors.

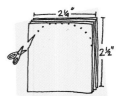

3 Separate the pieces into two pairs. Place the layers of one pair right sides together and pin. Sew a running stitch or whipstitch around the curved edge of the fabric, leaving the short straight edge open. Repeat on the remaining two pieces, remove all pins, and turn the mitten pouches right side out.

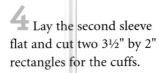

4 Lay the second sleeve flat and cut two 3½" by 2" rectangles for the cuffs.

5 Fold both strips in half lengthwise (long sides together), wrong side in. Then fold both strips in half crosswise (the opposite way) and pin. Sew a running stitch or a whipstitch along the short edges to create a double-thick loop. Remove the pins.

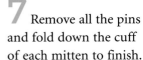

variations

■ If the mittens turn out too plain, you can iron on the little prizefighter's first initial to personalize them.

■ Increase the measurements to make bigger mitts for growing babies.

6 Insert one mitten pouch inside one of the loops, lining up the raw edges, and pin around the opening. Sew a whipstitch around the pinned edge. Repeat with the other pieces to make the second mitten.

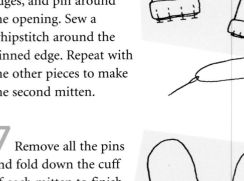

7 Remove all the pins and fold down the cuff of each mitten to finish.

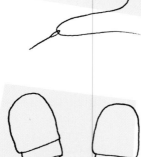

Generation T

50 **too cool for drool**
(burp cloths)

Whether you're babysitting or parenting, there comes a point when your entire day seems to revolve around burping baby—when every nursery rhyme starts sounding like, "Hey Spittle, Spittle; the cat and the fiddle. . . ." Back when I was a lot smaller and had a lot less control over my salivary tendencies, my parents used cloth diapers for me to drool all over—hey, they're very absorbent! But these are different times, and if you have to wear the darn thing on your shoulder all day, it might as well look fashionable. So toss one of these over your shoulder, start bouncing and patting baby's back . . . and it's sort of like you're at the rock show, moshing—*very* gently.

LEVEL 3

ingredients
(makes a set of 4 burp cloths)

- **3 T-shirts (L or XL)**
- **ruler**
- **chalk marker**
- **scissors**
- **straight pins**
- **needle**
- **thread**

1 Lay the T-shirts flat and mark two 10" by 16" rectangles across the front of all three T-shirts. Cut out the rectangles through both layers. You should have twelve rectangles (four per T-shirt).

2 Layer the rectangles into groups of three, with the top and bottom layers facing right side out. Pin each of the four "sandwiches" together.

3 With your scissors, round off the corners of each set of rectangles. Then mark the midpoint of the 16" sides. At the midpoint, mark about 1½" in from each side. Draw concave arcs into each side so that the peak of the arcs pass through the mark to make a figure-eight shape, as shown.

4 Cut along the marked edges, through all layers, with each of the sets.

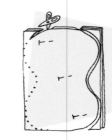

5 Pin around the edges of each set and draw two parallel lines 4" apart, centered along the length of the sets. Sew a running stitch around the pinned perimeter of each set (going through all three layers). Then sew along all the marked lines.

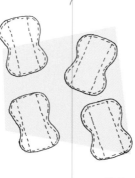

6 Remove all the pins. Toss one burp cloth over your shoulder—the curved edge should fit nicely around the base of your neck. A set of four makes a nice gift (tied together with a T-shirt ribbon, of course), but you might have to double the recipe to get through a whole burpy day!

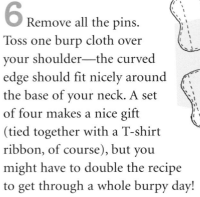

51 **tutu for now!**
(baby tutu)

Baby's first ballerina outfit can never come too early. Here's a simple way to use material from one adult T-shirt (why go the way of irritating tulle when you can give her soft 100% cotton?) to build a tutu onto baby's regular onesie. Just in time for her to bounce out her first dance steps on your lap!

LEVEL 4

---

ingredients

- **1 baby onesie**
- **1 T-shirt**
- **scissors**
- **needle**
- **thread**
- **seam ripper**

1 Lay the onesie flat and measure across the waist, then multiply by 2 to get x".

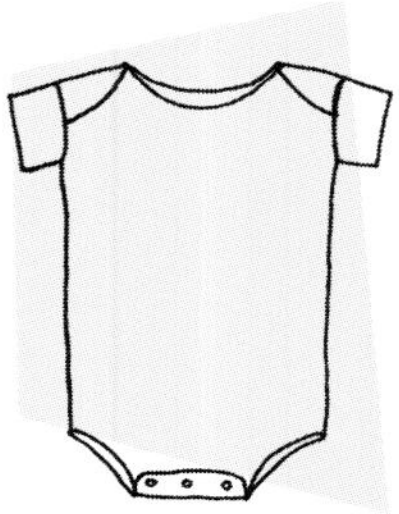

2 Lay the T-shirt flat, cut off the hem, and cut a 6" tube from the bottom of the T-shirt.

3 Cut through one side of the tube to make a long strip. Multiply x by 3 and mark that measurement from one end of the strip. Cut off the excess fabric.

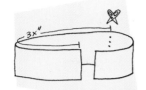

4 Fold the strip in half lengthwise, wrong sides in, pressing one long edge against the other. Pin and sew a basting stitch along the edge.

5 Gently gather the fabric evenly over the thread until the ruffled strip is about x" long.

6 Center the ruffle over the front of the onesie and pin the basted edge, waist high, to the fabric below it. Flip the onesie over and pin the rest of the ruffle to the back, overlapping the ends slightly.

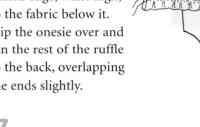

7 Sew a zigzag stitch over the pinned area, being sure not to sew through both layers of the onesie.

8 Remove the pins (every last one!), use a seam ripper to remove the basting stitch, and snap the onesie onto your littlest prima ballerina.

variations

■ Add rows of miniature ruffles just to the tush part of the onesie for a baby bustle!

■ Add side ruffles over each leg hole for an abbreviated tutu.

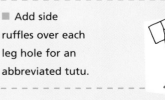

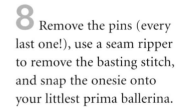

52 hangin' stuff
(stuffed mobile)

In the early twentieth century, artist Alexander Calder awed us by eliminating the need for a canvas when he hung art in the sky and invented the mobile. Since then, parents have been cultivating art appreciation in their babies by hanging nursery rhyme and celestial-inspired mobiles over their cribs. In the spirit of DIY, make that delightful tradition your own. Use old T-shirts to customize a mobile for the little one—lull him to sleep with traditional clouds and moon and stars, teach him to count with sheep, or start him rocking early with skulls and crossbones.

LEVEL 4

- -

ingredients

- -

- **paper**
- **pen or pencil**
- **1 T-shirt (or a combination of scraps)**
- **straight pins**
- **scissors**
- **needle**
- **thread**
- **poly-fill stuffing**
- **2 metal hangers**

1 Choose five related (or unrelated!) shapes and draw them at about the same size on a piece of paper. Cut out the shapes and pin them onto the T-shirt.

2 Measure and mark ¼" around each shape and cut through both layers. Remove the paper pattern, keeping the two layers pinned together, right sides out.

3 Cut off the bottom hem of the T-shirt and remove the stitching. Then cut a 1" loop off the bottom of the shirt.

4 Stretch out both loops and cut four equal strips from each.

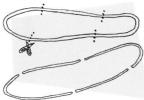

5 Tuck the end of one strip between the two layers at the top of one shape. Sew a running stitch or a whipstitch around the perimeter of the shape, making sure to catch the strip in the stitching and leaving 1½" unsewn at the bottom. (Hint: Use contrasting thread for visible stitching.) Repeat for all shapes.

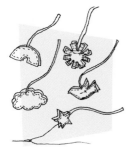

6 Remove the pins and push stuffing through the open end of each shape, stuffing the corners first.

7 Stitch the openings of each shape closed and set aside.

8 Hold the hangers together, then rotate one 90 degrees so the hangers are crossed. Twist one of the hooks so it aligns with the other.

9 Wrap a strip of fabric around each of the two intersections, crisscrossing through the wires to keep them secure.

10 Tie four of the shapes to each of the four hanger corners. Tie the fifth to the intersection so it hangs from the center of the mobile. Tie the last strip of fabric in a bow around the hook or use it to hang the mobile from the ceiling.

variations

■ To make a **NO SEW** version, cut your shapes bigger and knot them closed like the pillows in Pillow Talk (page 98).

■ Instead of shapes, make different-colored no sew pom-poms (see Pom-Pom Circumstance, page 158) to hang from each corner.

53 **baby back bib**
(bib)

C inderella's Fairy Godmother is a true maverick of all things DIY. I mean, she does repurpose a pumpkin into a magnificent stagecoach and four dirty mice into gleaming white horses after all! I know, I know—you don't have a magic wand. But you *do* have a pair of scissors, and since this bib is a no sew project, it'll be ready faster than you can say *bib*-bidi-bobbidi-boo! This bib will protect even the messiest child's clothing from spills and stains that will take more than talking mice and birds to remedy—and *that* is pure magic.

LEVEL 2

ingredients

- 1 T-shirt
- chalk marker
- ruler
- scissors

1 Lay the T-shirt flat and measure the distance from one neckband seam to the other across the neck hole to get X". Mark X" across the center of the shirt front 8" to 9" down from the shoulder seams on either side of the neckband. Draw vertical lines from the shoulder seams down to the X" line.

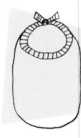

2 Cut along the marked lines through just one layer. Where the mark ends, continue cutting around the back of the neckband, just outside the seam.

3 Round the corners of the rectangle with scissors and snip through the center back of the neckband to make two ties. (*Note:* If you are working with a smaller tee, leave the neckband intact so it can be slipped over baby's head.)

variation

■ For better absorbency, add a second panel of fabric behind the first. Simply cut through two layers in step 1. Sew a running stitch around the raw edges of the bib to keep it from curling.

4 Gently tie around baby's neck to keep the outfit underneath free from spills. Remove after mealtime and drop it in the wash!

54 pom-pom circumstance
(toddler hat)

GREEN TEE

As fast as he's growing, your toddler nephew may still be too small to hit the slopes this winter—so gear him up instead for childhood's favorite autumn pastime. With this colorful, lightweight hat he'll be able to conquer the leaf piles out front (and you'll be able to keep an eye on him!) while staying warm on cool fall days.

LEVEL 4

ingredients

- **2 T-shirt sleeves (L or XL, same or contrasting color)**
- **ruler**
- **scissors**
- **straight pins**
- **chalk marker**
- **needle**
- **thread**

1 Cut out the bottom seam of one sleeve and lay the fabric flat, right side up, with the hemmed edge at the bottom. Measure the circumference of the child's head and mark that length (x") along the hemmed edge of the fabric.

2 Measure and mark 7½" up from the hemmed edge at several points and draw a straight line through those marks. Cut along the line and remove the excess fabric.

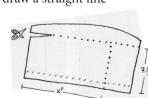

3 Fold the rectangle in half crosswise, short sides together, and right side in. Pin along the open side edge and sew a running stitch along the pinned edge. Remove the pins.

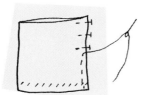

4 Take the second sleeve and cut ¾"-wide strips. Stretch out the strips and then cut them into thirty 3½" to 4" pieces.

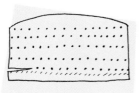

5 Gather the thirty pieces, as shown, and tie a longer strip *tightly* around the center of the bunch in a double knot.

6 Lay the tube from step 3 flat, the seam centered in the back. Holding on to the knot ends, insert the pom-pom through the open edge opposite the hem, aligning it with the back seam. Pin the knot ends in position between the open edges, and continue pinning along the entire edge.

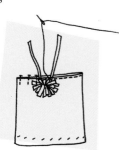

7 Sew a running stitch along the pinned edge, making sure to catch the knot ends in the seam. Remove the pins and trim the strips.

8 With the hat still inside out, pinch the sewn corners together and secure them with a few tight whipstitches to give the hat shape.

9 Turn the hat right side out.

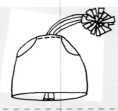

variations

■ Insert the pom-pom farther from the edge in step 6 to make it dangle.

■ Use scrap strips for a multicolored pom-pom.

■ Make a hat for yourself, measuring your head's circumference along the bottom hem of the T-shirt and measuring about 9" up.

55 **mighty my tee** (superhero cape)

NO SEW

I t's a rainy afternoon and the kid you babysit is bummed because she can't meet her friends, imaginary or real, for adventures on the jungle gym or at the park. Never fear, superfun is here! Create adventures inside when you turn her into a superhero. With this T-shirt cape, she'll be more powerful than a (Thomas the Tank Engine) locomotive, able to leap tall furniture in a single bound, and fight for truth, justice, and DIY faster than you can say "Shazam!"

LEVEL 1

ingredients

- **1 T-shirt**
- **ruler**
- **chalk marker**
- **scissors**

1 Lay the T-shirt flat, back side up. Mark a straight diagonal line from the bottom left corner to a point 2" left of the neckband. Mark a second diagonal line from the bottom right corner to a point 2" right of the neckband.

(back)

2 Continue the diagonal lines over each shoulder until they intersect at the front of the neckband.

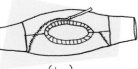

(top)

3 Cut along the chalk markings, through just one layer, and around the neckband in the front.

(back)

4 Slip the neckband over your little superhero's head. Make sure the cape is short enough that it won't be accidentally snagged or stepped on. Now it's up, up, and away! *Optional:* Across the back of the cape, iron on (or cut out and stitch) letters to personalize the cape with her name, a title ("Super Sister" or "Big Brother"), or an appropriate word ("Shazam!").

56 jumper for joy
(toddler jumper)

Any little girl will love the freedom this dress allows as she toddles around, exploring the park on a beautiful summer day. Mom will love this dress, too, because it's so easy to make that she can have more than one stashed in the diaper bag for when that ice cream scoop comes toppling off her girl's cone and down her front.

LEVEL 3

ingredients

- **1 T-shirt**
- **scissors**
- **chalk marker**
- **straight pins**
- **needle**
- **thread**

1 Turn the T-shirt inside out and lay it flat. Cut off the sleeves just inside the seams and cut out the neckband.

2 Deepen the neck hole about 2" to 3", cutting through both layers. Measure and mark about 15" down from the bottom of the neck hole. Cut horizontally across the bottom of the shirt at that measurement.

3 Center 13" along the bottom and make a mark at either end.

4 Mark diagonal lines starting 2" from either side of the neck hole down to the bottom marks (creating an A-line). Cut along the marked lines through both layers.

5 Mark the sides about 2" below the bottom of the neck hole (this will be the bottom of the armhole). From these marks to the top outer edge of the straps, cut out slight arcs, gently mimicking the curve of the original sleeve seam.

6 Pin along the sides from the bottom of the armhole to the bottom of the dress. Sew a running stitch along the pinned edges. Remove the pins and turn the dress right side out.

variations

■ Make it shorter for a sweet little tank top!

■ For a younger baby, make a snuggly onesie: Make the "skirt" narrower (no need for as much leg room for walking), run a drawstring through the bottom hem (casing), and gather it closed in a bow. Just make sure to keep all strings trimmed short to avoid a choking hazard!

7 Cut through the straps at the top, stretch them a little, and tie the paired strips in double knots at the top of each shoulder.

8 Slip it on her and re-tie the knots if necessary to adjust the height of the dress so it fits at the neck and under the arms.

57 **antsy pants**
(baby or toddler pajama pants)

Forget that someone named Bob in square pants; these are T-shirt pants. That's right: T-shirt pants. Take an old rock shirt—like that Clash shirt that you've been holding on to—and breathe new life into it by turning it into these karate-style pants. It's a win-win-win situation: The T-shirt gets new life; the little karate kid gets an early start on rock appreciation; and you get to feel that special pride when his great duds make him the envy of the other kids in playgroup.

Note: If your child is too squirmy for measuring (step 2), take a pair of his pants, fold them in half, lining up the outer leg with the double folded tube edge in step 3, and trace—then skip to step 8.

LEVEL 4

ingredients

- 1 T-shirt (L or XL)
- ruler
- scissors
- chalk marker
- straight pins
- needle
- thread
- safety pin

1 Lay the T-shirt flat, cut off the bottom hem, and remove the stitching. Cut through the loop to make a drawstring, and set aside.

2 Measure your child from waist to foot to get x". Mark that measurement (x") up from the bottom of the T-shirt on both sides. Mark and cut across the T-shirt, creating a tube.

3 Fold the tube in half lengthwise, bringing one folded edge over to align with the other folded edge (so that one side has two visible folds and the other has one visible fold).

4 Measure and mark 8" from the double-fold edge. Extend the mark vertically, cut along the line, and remove the excess fabric.

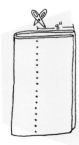

5 Make a mark (A) 7" down from the top along the cut edge. Measuring from the double-fold side, mark (B) 7" along the bottom edge.

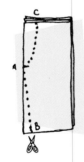

6 Measure around your child's waist, add 2", and divide by 4 to get y". (Example: If your child's waist is 18", add 2 to get 20" and divide by 4 to get 5".) Measure y" from the double-fold side, along the top edge and mark (C).

7 Draw a diagonal line to connect A and B. Draw a concave arc between A and C, as shown. Cut along both lines (through all four layers) and remove the excess fabric.

8 Unfold the two panels and place them together, right sides facing. Pin and sew a running stitch along the curved edges. (This will be the crotch seam.) Remove the pins.

continued ▶

9 Rotate the new "tube" you've created so that the seams are in the center, as shown. Pin the edges of the upside down "V," and sew with a running stitch.

10 Fold and pin the top edge down about 1¼". Sew a running stitch or backstitch 1" from the folded edge. Remove all pins and turn the pants right side out.

11 Make two small snips (through only the top layer of fabric) 1" apart at the center front of the waistband casing. Attach a safety pin to one end of the drawstring and thread it through the waistband.

12 Pull the pants up around the child's waist, tying the drawstring in a bow.

variations

■ If the pieces you cut from your shirt are plain, embellish the legs or bum area with iron-on letters or logos.

■ Crop the pant legs for a pair of shorts.

58 the little empress
(toddler dress)

She's read about Cinderella, the Paper Bag Princess, Rapunzel, and Sleeping Beauty. Help her find her very own royal persona by transforming one of Daddy's XL T-shirts into this poufy, empire-waist dress for Daddy's little girl. Before you know it, the princes will be lining up outside the castle gate for a chance to slay a dragon for her affection.

LEVEL 4

ingredients

- **1 T-shirt (L or XL)**
- **ruler**
- **scissors**
- **measuring tape**
- **chalk marker**
- **straight pins**
- **needle**
- **thread**

1 Turn the T-shirt inside out, lay it flat, and cut off the hem. Trim off the stitching on the hem and cut through one layer of the loop to make a drawstring. Set it aside.

2 Depending on how long you want the skirt, mark a horizontal line 8" to 15" up from the bottom of the shirt. Cut along the line to make a tube (the skirt). Set aside.

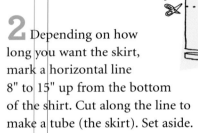

3 Measure around the child's chest with a measuring tape and divide by 2 to get x". Mark a rectangle 5" by x" across the remainder of the T-shirt.

4 Cut out the rectangle through both layers and pin along the 5" edges. Sew a running stitch with a ½" seam allowance or a whipstitch along both pinned edges to create the bodice. Remove the pins.

5 Measure the circumference of the bodice (it should be the child's chest measurement minus 1") and divide by 6 to get y". Make marks y" apart around the bottom edge of the bodice.

6 Measure the circumference of the tube you cut in step 2 (the skirt) and divide by 6 to get z". Make marks z" apart along the top edge of the skirt.

7 Sew a basting stitch along the top edge of the skirt. Gather the fabric evenly over the thread so that the gathered circumference of the skirt matches the circumference of the bodice.

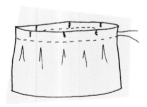

8 Rotate the inside-out bodice so that the marks are facing up (the bottom edge is temporarily the top edge). Turn the skirt right side out and insert it through the bodice, lining up the top edge of the skirt with the bottom (marked) edge of the bodice. Line up the six corresponding chalk marks to make sure the gathers are even. Pin in place and sew a zigzag or a whipstitch along the pinned edge.

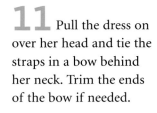

9 Remove the pins and fold the bodice up (right side out). Poke or snip two holes 4" to 5" apart and 1" down from the top center edge.

10 Thread the drawstring you created in step 1 into one hole, from outside to inside, and out through the adjacent hole. Pull the drawstring until it is centered in the tube.

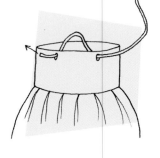

11 Pull the dress on over her head and tie the straps in a bow behind her neck. Trim the ends of the bow if needed.

variation

■ Use pieces from two different T-shirts for the skirt and bodice.

59 shake it up baby
(fringe dance skirt)

NO SEW

What better way to fight those dreary-day blues than by imagining you're in a warm tropical place? Together with your young charge (she can help pick out the colors), you can refashion a single T-shirt into this easy-to-make fringe dance skirt and hold a luau at home with the music turned up— let's hula!

LEVEL 1

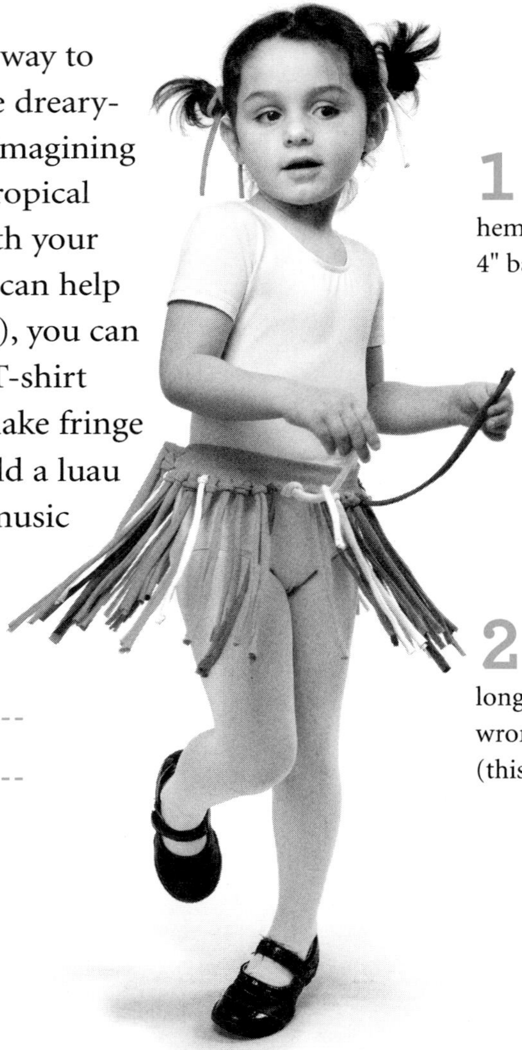

---

ingredients

- **1 T-shirt (or lots of T-shirt scraps)**
- **scissors**
- **ruler**
- **chalk marker**

1 Lay the T-shirt flat and cut off the hem just above the seam. Then cut off a 4" band from the bottom of the shirt.

2 Cut through the band to make a long strip. Fold it in half lengthwise, wrong sides in, with the fold at the top (this is the waistband).

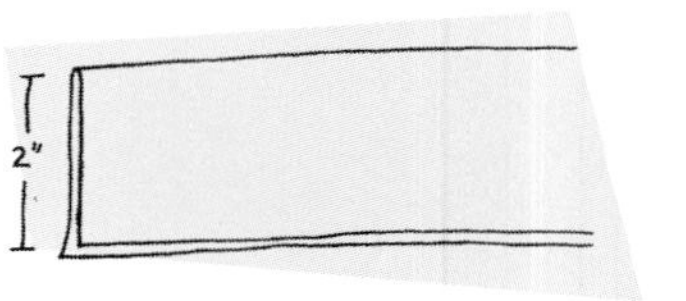

3 Cut a long 1"-wide strip, spiraling up from the bottom of the shirt and stopping at the sleeves. *Optional:* Alternatively, collect or cut scrap strips from sleeves.

4 Cut 10"-long pieces from the strip and stretch them out.

5 Measure the waist of the little booty-shaker and center that measurement (x) along the folded waistband, marking both ends.

6 Snip or poke small holes through both layers of the waistband ½" from the bottom and about ½" apart between the two marks you made in step 5.

variation

■ Alternate or use pieces of ribbon for the skirt fringe.

7 One at a time, take a strip you cut in step 4, fold it in half, and push the loop about 2" through a hole on the waistband. Pull the two ends through the loop and tighten in a cow hitch knot.

8 Tie the waistband in the back with a bow and let her twist and shout!

60 let's get animal
(stuffed animal)

Every kid has a favorite snuggly—a teddy bear or blanky—that he or she carries daily from the crib, to the park, to the store, to the potty, to infinity and beyond. It's a child's confidant, comforter, and companion—and it's bound to pick up a few germs here and there. Make a stuffed animal from a trusty old T-shirt, and it will withstand the frequent washings it no doubt will require. A child's snuggles and hugs (and the spin cycle) will gently soften the T-shirt fabric animal a little more every day. With enough T-shirts on hand, you can make a whole menagerie.

LEVEL 4

---
ingredients

- **1 T-shirt**
- **paper**
- **pen or pencil**

- **straight pins**
- **scissors**
- **needle**
- **thread**
- **stuffing or T-shirt scraps**

1 Sketch or trace the shape of his favorite animal on a piece of paper (it doesn't have to be exact). Note key features like horns, big ears, a trunk, or an extra-long neck. Make sure legs and other features are all wider than your thumb (so that you can easily fill them with stuffing later).

2 Cut out the shape to make a pattern and pin it onto your T-shirt. Cut around the edges of the pattern through both layers. Carefully remove the pattern and keep the two layers of fabric pinned together.

3 If your animal has a long tail (lion, monkey, horse, etc.) that was not included in your sketch, create it using a strip of fabric and pin it in the appropriate place between the layers of fabric (fringe the ends for a lion's tail or fringe the whole length for a horse's mane).

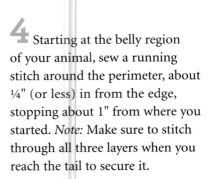

4 Starting at the belly region of your animal, sew a running stitch around the perimeter, about ¼" (or less) in from the edge, stopping about 1" from where you started. *Note:* Make sure to stitch through all three layers when you reach the tail to secure it.

5 Fill your animal with stuffing or fabric scraps, filling the legs and ears and other extremities first, and sew the opening closed. Remove all the pins. You're all done— unless your furry friend would like some optional add-ons.

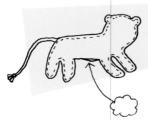

6 Create a lion or horse mane by cutting ½" fringe into a 1½"- to 2"-wide strip of fabric (the strip should be long enough to go around the entire head twice for a lion's mane and long enough to stretch the length of the neck twice for a horse's mane). Cut each long strip into two equal strips and pin each one in place onto both sides of the animal. Sew a running stitch to attach it. Be sure to remove all pins and trim all threads before giving the stuffed animal to a child.

variation

■ If animals aren't your style (or your drawing tends to the abstract), outline the shape of a friendly monster!

Generation T

61 **mop top** (rag doll)

NO SEW

GREEN TEE

Remember making these dolls out of yarn or embroidery floss when you were a kid? What a great way to spend an afternoon. Making a mop top doll for the kid you babysit (while she naps!) will let you relive the memory. With permission, make it more special by using a mix of old T-shirts from both parents' drawers—ones that they don't wear anymore— along with one or two old shirts that the little sprout has so rapidly outgrown.

LEVEL 2

ingredients

- **1 T-shirt (L or XL) or a colorful handful of scrap hems from a mix of T-shirts**
- **scissors**

1 Cut or collect an odd number of between twenty-five and thirty-one 1"-wide strips made from loops from the bottom of T-shirts. Set aside one strip.

2 Even out the ends on one side and cut the opposite ends to match the shortest piece. Fold the cluster of strips in half.

3 Tie the single strip in a double knot around the halfway fold. Trim off the ends of the single strip to use later.

4 Tie another length of the single strip around the entire cluster about 2" down from the top to create the head.

5 Separate two groups of six to eight pieces from the sides of the head. Gather the pieces into miniclusters (they don't have to be even) and braid them to create arms. When they reach a desirable length, tie a piece of strip around each in a tight double knot to make wrists. Trim the end of each arm about 1" beyond the ties.

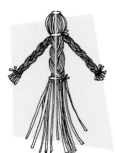

6 Braid the torso about 2" shorter than the arms. Tie a strip around the waist.

7 Split the strips into two clusters for the legs. Braid each leg and tie it at the ankle when it's reached its desired length. Trim the ends about 1" to 1½" beyond the tie.

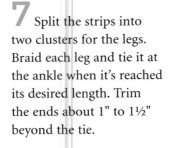

variations

■ Stop after step 4 and trim the ends unevenly for a jellyfish!

■ Instead of braiding each limb (and the torso, too), just tie the strands at each intersection as shown.

■ Experiment by tying the ties differently to make a mermaid.

■ Stop at step 6 so your doll can wear a skirt instead of pants.

■ Instead of folding the strips over to make it double-thick, tie the ends at the top so your doll has crazy hair.

62 brought to you by the letter T
(pillow)

W hether it's through direct conversation or songs about buying letters on *Sesame Street,* it's never too early to introduce a child to language. Now you can personalize your little one's bedding with a letter pillow and expose him to letter and word recognition when he's waking up or drifting off to sleep. The pillow might feature a baby's initial (A is for Alice), spell out his full name with three cushions (M-A-X spells Max); or offer a gentle reminder that this N-is-for-Nap is brought to you by the letter Zzzz. . . .

LEVEL 3

ingredients

- 1 T-shirt
- chalk marker
- straight pins
- scissors
- needle
- thread
- stuffing

1 Lay the T-shirt flat and draw a large block letter (upper or lowercase) about 8" tall across the front of the shirt. Pin the layers together to keep them from shifting. *Optional:* If there's room on the shirt (and you have the time), add more letters (spell out the child's name or go with "ABC," "Baby," etc.).

2 Through both layers, cut out the letter shape about ¼" outside the lines.

3 Sew a running stitch or whipstitch along the edges of the letter, leaving about 2" open to stuff it.

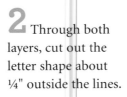

variations

■ Make a traditional rectangular pillow and add a pocket with a shape hidden inside.

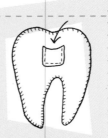

■ Make a tooth-shaped pillow from an old T-shirt or jersey pajama top, and add a tiny pocket—small enough for that first tooth but big enough for some large bills, of course!

■ Make smaller letters and string them together in a mobile (see Hangin' Stuff, page 154).

4 Remove the pins and stuff the letter, using a pencil or pen to push the stuffing into the corners if needed.

5 Stitch closed the remaining 2".

6 Snuggle up with baby and a good book.

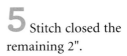

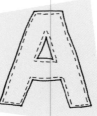

63 roll it, patch it, mark it with a tee!

(patchwork quilt)

A fleece-wear designer friend made these miniquilts with her fleece fabric scraps—she's also made them with old sweatshirts and babies' onesies. Let's add old T-shirts to the mix. Perfect for comforting a newborn, this patchwork quilt of revived tees is all about new life.

LEVEL 2

- -
ingredients
(makes a 35" to 41" square quilt)
- -

- **forty-two 9" by 9" T-shirt squares**
- **ruler**
- **scissors**

1 Cut or gather forty-two scrap 9" by 9" squares. (If you limit the colors in the quilt, you can make it using between seven and eleven large T-shirts.)

2 Cut 2" squares from the corners of each quilt square. About ½" apart from each other, cut an equal number of 2"-long slits about ½" apart into the edges of each square (to create fringe).

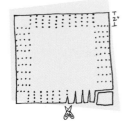

3 Lay out squares in the order you'd like them to appear. Going left to right, tie the right fringe from the first square to the corresponding fringe on the second square in a double knot. Tie the right fringe on the second square to the corresponding left fringe on the third square. Continue in this manner until all seven squares in the row are knotted together.

4 Repeat step 3 with row two, three, four, and so on, until all squares are knotted in rows.

5 Going top to bottom, tie the bottom fringe of row one to the top fringe of row two. Then tie the bottom fringe of row two to the top fringe of row three. Continue until all seven rows are knotted together.

6 Spread out the blanket, trim off the outside fringe around the perimeter, and gently round the corners.

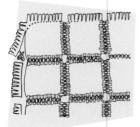

7 Shake out the blanket of T-shirt dust and it's snuggle time!

variation

■ At a baby shower, ask each guest to bring a 9" by 9" square to tie on to make a baby quilt during the Tee Party.

64 materni-tee

NO SEW

(maternity shirt)

Just because you have a bun in the oven doesn't mean you have to give up your hip aesthetic for the blousy calicos that your mother wore. Shop for bigger sizes (in this case, "shopping" might mean raiding Daddy's dresser drawer), and grab some scissors! Just be careful with all of those sharp objects . . . I know your hormones are raging these days.

LEVEL 2

- -

ingredients

- -

- **1 T-shirt (L or XL, depending on stage of pregnancy)**
- **scissors**

- **3 T-shirt strips, 22" to 24" long (or 48" ribbons)**
- **ruler**
- **chalk marker**
- **safety pin**

1 Lay the T-shirt flat, cut off the bottom hem, and cut out the neckband. Cut 3" off the end of each sleeve, parallel to the sleeve hem.

2 Try on the shirt and make a mark on the front just below your bust. Remove the shirt and extend the mark horizontally across it. Mark two more lines below and parallel to the first and 1" apart. Continue the lines around the back so you have three parallel rings drawn around the shirt.

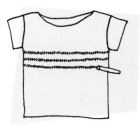

3 Snip or poke holes about 1¼" apart along the top ring for an odd number of holes in total.

4 Repeat on the second ring, staggering the holes, so that the first hole falls between the first two holes of the first ring, and so on. Repeat step 3 on the third ring, lining up the holes with those along the first ring.

5 Stretch out one of the T-shirt strips, attach a safety pin to one end, and thread it down through one of the holes along the first ring just right of center. Weave it in and out until you thread it out the last hole.

6 Repeat step 5 with the remaining two laces on the remaining two rows, staggering the starting point just right of the one of the ring above it.

7 Try on the top, pulling each pair of drawstrings comfortably tight below the bust and tying them in a knot or a bow. Trim the ends and adjust the gathers toward the front.

variations

■ Post-baby, you can still wear this style! Simply start with a smaller shirt and mark the three lines a little lower, around your natural waist.

■ For another maternity option, see the Tie, Tie Again dress on page 75. Wear it as a shirt.

65 come to gather, right now, over tee

(maternity shirt)

The key to maternity-wear is in the empire waist, and this design is no different. The gather keeps the fabric cinched and fitted right below the bust (you have, amazingly, an ample bosom for possibly the first time in your life, so celebrate it) and loose-fitting *around* the belly (just because you can feel him kicking up a storm in there, doesn't mean the rest of the world needs to see his Beckham skills quite yet).

LEVEL 3

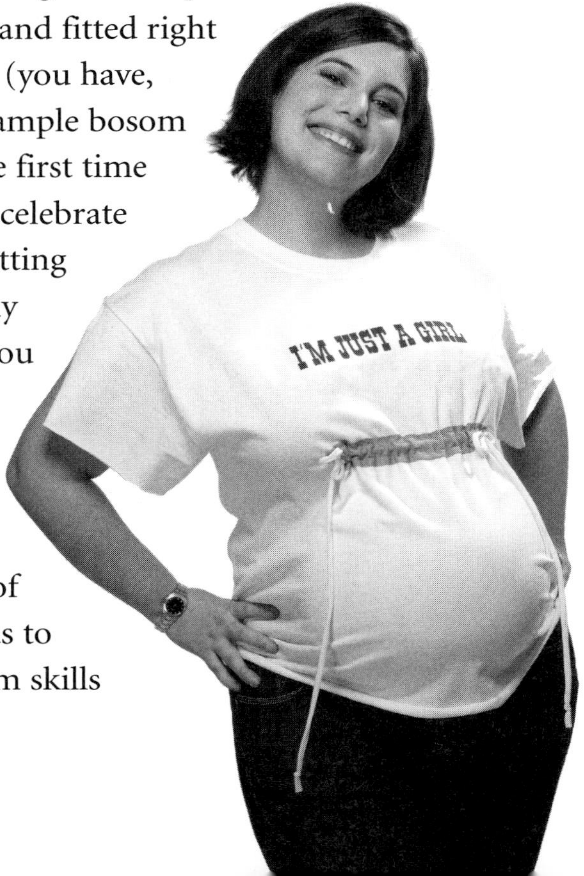

---

ingredients

- ■ **1 T-shirt (baggy)**
- ■ **scissors**
- ■ **straight pins**
- ■ **needle**
- ■ **thread**
- ■ **safety pin**

---

1 Lay the T-shirt flat and cut off the bottom hem. Cut off the stitching from the hem and cut through one layer to make a drawstring cord. Set aside. *Optional:* Cut the hem from a different T-shirt to preserve more of the length of the original T-shirt.

2 Cut a 1¼" strip off the bottom of the shirt. Cut through one layer of the loop to make a strip and trim it to 10". Pin it centered (equidistant from the side edges) onto the T-shirt just below the bust. *Optional*: As above, cut a 10" by 1¼" strip from another T-shirt to preserve the original length of the T-shirt.

3 Sew two rows of running stitches ¼" from each edge of the strip, securing the strip to only the front layer of the shirt. Remove the pins; you've created a drawstring casing.

4 Attach a safety pin to one end of the cord (from step 1) and thread it through the casing (from step 3).

5 Remove the safety pin, even out the ends, and tie an overhand knot at each end of the cord.

6 Pull the ends of the cord together, gathering the fabric over them and either a) tie the ends together, or b) tie each end at the side of the casing in a small bow.

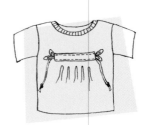

7 Mark and cut a line 3" from and parallel to the sleeve hem, as shown. Remove the excess fabric and repeat on the other sleeve.

8 Cut along the top of each sleeve to create a fluttery effect.

9 Try it on, adjusting the drawstring over your growing bump.

variation

■ Add similar casings onto the back or each side to cinch the fabric away from the middle.

Chapter 5

Pet Central

Heavy Petting

- -

From tee-riffic toys to style-leash accessories, here are six surprising ways to personalize your pooch and pretty up your kitty.

From socialites carrying microdogs in their purses to muscled men wearing pythons wrapped around their shoulders as they cruise the boardwalk, these days the pet *is* the fashion accessory. Not only do pets dress up their human's outfit, they're interactive and bring personality to the occasion even when you're not feelin' it. So why not give 'em their own gear? By now they've earned the right to have some accessories of their own, and not that stuff sold at the register in the hardware store. Show your pet how much you appreciate him by making him something that both of you will love.

While poodles in dorky sweaters have given pet clothing a bad name, your mutt in his badass bandana will be too cool to dispute. Everyone secretly anthropomorphizes their pets, so why not pretend our pets resemble DIY-loving indie rocker humans? Using T-shirts and T-shirt scraps, you can personalize your pooch's wardrobe, or give your kitty something new to bat around.

Most of these projects are fun and simple, good for the lazy Saturday when you're overcome with how cute your cat is when she stretches and just have to make her a new toy (or if you're more ambitious, a new bed). Repurpose old tees to make a never-before-seen dog lead, in a Lead of Their Own (page 196). And it isn't just the mammals that need the love. Make a tropical-themed place mat for a friend's fishbowl (see A Time and a Place Mat, page 100) or a

blanket (see Ants Go Marching, page 256) to toss over the birdcage. But these aren't the only projects you can adapt—alter the doggy vest to make a harness leash for your pet ferret so that he, too, can take you for a walk around the block.

Pets are so often already miniature resemblances of their owners—you know, the mustachioed owner with his schnauzer; the old hippie with his bearded collie; the permed and teased-out blonde with her pure-bred white Persian kitty. Go the distance and complete the picture: Wear matching T-shirts! Okay, how about at least projects cut from the same cloth?

The next time you get on a refashioning kick, don't stop at making a tank top for yourself— make a vest for your dog at the same time. Turn your next walk through the neighborhood into a tandem runway show.

What's on Your Playlist:

"A Horse with No Name"
—*America*

"Puff the Magic Dragon"
—*Peter, Paul and Mary*

"Hound Dog"
—*Elvis*

"Rock Lobster"
—*B-52s*

"Blackbird"
—*The Beatles*

"The Lion Sleeps Tonight"
—*Various*

"Rockin' Robin"
—*Michael Jackson*

"Wild Horses"
—*Rolling Stones*

"Werewolves of London"
—*Warren Zevon*

"Octopus' Garden"
—*The Beatles*

"White Rabbit"
—*Jefferson Airplane*

Generation T

GREEN TEE

66 caterpillar thriller
(knotted cat toy)

NO SEW

Cats have to scratch, right? And what cat doesn't feel at home sleeping atop your freshly washed and folded laundry? It's cute . . . for a second. Then you start to worry that he's going to shred your pillowcases. Who can blame him for deconstructing? Cotton, assuredly, is a soft treat. Go ahead and give your furry feline friend what he really wants: a knotted T-shirt of his own to scratch, stretch, attack, cuddle . . . and chew on.

LEVEL 1

ingredients

- **1 to 3 T-shirt sleeves (L or XL, assorted, for color variety)**
- **ruler**
- **scissors**

1 Cut three 1¼" by 18" strips from scrap sleeves and stretch them into cords about 24" long. *Note:* Thinner strips make a thinner "caterpillar."

2 Tie the three ends in an overhand knot and braid the strips together leaving about 2" at the end.

3 Finish the braid so that the two strips you want visible are on the outsides (the middle strip will be covered). Tie the outside strips together, as shown.

4 Hold the end of the middle cord with one hand while pushing against the bottom of the braid with the other.

5 Trim the middle piece off and tightly tie the three ends together. *Optional:* Twist the toy slightly to create a double-helix design.

variations

■ If you want to keep control of playtime, leave the middle piece long to dangle the caterpillar in front of Tiger . . . good times for all.

■ Make a longer one for yourself and wear or use as a bracelet, headband, keychain, or belt!

67 mouse padded
(stuffed cat toy)

GREEN TEE

Don't want real mice in your apartment? This feline's friend is a great compromise. Grab a tee you're no longer into—it doesn't fit, it's got a few holes, or you realize you actually hate that band—and cut and sew it into the mouse toy your cat's going to love. And if you fill the toy belly with catnip, your cat will be transformed, too, dropping his trophy at your feet for a head scratch. *Bonus:* When it's not being chased, this mouse won't chew a hole in the wall.

LEVEL 4

ingredients

- **4" by 4" square T-shirt scrap**
- **1"-wide strip (between 5" and 12" long in a contrasting color)**
- **chalk marker**
- **scissors**
- **needle**
- **thread**
- **scrap fabric or stuffing**
- **catnip (optional)**

1 Fold the 4" by 4" square in half, right side in. Draw a half of a heart from the folded edge, as shown, maximizing the size of the fabric. Cut along the chalk mark.

2 Starting at the tip, sew a whipstitch along the raw edge, leaving ¾" open (unstitched). Turn the "body" right side out through the ¾" opening.

3 Cut two ¾" circles from the remaining fabric square and set aside.

4 Cut four circles from the strip: two ¼" in diameter and two ½" in diameter. Snip the ends of the strip to even them out and tie a knot at one end.

5 Place one of the ½" circles onto a ¾" circle, right sides facing up, and sew a simple running stitch around the perimeter of the smaller circle, affixing it to the larger. Repeat with the other two circles of the same sizes. These are the ears.

6 One at a time, pinch each ear piece at one side, pin, and stitch it about 1" back from the nose and ½" from the top seam.

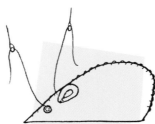

7 Pin and stitch the eyes (the ¼" circles) about ½" back from the nose and ⅓" from the top seam.

variation

■ Have some big cat urges of your own? Satisfy your feline alter ego by supersizing the pattern to make a pair of mousy throw pillows you can both snuggle up to.

8 Fill the mouse body with scrap fabric or stuffing through the opening. Insert the unknotted end of the strip at the bottom of the opening and, as you stitch the hole closed, sew the strip into place as a tail. *Optional:* Shorten the tail for an independent play toy or keep it long so you can hold on to the knot and play with your kitty!

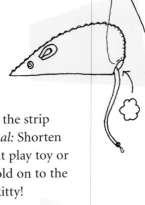

9 Before you hand off your kitty toy, make sure everything is attached securely so that an overzealous kitten doesn't inadvertently remove an ear or tail!

68 t-shirt's pet
(pet bed)

This sweet bed will fit a feline or a small canine—or both together if they're friendly! Princess can dig her claws in and Fido can snuggle his nose in. Encourage your pets off the sofa by giving them a more appealing spot they can call their own. Use graphic T-shirts to catch their eye and the softest fabric to make their cat nap dreamy.

LEVEL 4

ingredients
(makes a bed about 3' in diameter)

- **4 T-shirts**
- **ruler**
- **chalk marker**
- **scissors**
- **measuring tape**
- **straight pins**
- **needle**
- **thread**
- **3 bags poly-fill stuffing or T-shirt scraps**

1 Lay the T-shirts flat and cut off the hems. Then mark and cut a 16" to 20" square from each T-shirt through both layers.

2 Layer the squares together into groups of four and mark and round off one of the corners by cutting a wide arc between two opposite corners, as shown, creating a quarter-circle wedge.

3 Separate the eight wedges and arrange them, right sides down, into two large circles as shown, alternating the panels.

4 Pin two wedges, right sides together, along one of the straight edges to make a half-circle. Sew a running stitch or whipstitch along the pinned edge. Repeat on the other three pairs. Remove all the pins. (You should have four half-circles.)

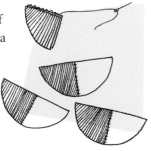

5 Pair off the two half-circles, right sides together, and pin and sew along the straight edges to create two circles.

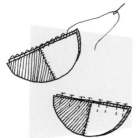

variations

■ If you don't have pets, you can make cushions for sitting in an Asian-style living room.

■ Make smaller circles for chair cushions or throw pillows.

6 Remove the pins and unfold the circles.

7 Place the two circles together, right sides facing, and pin around the edges. Sew a running stitch or a whipstitch around the pinned edges, leaving about 3" open.

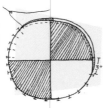

8 Remove the pins, turn right side out through the opening, and fill the pillow to your desired plumpness with stuffing or T-shirt scraps.

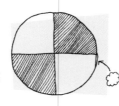

9 Stitch the opening closed with a hidden whipstitch. *Optional:* Stitch a knot through the center intersection, puckering the center of the circle cushion. Stitch through it a few times to make it secure.

69 bandana-rama

NO SEW

(doggy bandana)

Your dog is a faithful friend, a sidekick who will follow you anywhere. Heck, he even runs at your side during your weekly jogs. Why not make him his own bandana and let him stand out from the pack? You'll be able to spot him at the dog run *and* he'll be the hippest pooch on the block.

LEVEL 1

ingredients

- 1 T-shirt
- ruler
- chalk marker
- scissors

1 Lay your T-shirt sideways, so one of the sleeves is on top.

2 Mark an isosceles triangle whose base is above the hemline and extends from the back fold, approximately 11" by 20" by 23".

3 Cut through both layers along the chalk lines and unfold the fabric. *Optional:* Use iron-on letters to write your dog's name across the front of the bandana.

4 Tie the long ends around your pooch's neck with a double knot for a little identifying color.

variation

■ Why leave it all to the dogs? You can make a cute bandana scarf for yourself while you're at it! Hang it around your neck or wear it on your head.

T-shirt Origami

Japan-created, Martha-approved. Here's a no-fail way to keep your T-shirts folded and organized (you know, before you take your scissors to them).

1. Rotate the T-shirt to the side so the neckband faces left. Pinch the fabric through both layers at A with your left hand and at B with your right hand, drawing an invisible line about 2" from the edge of the neckband. With your left fingers, fold A to C crossing over B (B becomes the fold). Uncross your arms and shake out the shirt.

2. Pinching A and C in the left hand and B in the right hand, fold the visible sleeve underneath the shirt, as shown.

3. Lay the folded T-shirt flat, rotate it 90 degrees so the neckband is correctly oriented, and repeat (for the rest of your dresser drawer!).

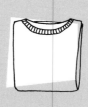

70 dog's vest friend
(small doggy tee)

Sure, you can force a people T-shirt onto your pup, but why not something custom-made for your canine? In this vest he'll strut his stuff— having all the other little doggies at the dog run saying, "Bow . . . *wow!*"

Note: Not all doggies like to be dressed up, so know your dog and know thyself and make sure dressing him up is about his happiness rather than your delight in seeing little Dexter as the duke of dogtown.

LEVEL 5

ingredients

- 1 T-shirt
- measuring tape
- chalk markers
- scissors
- straight pins

1 Measure your dog from neck to base of tail (x). Mark and cut horizontally across the T-shirt x" down from the center of the neckband.

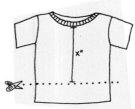

2 Mark two parallel lines extending from either side of the neckband to the bottom of the shirt. Mark two parallel lines horizontally across the shirt at the neckband and 2" below it.

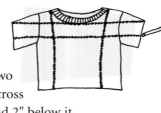

3 Cut through both layers around the shape created by the outermost lines and cut off the neckband.

4 Cut a 2" to 2½" tube from the bottom of the shirt you cut off in step 1. Cut through the tube at each side to create two equal strips.

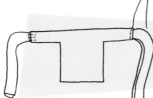

5 Fold the two strips in half and insert the ends between the layers of fabric at "arms."

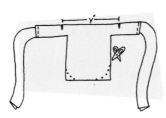

6 Measure the distance around your dog's neck (y") and center it across the top edge. Round the two bottom corners with your scissors.

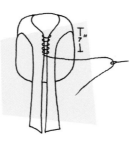

7 Fold so the two end points of y meet, right sides in, and sew 7" down the side strips, creating a neck hole and the torso.

8 Sew a running stitch around every edge, leaving a ¼" seam allowance.

9 Pull it over your dog's head. Fold the strips at a right angle and wrap them over the dog's back.

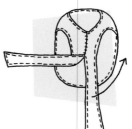

10 Tie in a bow. Remove and trim and refinish the ends if needed.

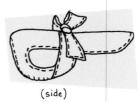

(back)

(side)

variations

■ A big dog can wear a T-shirt the same as you do: Find a T-shirt with a neckband that fits comfortably around your pet's neck and tie a knot at the bottom of the tee (at either his back or his belly) so it doesn't hang and get tangled in his legs.

■ Every dog appreciates a little personalization—she learned her name after all, so let her flaunt it with appliquéd letters atop the vest.

■ It's Superdog! Make a puppy cape!

71 a lead of their own
(dog lead)

NO SEW

Remember wrapping bits of your friend's hair in embroidery floss during recess and at sleepovers? My friends and I called them "happy sticks"—some called them (more obviously) hair wraps. Whatever you called them, all you need to remember is the technique. With a few T-shirt strips, you can fashion a long one (sans hair) to use as a very hip, sturdy dog lead. How very style-leash!

Note: A slip *lead* is not a standard dog *leash*. If used incorrectly, a lead can cause choking, so if your dog likes to pull, be extra cautious when using a lead to make sure he or she is never in distress.

LEVEL 2

ingredients

- **2 T-shirts (contrasting colors)**
- **scissors**
- **ruler**
- **safety pin**

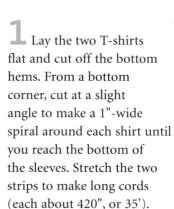

1 Lay the two T-shirts flat and cut off the bottom hems. From a bottom corner, cut at a slight angle to make a 1"-wide spiral around each shirt until you reach the bottom of the sleeves. Stretch the two strips to make long cords (each about 420", or 35').

2 Align the two cords and fold them in half to make a loop. Tie the looped end in an overhand knot about 2" from the fold. (You should have four dangling ends about 210", or 17½', long.)

3 Safety pin the knot to your pant leg or a pillow to keep it secure. Spread the four strips out, alternating them.

4 Wrap the first strip (A) around the three other strips (B, C, D), and pull it through to make a single knot. Repeat, keeping the three strips taut as you pull A tightly around them and slide it up to the top.

5 Continue making knots with A in this manner until you reach a desired length for segment A.

6 Now select strip B and wrap and knot it around the other three strips (C, D, A) to match the segment length of strip A.

7 Repeat with strips C and D, and repeat the pattern as necessary until the rope reaches about 50" to 60" in length.

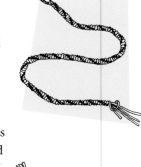

8 Thread the loose ends through the end loop and tie them four times in an overhand knot to create a knobby handle. Trim the ends. Wrap the slip lead around your pooch's neck and shoulders, pulling it so that it rests comfortably around her neck.

variations

■ Use this knotting technique to make bracelets, a belt, or a headband.

■ Alternatively, use the looping technique from the Sweatin' to the Oldies sweatband (see page 240) to make a dog lead.

■ Or, add more strips to thicken the cluster and braid or macramé (see Mad About Macramé belt, page 83) the strips instead.

Chapter 6

Mr. T

Be the Best You Can Tee

Cuff links, spats, ties, and tees—get ready, get set for 15 sweet projects you can make just for him.

A h, guys and their T-shirts. That unbelievable bond. In the first chapter of T-shirt history, the T-shirt was an exclusively male apparel item. Besides being a member of the boys-only club, the tee was hidden as an undergarment, or part of standard sailor-issued gear, not likely to be seen by mere civilians. But it wasn't shy for long.

The T-shirt kicked it into high gear with several noteworthy onscreen appearances, costaring alongside the smoldering likes of Marlon Brando, Paul Newman, John Wayne, and James Dean, all of whom set the standard for the relationship between men and their white T-shirts.

Years later, there were statements to be made, and a plain white T-shirt was, well . . . too plain. Silk-screening was just the process to get the word out (think "I'd Rather Be Skiing," "Don't Mess with Texas," and

"Save the Whales"). Now there are opportunities beyond cool screen-printed tees. Many guys are layering up: More often than not, I've noticed that they like to *add* things (patches, pins, layers) to their T-shirts. Sure, there are a few who cut off the sleeves to go to the gym. Or the Sid-wannabes who shred and slash their tees to a cobweb-style effect. The fact is, guys treasure that first T-shirt they bought at a rock show and hold on to it until well after it's been stretched beyond recognition and worn to rock-royalty perfection. Their T-shirts are loyal shrines to their favorite band (The Rolling Stones), bar, team (Sox, anyone?), or quirky hipster coffee shop. And they wear these "marks" with pride, irony, and devotion.

Turn the pages to find a number of T-shirt designs to celebrate that layering effect that is so appealing, plus some traditional guy accessories (spats, cuff links, a tie), all easily made from parts of a T-shirt.

Here's to injecting a little testosterone into the T-shirt. This is T-shirt refashioning with, for, and by the dudes of the world. That said, all of these designs are fairly gender-neutral—the T-shirt is a pretty universal, unisex garment, which is one reason it's become so iconic. So if you find a style that suits you, don't be shy: Just follow your measurements, make it, and wear it! Embrace the likes of Annie Hall and Iggy Pop and blur the lines of gendered fashion.

What's on Your Playlist:

"Mister Sandman"
—*The Chordettes*

"Mr. Roboto"
—*Styx*

"Mr. Bigstuff"
—*Jean Knight*

"Mr. Brightside"
—*The Killers*

"Mr. Tambourine Man"
—*Bob Dylan*

"Big Shot"
—*Billy Joel*

"Sir Duke"
—*Stevie Wonder*

"Man in Black"
—*Johnny Cash*

"Brown-Eyed Handsome Man"
—*Chuck Berry*

"Secret Agent Man"
—*Johnny Rivers*

"Candy Man"
—*Sammy Davis Jr.*

"Old Man River"
—*Paul Robeson*

72 mohawk mo' rock!
(hat)

NO SEW

Perhaps you've covered your tats well enough to get that investment-banking gig, but your inner punk soul is crying to step out. A real mohawk might take a little too much hair product to keep in place—never mind that HR wouldn't approve. Okay, so this hat is not quite the mohawk of your youth, but at least you can wear it, wash it, and wear it again. *And* it'll let you rock out on the subway, bus, or car ride into the office until you have to go from Peter Pan to J. P. Morgan.

LEVEL 2

ingredients

- **2 T-shirts (L, in different colors)**
- **measuring tape**
- **chalk marker**
- **scissors**

1 Measure the circumference of your head at its widest. Divide by 2 to get X".

2 About 10" from the top of one shirt (preferably with a logo), draw a horizontal or slightly diagonal line X" long across the front of the shirt. Draw an arc across the logo that connects the ends of X and extends 10" at its highest point. From the bottom of X, draw a long 3"-wide rectangle to the bottom of the T-shirt.

3 Cut out the shape marked in step 2 through both layers and place the pair across the front of the second T-shirt. Pin and cut around it through both layers of the second T-shirt.

4 Remove the pins and layer the two pairs so that the right side of the backs of the T-shirts are in the middle and facing, and the right sides of the front of the tees are facing out. Line up the edges and use the tips of your scissors to snip small holes through all four layers ¾" in from the edge along the arc and about 1½" apart.

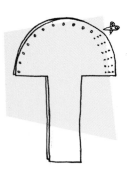

5 Count the number of holes you made in step 4 and cut an equal number of 1½" by 5" strips from both T-shirts.

6 Take one strip, fold it in half, and push the looped end halfway through the first hole from step 4. Pull the two ends through the loop to create a cow hitch knot that wraps around the edge and connects the sides of the hat together.

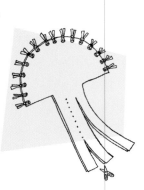

7 Alternating color strips, repeat step 6 with all holes until both sides of the hat are connected.

8 Cut lengthwise along the 3"-wide strips at the bottom of the hat to create three pairs of dangling fringe on each side.

9 Braid the strips together on each side and knot (or tie a scrap strip around) them at the end. Trim the mohawk fringe to your liking and rock out!

variation

■ Make the fringe extra long for a mane.

73 **moth-eaten chic** (t-shirt)

NO SEW

A friend, in a rare expression of creativity, saw a shirt like this and said, "I could *so* make that. You know, actually, I think I already have. . . ." As someone who wears punk pins on a regular basis, he has a slew of old T-shirts riddled with holes from years of pinning. Now you can get the look in a matter of minutes.

LEVEL 1

ingredients

- **1 T-shirt**
- **scissors (make sure the tips are sharp) or razor**
- **1 cardboard box flap**
- **chalk marker**

1 Take one T-shirt, turn it inside out, and insert the cardboard flap between the front and back layers.

2 Being sure to cut through only the front of the shirt, use the points of the scissor blades to poke or snip a small hole no larger than ¼" through one side of the chest region of the T-shirt.

3 Using chalk, mark a circle of six to eight dots with a 2" radius from the first hole. Then poke or snip at each of the dots, as shown.

4 Using the same number of holes you made in step 2, make a wider circle (about 3" farther) outside the first circle. Continue increasing the size of the circles as you move farther and farther to the edges of the shirt. (Soon the circles will increase so much that they won't be complete.)

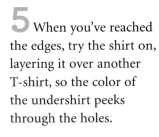

5 When you've reached the edges, try the shirt on, layering it over another T-shirt, so the color of the undershirt peeks through the holes.

variations

■ Make your "explosion" of holes originate at the bottom of the shirt, or just below the center of the neckband.

- -

■ Poke holes in different patterns—a heart, the Big Dipper (or the constellation that represents your astrological sign), an ironic Nike swoosh. Poke holes in the shape of letters, and send messages in dots. (Or better yet, send your message in reverse Braille, and let someone read you!)

74 **dart attack**
(t-shirt)

Somewhere between a dartboard and abstract art (a circular study for painter Josef Albers, perhaps?), this shirt incorporates two or three different-size circle patches that fit inside each other. It's visually appealing and the perfect cover for a corny or horrifying logo that you'd rather not advertise across your chest. Rotate the circle patches to create more abstract renditions of traditionally recognized words or images, or work with plain colors—shades of red or alternating orange and blue. Everyone will know the way to your heart when you're wearing this DIY dartboard.

LEVEL 3

ingredients

- ■ **1 T-shirt (regular fit)**
- ■ **2–3 scrap T-shirts**
- ■ **chalk marker**
- ■ **straight pins**
- ■ **needle**
- ■ **thread**

1 Lay the base T-shirt flat. From your scraps and other T-shirts, decide which colors and patterns best complement the background tee.

2 Trace (graduated mixing or measuring bowls make great patterns) and then cut three circles with diameters of 8½", 6", and 3½", respectively, from two or three scrap T-shirts.

3 Arrange the circles, layering them in descending size order, onto the front of the base T-shirt about 2" from the bottom of the neckband. Try rotating the circles so text or graphics don't necessarily read right side up.

4 Pin the circles in place and use a running backstitch to sew along the pinned edges, starting with the outermost circle and working your way in.

5 Remove the pins, pull it on, and hit the town—just watch out, you're now a target on the move.

variations

■ Want to be a rebel and "color outside the lines"? Add more decorative stitching (in contrasting thread color) across the T-shirt.

■ Experiment with other graduated shapes—squares, rectangles, ovals, stars, or a combination.

■ Live life dangerously and apply the target to the back.

75 #1 in my heart
("foam" finger)

Rooting from the couch or from the stadium, you need more than a bag of chips or a hot dog to show support for your team. Give 'em the spirit finger. If you use one of your team's T-shirts to make it, your prop has the added bonus of featuring the name of the team or of your favorite player. And maybe, just maybe, your "#1"-of-a-kind finger—the only jersey one in a sea of foam—will get you featured on the JumboTron.

LEVEL 4

ingredients

- **3 T-shirts**
- **ruler**
- **scissors**
- **chalk marker**
- **straight pins**
- **needle**
- **thread**
- **poly-fill stuffing**

1 Lay one T-shirt flat and cut a 12" by 18" rectangle through both layers.

2 Place your fist facedown against the rectangle, centered about one third up from the bottom, and trace a giant fist about 3" to 4" around yours.

3 Sketch a 4½"-wide by 8"-tall "index finger" that extends from the top of the traced fist (over to one side, please—no massive middle fingers!).

4 Cut around the shape, through both layers, and use it as a pattern for the other two T-shirts. Cut shapes out from those two T-shirts as well.

5 Sandwich the pieces together into two piles of three and pin them. Choose which one you want to be the front of the hand, and sketch the finger and thumb lines, as shown. Draw a 5" to 5½" line centered ½" from the bottom edge.

6 Flip over the second pile and draw small lines for the knuckles in the back. Make another 5" to 5½" line centered ½" from the bottom edge.

(back)

7 Sew a running stitch along the lines you drew in steps 5 and 6 (through only 3 layers at a time).

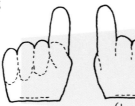 

(back)

variations

■ For a version using just one T-shirt, use a lot of stuffing to keep the hand upright. And sew a lone mitten into the base so your real hand doesn't mingle with the stuffing of the big hand.

■ Make a fist for your next rally, a sign language "I love you," a Hawaiian "hang loose," or a rockin' "rock on."

8 Sandwich the two (front and back) pieces together and pin. Starting at one end of the stitched line at the bottom, sew a running stitch (through all six layers) along the outer edge, stopping at the other end of the bottom stitched line. Remove the pins.

9 Stuff the hand, finger first. Then slip your hand in through the opening at the bottom, and it's root, root, root for the home team!

(back)

76 baby, i got your number

(t-shirt)

This one's best made with scraps—though iron-on numbers can help fill in the missing pieces faster. Show off your grasp of elementary math with a 1 through 10 homage to *Sesame Street*'s Count von Count (cue the thunder and maniacal laughter).

LEVEL 3

ingredients

- **1 T-shirt**
- **10–20 T-shirt scraps with numbers**
- **scissors**
- **needle**
- **thread**

1 Collect or cut numbers 1 through 10 or 20 from scrap pieces of T-shirts.

2 Lay the base T-shirt flat and arrange and pin the numbers to the front layer only. Have them read left to right, spiral them out from the center, or go backward.

3 Sew the numbers onto the shirt with a running stitch or whipstitch. Remove the pins.

variation

- If you're coming up short with the numbers, use your phone number (8-6-7-5-3-0-9-style), birth date, age, or graduation date.

77 heart on your sleeve
(t-shirt)

Where do you wear your heart? With this design, there's no question—it's out there for the world to see. Embellish it with your sweetheart's name, the classic "Mom," or leave it open for discussion . . .

LEVEL 3

---

ingredients

- **1 T-shirt (regular fit)**
- **1 T-shirt sleeve**
- **chalk marker**
- **ruler**
- **scissors**
- **straight pins**
- **needle**
- **thread**

1 Lay the T-shirt sleeve flat. Along the long edge (opposite the seam in the underarm), mark half of a heart whose line of symmetry is about 3" to 3¼" tall, as shown.

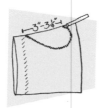

2 Cut through both layers, along the chalk mark, leaving the fold intact.

3 Unfold the fabric and place the heart onto the sleeve of your T-shirt so that it faces to the side (like a standard tattoo). Pin it in place.

4 Use a running stitch to sew around the perimeter of the heart. Remove the pins. *Optional:* Personalize the heart with iron-ons.

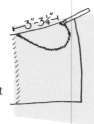

(side)

78 cuff love GREEN TEE
(button wrist cuff)

I was inspired to make this bit of man-jewelry one morning while doing some amazing people-watching at a local coffee shop. As the young man sitting near me casually sipped his latte and bravely attempted the *Times* crossword puzzle from the day before, it struck me that his buttoned jersey wrist cuff (part casual hipster, part incognito superhero) was the perfect Sunday-morning accessory.

LEVEL 3

ingredients

- 2 T-shirt sleeves
- tape measure
- chalk marker
- scissors
- needle
- thread
- 1" button

1 Measure the circumference around the wrist and add 2 to get x".

2 Cut out the bottom seam of two T-shirt sleeves and lay the fabric pieces flat.

3 Layer the fabric pieces over each other, wrong sides together. Pin them in place in the center to keep them from shifting. Mark and cut a 3" by x" rectangle through both layers.

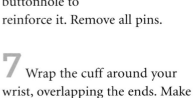

4 Sew a running stitch around the perimeter of the rectangle, about ¼" in from the edges. Check that the cuff fits well around your wrist with a 1" to 2" overlap.

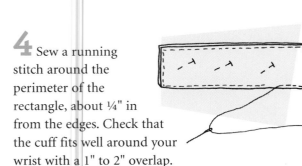

5 On one end, ½" from the edge, mark and cut a ¾" slit equidistant from and parallel to the long sides (this is the buttonhole).

6 Sew a tiny whipstitch around the edges of the buttonhole to reinforce it. Remove all pins.

7 Wrap the cuff around your wrist, overlapping the ends. Make a mark through the buttonhole onto the fabric below.

8 Stitch the button on at the mark.

9 Wear or continue to decorate with stitching, more buttons, or iron-ons.

variations

■ Make two cuffs for a Chippendales sort of vibe.

■ Add a row of buttons to make a cuff that's adjustable.

79 **tattoo you** (t-shirt)

Combine the best of two T-shirts in tattoo-style splendor. Cut the design from the most threadbare tee and apply it to another. Marry like themes or go for opposites-attract: well-rocked Ramones meets well-run marathon tee; bowling title meets baseball team. Punk meets pop— now play nice!

LEVEL 3

ingredients

- **2 T-shirts (preferably with designs/logos; the base shirt must fit well)**
- **scissors**
- **straight pins**
- **needle**
- **thread**

1 Lay the logo-ed T-shirt flat. Cut, through just one layer of fabric, about ¼" around the perimeter of the design(s) you'd like to apply to the base shirt.

2 Lay the base T-shirt flat and experiment with placing the cutout shape(s) across the front, back, or sides. Try overlapping the piece(s) with existing patterns and logos on the base tee, or keep them separate.

3 Pin the piece(s) in place on the base T-shirt. Use a running stitch to sew along the pinned edges. Remove the pins.

4 Sew some reinforcing seams through the patch to prevent the fabric in the center from puckering or bubbling out. Slip the shirt on and show off your new "ink."

80 spat's all, folks
(spats)

GREEN TEE

The FBI broke up the glory of organized crime, and you were most likely born too late to swing with Satchmo or Cab Calloway. But you can still indulge your hepcat with these glorified gators. Slip them on over your shoes and strut down the street with your hat cocked like you're the mayor of *Spat*ican City.

LEVEL 3

ingredients

- **2 T-shirt sleeves**
- **scissors**
- **chalk marker**
- **needle**
- **thread**
- **8 to 10 medium-size buttons**

1 Pull a sleeve over the foot, hem first. Put on a pair of shoes and align the underarm seam with the front of the foot.

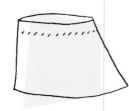

continued ▶

A cool cat with cool spats.

4 Remove the sleeve and sew four buttons, evenly spaced, along the traced line.

5 Snip four small slits (slightly shorter than the diameter of the button) along and perpendicular to the pinched front edge, through both layers, so that they line up with the buttons. *Optional:* For a more structured buttonhole, sew a tiny whipstitch around each slit.

6 Repeat steps 1 through 5 on the opposite sleeve. Slip the spats on and button them up. *Optional:* If they're riding up, add a T-shirt strap across the bottom to keep them planted.

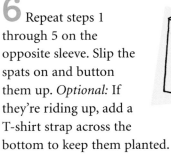

2 Pinch the top of the sleeve firmly (but gently) around the ankle.

3 Fold the pinched part down to the outside of the foot and trace the folded edge along the side of the sleeve, as shown.

variation

■ Use punk pins in place of buttons for an entirely **NO SEW** experience.

81 ranch dressing
(bolo tie)

GREEN TEE

NO SEW

The bolo tie design is derived from a Spanish throwing weapon, but its dark beginnings didn't stop it from being made the official neckwear of New Mexico in 2007. Why suit up with a boring traditional necktie when you can live dangerously? It's like being James Bond . . . if Bond were from the Southwest.

LEVEL 2

1 Cut off the hem of a T-shirt and then cut three ½" loops off the bottom. Snip through each loop to make three long strips.

2 Stretch out the strips and tie the ends together in a tight overhand knot. Braid the strips together to make a long cord.

3 Knot the ends in another overhand loop and trim off any excess fabric. Loop the braided length in half and attach the punk pin *around* the two cord ends.

(back)

4 Slip the loop over the head and slide the pin up the cords so it sits tightly against the collar.

---

ingredients

- **1 T-shirt or 3 T-shirt laces**
- **scissors**
- **punk pin**

Generation T

82 exquisite corpse (t-shirt)

So you have the Mickey Mouse T-shirt from your trip to Disney World fifteen years ago, the robot T-shirt from—well, you just happen to like robots—and the dinosaur T-shirt from that visit to the Museum of Natural History. Oh, what to do? In the spirit of the French surrealists' *cadavre exquis,* imagine what a T. rex would look like with Mickey ears and robot legs. Or a robot head with short arms, a tail, and scrawny mouse legs. It's a build-your-own adventure!

LEVEL 3

- - - - - - - - - - - - - - - - - - - -

ingredients

- - - - - - - - - - - - - - - - - - - -

- ■ **3 T-shirts**
- ■ **scissors**
- ■ **straight pins**
- ■ **needle**
- ■ **thread**

1 Lay all three T-shirts flat and decide which T-shirt makes the best base (choose the best color or the one that still fits).

2 Carefully cut ¼" around the perimeter of the graphic(s) on each of the two remaining T-shirts. Arrange them over the image on the base T-shirt.

3 Trim off any excess fabric and pin the pieces to the front of the base T-shirt. Use a running stitch to outline the entire "body," making sure to go through both layers of fabric when you reach the appliqués so that they are secured to the base T-shirt. Stitch any overlapping raw edges of the appliqués to the shirtfront.

4 Sew some reinforcing seams through the appliqués to prevent the fabric in the center of your shapes from puckering up. Remove the pins and try on this exquisite corpse!

All the News That's Fit to Screenprint

Every six weeks, T-post, an enterprising company in Europe, sends a new T-shirt with a news story printed on it to subscribers' homes or post office boxes. The design is based on a current news item, and the story itself is printed on the inside of the shirt. So instead of recycling your news at the end of the day, you wear it. And when that gets old, you refashion it and wear it some more! Check out t-post.se to subscribe.

variation

■ If all three of your T-shirts are too small, too big, or too ragged, cut out each of the graphics and sew them onto an entirely new T-shirt.

83 **urban cowboy** (t-shirt)

Go west, young man! (Okay, you can stay planted along the eastern seaboard, but go western with your closet.) So, you've been eyeing that snap-up cowboy shirt in the vintage store, but you don't have the funds to buy it? Why not make your own? Yoke up a favorite tee and hit the local saloon in this ranch-inspired top. Just do us all a favor and leave the chaps at home.

LEVEL 4

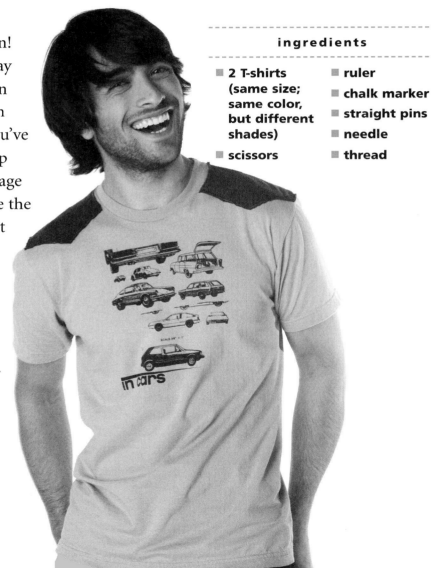

ingredients

- **2 T-shirts (same size; same color, but different shades)**
- **scissors**
- **ruler**
- **chalk marker**
- **straight pins**
- **needle**
- **thread**

1 Set aside the lighter shirt, which will be the base shirt. Lay the darker shirt flat. Measure and mark three points down the front from the top shoulder seam: 3" down along the neckband, 3" down along the side sleeve seam, and 4" down between them. Repeat on the opposite shoulder and connect the points with your chalk marker.

2 Flip the shirt over. Make a mark 5" down from the top shoulder seam along each sleeve seam. Make a third mark 6½" down from the center of the neckband. Connect the points.

(back)

3 Cut, through only one layer at a time, along the chalk lines you drew in steps 1 and 2.

4 Remove the panel from the darker shirt and pin it in place around the back neckband and over the shoulders of the lighter shirt.

5 Starting on one of the front portions, sew a running stitch along the pinned edges.

6 Continue sewing around the pinned edges to the back, completely securing the darker yoke to the base T-shirt.

(back)

7 Remove the pins and wear.

84 the missing links (cuff links) GREEN TEE NO SEW

An easy gift to make from scraps, here's the perfect accessory to remind him that even when he's all buttoned up and starched in that stiff-looking penguin suit, his T-shirt isn't so far away.

LEVEL 1

ingredients

- 1 T-shirt sleeve
- scissors
- clear nail polish (optional)

1 Mark and cut two 2" by 5½" strips from a T-shirt sleeve.

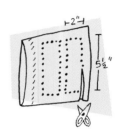

2 Take one strip and tie one end in a tight— *tight!*—overhand knot.

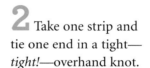

3 Tie the other end in a second overhand knot about ¼" from the first. As you tighten the second knot, coax it into place at the end of the strip.

4 Repeat steps 2 and 3 with the second strip. Trim off the ends very close to the knots. *Optional:* The knots should stay in place but, for security, paint on some clear nail polish over the ends and let dry.

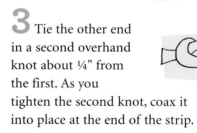
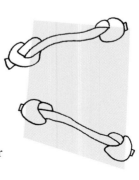

85 slash 'n' burn
(t-shirt)

Malcolm McLaren found the inspiration he was looking for in NYC musician Richard Hell's apathetic attitude and torn and safety-pinned clothing. Johnny Rotten solidified the look back in England, and before you knew it, the "punk look" was being bought and sold to kids willing to fork over the cash. Isn't that ironic . . . and a little *not* punk?

LEVEL 1

ingredients

- **1 T-shirt**
- **scissors, seam ripper, or razor blade**
- **1 flap from a cardboard box**
- **safety pins**

1 Lay the T-shirt flat and insert the cardboard flap between the front and back of the shirt. Cut slits haphazardly through just the front side of the T-shirt. Try cutting small snips and tearing them larger with your fingers.

2 Turn the shirt over and repeat on the back. Remove the cardboard. *Optional:* Wash and dry once before adding the pins.

(back)

3 Close some of the slashes with safety pins; place them evenly for a primmer version of punk, or set them riotously askew. Try it on and make any adjustments.

86 **go-go gadget**
(cord caddy)

The Age of Electronics might keep you tuned in, turned on, plugged in, and uploaded, but all of those chargers and cords under your desk or at the side of your bed definitely keep you tied down. In these days of watching carbs, say good-bye to wire spaghetti. Embrace your inner geek and get this stuff organized!

LEVEL 3

ingredients

- **1 T-shirt (M or L)**
- **ruler**
- **chalk marker**
- **needle**
- **thread**
- **scissors**
- **wooden or wire hanger**

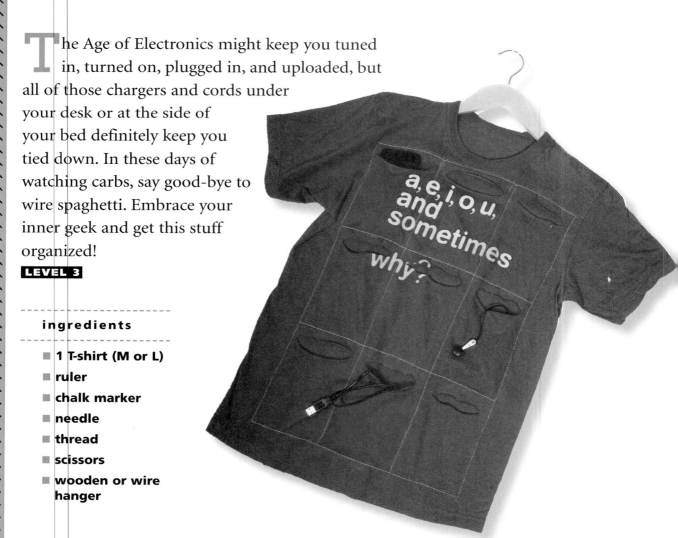

1 Lay the T-shirt flat and draw horizontal lines across the T-shirt just above the hem and just below the neckband. Draw two more lines parallel to, equidistant from, and between the first two.

2 Sew a running stitch or backstitch along the lines connecting the front and back layers of fabric, creating three equal rows.

3 Measure across one of the rows and divide by 3 to get x". Make marks every x" along the rows. Extend the lines vertically to make three columns.

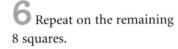

4 Sew a running stitch or backstitch along the four vertical lines through both layers. You should have a stitched grid with nine boxes.

5 On the first rectangle (upper left corner), mark and cut a slit *through only the front layer* about 1" down from the top seam and ½" from the side seams.

6 Repeat on the remaining 8 squares.

7 Insert a hanger (preferably wooden if your gadgets are heavy, otherwise bend a wire one to fit) through the neckband of the shirt. Hang it on the back of a closet door and fill each pocket with cords, chargers, and spare batteries. *Optional:* If you're feeling adventurous, label each pocket with iron-on letters: flash drive, MP3 player, FireWire cable, digital camera, printer cords, scanner cords, USB cords, etc.

variation

■ Ladies can also sort and store jewelry, lingerie, or other gadgety and nongadgety accessories.

Chapter 7

Road Trippin'

Pimp My Ride

Head out on the highway with 14 top-down projects to decorate your car and yourself when you're on the go.

You've got your road buddy in the passenger seat and all the essentials packed and ready to go. The map's in the glove box and the chip bag's open and accessible, so roll down the windows, crank up your best travel mix, and feel the wind in your hair. These are projects to deck out your drive, and pack in your suitcase. They range from practical (a lightweight dress you can wear every day or a steering wheel cozy to protect your hands in the blistering heat) to playful (a faux air freshener shaped like a tree, a reversible checkers/backgammon game board). You don't want to leave home without them, and making them will get you primed for the journey ahead.

Kerouac immortalized the experience in *On the Road,* and countless movies have followed suit, celebrating cars, friends, and freedom. But your trip will be your very own. Take the road less traveled, as poet Robert Frost suggests. Do the unexpected, even if it takes longer. Tour the historic houses, go skinny-dipping after hours, take in a drive-in movie. Cruise along the wide-open highway for another stretch of road before stopping at the next small-town Laundromat along the way. Shake the dirt and sand out of your I-made-them-myself car floor mats, wash them, dry them, get your motor running, and head back out on the highway. (Then look for adventure and whatever comes your way!)

You don't have to travel across the country to get mileage out of this chapter,

either. These do-it-yourself projects are designed to take with you or wear whenever you're on the go . . . in the car, on the train, biking to the park for a picnic. *Even* if your trip is an hour's drive to your local state park (pack your sleeping bag!), or a subway ride to the beach (don't forget your beach caddy) or a short jaunt on your scooter to the corner deli (accessorize with gloves!), you can dress the part in inimitable DIY style. *Even* if you ride the bus or other public transportation most everywhere and most often, there are occasions when you book a rental car for the weekend—and rental cars can *always* use some spiffing up.

Whatever the scenario, the smart traveler is always prepared: Travel with an old T-shirt and scissors in your "to-go" bag at all times because you never know when the next traveling travesty will strike. Move over AAA; it's DIY to the roadside rescue.

87 cruise control
(car floor mats)

What a welcome mat is to your house, these floor mats are to your car. They make your passengers feel at home whether you're cruising across state lines or just across town. And they're a great gift for the new car owner, or for someone who just inherited his parents' Buick Skylark. Coordinate the color of the mats to match the color of your car, or liven up a gray interior with bright shag-a-delic fabrics. Slap down two in the front and two in the back, slide behind the wheel, and rev the engine. Congratulations—you just pimped your ride.

LEVEL 3

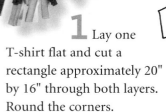

---
ingredients
(makes 1 driver's, 1 passenger's, and 2 rear floor mats)

- **4 T-shirts**
- **ruler**
- **chalk marker**
- **scissors**
- **needle**
- **thread**

1 Lay one T-shirt flat and cut a rectangle approximately 20" by 16" through both layers. Round the corners.

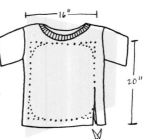

2 Keeping the two layers sandwiched together, mark and cut an arc that starts 5" inches in on the top and 8" down from the top (to make room for the wheel well).

3 Starting 1" in from the edges, mark and then snip horizontal and vertical rows of small holes about ¾" to 1" apart. Separate the two pieces.

4 Lay a second T-shirt flat and cut off the bottom hem. Cut into the bottom edge on an angle and level out the cut 1" from the bottom. Maintaining that 1" distance from the bottom edge, spiral around the bottom of the shirt until you reach the bottom of the sleeves (see step 1, page 107). Cut the resulting strip into several more manageable lengths (at least 12").

5 Attach a safety pin to the end of one strip and thread it down through the first hole of one piece leaving a 2" tail. Pull it back up through the second hole. Then thread it down through the second hole (the same hole you just pulled it through), leaving a 2" to 3" loop. Pull it up through the third. Then go down through

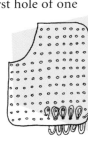

the third hole (leaving a loop) and up through the fourth, and so on, using new strips, as needed. When you're finished threading, snip through the ends of the loops to create shag fringe.

6 Using a running stitch, sew between the rows, securing each strip on the underside to the piece of fabric.

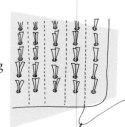

7 Repeat steps 5 and 6 on the other piece, making sure you turn the mat so that it is a *mirror* of the mat you just finished (that is, you want the cutout arcs to be on opposite sides).

8 Cut two 16" by 12" rectangles through both sides of the remaining T-shirt. Round the corners. Repeat steps 3 through 6 on both pieces.

9 Now step on the gas!

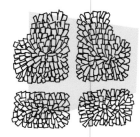

88 get fresh with me
(rearview mirror décor)

GREEN TEE

It's a truth universally acknowledged that your car will smell funkier at the end of a road trip than it did at the beginning. Sweaty socks, stale corn chips, a faint whiff of soda . . . they all add up to a slightly rank interior. Look like you've made the effort with this kitschy faux air freshener (and then roll down your windows to get a good cross breeze).

LEVEL 4

---
ingredients

- **4 T-shirt sleeves**
- **1 T-shirt strip (1" by 12")**
- **chalk marker**
- **scissors**
- **straight pins**
- **needle**
- **thread**
- **safety pin**

1 Mark and cut a 3" by 5" rectangle through both layers of one sleeve. Using one rectangle as a pattern, trace and cut 5 more rectangles through both layers (to make 12 rectangles total).

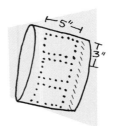

2 Stack and pin the layers together in two equal piles so that the right sides face out on the front and back of each set.

3 Cut off two adjacent corners of one set to make a point, as shown. Cut a 1" square out of the opposite adjacent corners.

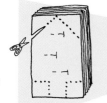

4 Mark and then make two 1" cuts 1" apart on each side of the set. Connect them with diagonal cuts parallel to those you made in the beginning of step 3, as shown. You should have a tree shape.

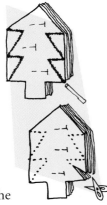

5 Repeat steps 3 and 4 on the second set.

6 Mark and cut a 2½" slit (through all layers) from the center bottom of one of the sets. On the opposite set cut a 2½" slit from the center top (through all layers).

7 Sew a running stitch, close to the edge, around the entire perimeter of each set. Remove the pins.

8 Slide the slits into each other, connecting the two pieces in a cross-section.

9 Snip two holes in the top tips of the second set (the one with the slit through the top), as shown. Attach a safety pin to one end of the 1" by 12" T-shirt strip from step 1 and thread it through both holes.

10 Tie the ends in a knot and hang the freshener from your rearview mirror. *Optional:* Soak or spray the freshener with a scent you actually like so it releases the scent as it sways in the breeze.

89 steering committee
(steering wheel cozy)

NO SEW

Whether you're battling cold New England winters (freezing steering wheel) or steamy Southern summers (scorching steering wheel), a steering wheel cozy will protect your hands from the extremes. I designed this for my sister who travels a lot between climates, from home in the North to school in the South. And it's a bit of fun interior décor that keeps her in good spirits when she's stuck in traffic on I-95.

LEVEL 2

ingredients

- **1 T-shirt**
- **scissors**
- **measuring tape**
- **safety pin**

1 Lay the T-shirt flat and cut off the bottom hem. Cut a 2½" tube from the bottom of the T-shirt and cut through one side to make a long strip. Cut a 1"-wide drawstring from the bottom of the T-shirt or use the hem, after removing the stitching. Stretch it out and snip through one side.

2 Measure the outer circumference of your car's steering wheel. Mark that measurement along the 2½"-wide strip from step 1 and snip off any excess.

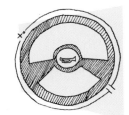

3 Wrap the strip around your steering wheel to make sure it fits.

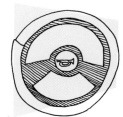

4 Mark and snip an equal number of holes down each side of the strip, ½" in from the edge and about 1¼" apart.

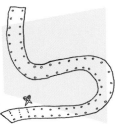

5 Lay the strip over the steering wheel, right side out. Attach the safety pin to one end of the drawstring and thread it through a hole near one of the braces, from the outside to the inside. Then thread it, from inside to outside, through the corresponding hole on the opposite edge. Pull the drawstring through, leaving a 7" tail at the end.

6 Continue threading the drawstring through the pairs of holes as if you were making a whipstitch. You are basically "sewing" the cozy to the wheel.

7 When you reach the next brace, "sew" your drawstring only around the outer edge of the cozy, where the holes are, then resume the full technique in step 6.

8 Once back at the original brace, pull the ends of the drawstring around the side of the wheel opposite the starting end and tie them securely in a small double-knotted bow. Snip the ends short so there is no danger of them tangling. As long as it's fitted and doesn't shift, the lacing will help with your grip on the wheel.

variation

■ Instead of the whipstitch technique, secure the cozy by crisscrossing the two ends of the drawstring as if you were lacing a shoe.

90 life, glove, and the pursuit of happiness

(gloves)

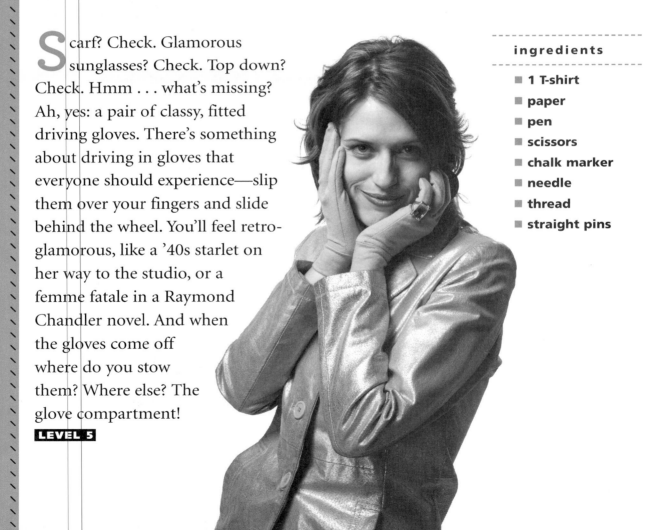

Scarf? Check. Glamorous sunglasses? Check. Top down? Check. Hmm . . . what's missing? Ah, yes: a pair of classy, fitted driving gloves. There's something about driving in gloves that everyone should experience—slip them over your fingers and slide behind the wheel. You'll feel retro-glamorous, like a '40s starlet on her way to the studio, or a femme fatale in a Raymond Chandler novel. And when the gloves come off where do you stow them? Where else? The glove compartment!

LEVEL 5

ingredients

- 1 T-shirt
- paper
- pen
- scissors
- chalk marker
- needle
- thread
- straight pins

1 Lay the T-shirt flat and remove the bottom hem. Then cut a 3½" strip off the bottom of the shirt. Turn the rest of the T-shirt inside out and set it aside.

2 Measure the distance around your wrist and add ½". Mark and cut that measurement twice along the strip so that you have two equal rectangles.

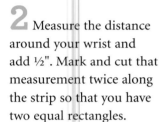

3 Fold each rectangle in half crosswise, right side in. Pin and sew a running stitch along the pinned edges. Remove the pins.

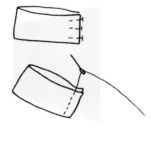

4 Fold the bottom edge of the tubes up to meet the top edge, wrong sides in. Pin the open edges together. (These will be the cuffs of the gloves.) Set them aside.

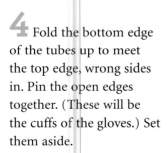

5 Gently stretch out your hand and trace its outline onto a piece of paper, extending down to include about 1" of your wrist. Cut out the pattern, adding about ½" around your hand and ¼" around the tips of your fingers.

6 Place the pattern on the front of the T-shirt (wrong side out) and trace around it.

continued ▶

Look Under *T* for *T-shirt*

Even though the garment wouldn't gain widespread popularity until the 1950s, its existence was made official decades prior: "T-shirt" became an official word in the English language when Merriam-Webster first included it in their dictionary in the 1920s.

7 Flip the pattern over and trace around it a second time (for the second hand) on the same T-shirt in the same manner as you did the first. (Unless you're going for the Michael Jackson look and only want one!)

8 Pin the two layers of the T-shirt together so they don't shift, and cut around the traced shape. Continue to pin the layers together around the perimeter of the hand, excluding the wrist.

9 Carefully sew a running stitch around the pinned edges with a ¼" seam allowance. Remove the pins and turn each glove right side out. Try it on; if it's too loose along the thumb, one of the fingers, or wrist, turn it inside out and restitch the seam with a wider seam allowance, making it fit a little tighter.

10 Slip a pinned cuff from step 4 over the bottom edge of a glove, lining up the open edges. Pin all three layers together. Sew a running or zigzag stitch around the edge. Repeat on the other glove.

11 Remove the pins and fold down each cuff. Slip your gloves on and go driving! (Or mini golfing, or dusting, or . . .)

91 mane-iac (scarf)

Who says fringe needs to be relegated to the ends of your scarf? This fringy spaghetti-string scarf has a ton of movement—the strings drape over your body and will billow out when the top's down and the window's wide open. Somewhere between Medusa's hair and a lion's mane, Mane-iac will make you feel like a wild woman on the hunt for adventure—it's a driving scarf for the twenty-first century.

LEVEL 1

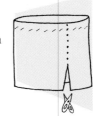

---

ingredients

- 1 T-shirt (L)
- scissors
- punk pin (or decorative brooch)

1 Lay the T-shirt flat and cut through both layers horizontally across the shirt just below the sleeves.

2 Rotate the tube so the hem is at the top. Cut vertically through it to create one wide rectangle.

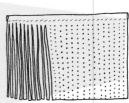

3 Starting at the left, cut long slits up from the bottom ½" apart, stopping at the hem. Pull at the fringe so the strips curl and separate.

4 Wrap twice, loosely around the neck and shoulders, securing with a punk pin.

92 **fender bender**
(racerback tank top)

Baggy, breezy, and a little bit tough, this racerback tank with a twist is biker chic at its best. So pull on your boots, hop on your chopper, and follow the signs to Route 66. And if all you have is a rusty Schwinn from a garage sale, you can still make it work: Tie some streamers to the handlebars (T-shirt scrap alert!), and pedal down your driveway like the outlaw you are.

LEVEL 3

1 Lay the T-shirt flat and cut off the sleeves just inside the seams. Cut out the neckband.

2 Expand the neck hole by measuring, marking, and cutting it about 3" to 4" deeper in the front. *Optional:* For added interest, cut a 3" vertical slit centered along the bottom front edge of the neck hole.

3 Cut off some fabric on the outside edge of the shoulder area to make the straps about 2½" to 3" wide.

4 Flip the shirt over and cut the armholes wider in the back (through only one layer), as shown, to create a racerback shape, making sure that the back piece is still 5" wide at its narrowest point.

(back)

5 Snip through the straps at the shoulder seams. Twist the back panel twice (one full rotation, so the right side faces out again). Align the shoulder straps again at the top and pin.

(back)

6 Sew a running stitch or whipstitch along the pinned edges. Remove the pins and layer over a sports tank or bandeau top. *Optional:* Get your seam ripper out and let down the hem for a little more length.

variation

■ Embrace the '80s even more by cutting the sleeves a little deeper, muscle tank–style, and wrap a contrasting T-shirt cord or cozy around the strap in the back to cinch it. Now get some parachute pants stat.

93 **double dare bolero**
(bolero cardigan)

Never travel without an extra layer (words of wisdom from moms everywhere). Whatever your destination, slip on this decidedly un-momlike bolero for evening strolls on the boardwalk or along the beach. You don't want to miss the best sunset ever because you had to run back to get a layer.

LEVEL 4

ingredients

- **3 T-shirts (1 fitted, 2 larger)**
- **scissors**
- **ruler**
- **chalk marker**
- **straight pins**
- **needle**
- **thread**

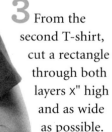

1 Lay the fitted T-shirt flat, cut off the bottom hem, and cut out the neckband. Widen the neck hole about 2" on either side.

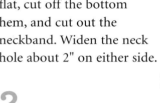

2 Mark and make a vertical cut through the top layer from the center of the neckline down to the bottom of the shirt. Measure the length of that cut edge (x").

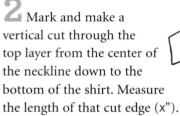

3 From the second T-shirt, cut a rectangle through both layers x" high and as wide as possible.

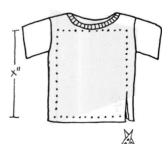

4 Pin one of the x" edges of each rectangle to a respective x" edge of the first T-shirt, right sides together. Sew along the pinned edges with a running stitch or whipstitch. Remove the pins.

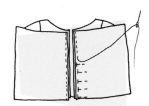

5 Draw diagonal lines from the right and left sides of the neck hole to the lower corners of the new panels, as shown. Cut along those diagonal lines, removing the excess fabric.

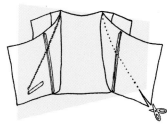

6 Lay the third T-shirt flat and cut off the bottom hem. Then measure, mark, and cut four tubes of equal height from below the sleeves.

7 Cut through the tubes to make strips. Pin the strips, right sides together, in a row to make one long strip. Sew along the short pinned edges and remove the pins.

8 With wrong sides in, fold the long strip in half lengthwise. Pin the edges and sew a basting stitch along the pinned edge. Remove the pins.

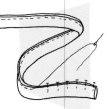

9 Gather the fabric against the stitches and pin the resulting ruffle evenly to the inside edge of the neck opening (which reaches from the corner tip of one front panel, around the back of the neck to the corner tip of the other front panel). Trim off any excess ruffle.

10 Sew a running stitch or a whipstitch around the pinned edge, being careful to catch all layers of the ruffle in the seam. Remove pins.

11 Try on the cardigan, loosely knotting the ruffled tips in the front.

variation

■ Use just two T-shirts and leave off the ruffle.

94 sweatin' to the oldies
(sweatband)

GREEN TEE

NO SEW

Here's a sweet macramé number to wear pulling weeds in the garden, working out to your mom's old Richard Simmons videos, or when driving with the top down in your vintage Corvette. Grab some scrap T-shirt strips and your crown can be decked out in no time.

LEVEL 2

ingredients

- Four ¾" to 1" loops (from the bottoms of T-shirts)
- scissors

1 Collect or cut four ¾"- to 1"-wide loops from the bottoms of T-shirts (in matching or mismatched colors). Cut through the loops and even the lengths. Loop the strips in half, and tie all eight ends in an overhand knot.

2 Safety pin the knot to a pillow or pant leg and make the fabric taut by looping each piece over the thumb and first finger of your right and left hands.

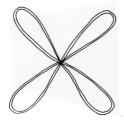

3 Switch the position of the left first finger loop with the right thumb loop by threading one loop through the other.

4 Switch the position of the right first finger loop with the left thumb loop by threading one loop through the other.

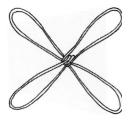

5 Repeat steps 3 and 4, continuing to alternate the loops. Loop the loops until your fingers are left with about 3" at the top. *Optional:* You can undo your work until step 2 and redo it to get the tension even.

6 Remove the loops from your fingers and loosen the overhand knot at the base. Remove the safety pin. Tuck all four loops through the loosened overhand knot and tighten.

7 Slide the band over your head to keep the hair out of your face or wear it aerobics instructor–style and work it out!

variations

■ Make a shorter cord for a bracelet cuff.

■ Make multiples and use them as handles for an overnight bag.

95 go west dress
(sporty dress)

My friend once drove for four days straight, from Colorado to California, wearing the same dress. She had other clothes, but it was hot in the desert, and the dress was so airy and comfortable that she didn't want to change. The Go West Dress is a tribute to her adventure and has that same casual won't-want-to-take-it-off feel. It's flared so you have plenty of legroom for driving, it's light and loose for battling the heat, and a no-fuss drawstring seals the deal.

ingredients

- **3 T-shirts**
- **scissors**
- **measuring tape**
- **chalk marker**
- **straight pins**
- **needle**
- **thread**

1 Turn one T-shirt (the one you want to use for the bodice) inside out and lay it flat. Cut off the sleeves just inside the seams, and cut through both layers across the top of the shirt just below the neckband. Measure the circumference of the bottom of the T-shirt and add 1 to get X".

2 Cut off the bottom hem. Fold the top front edge down about 1" and pin it. Repeat on the top back edge. Sew a running stitch along the pinned edges to create the drawstring casings.

3 Cut off the bottom hem of the second T-shirt and then cut 11" off the bottom to create a tube (the middle band of the dress). Cut through one side to make a rectangle.

4 Mark x" from one end of the rectangle and cut off the excess fabric beyond it.

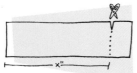

5 Fold the rectangle in half lengthwise, right side in, and pin along the open edge. Leaving a ½" seam allowance, sew a running stitch along the pinned edge. Remove the pins.

6 Turn the top of the dress right side out and insert it inside the middle band so the bottom edge lines up with the top of the band, right sides together. (Make sure the seam is oriented to the back or side.) Pin the two pieces together at the edges and sew using a zigzag stitch or whipstitch.

7 Remove the pins and fold down the middle band.

8 For the ruffle, lay the third T-shirt flat on its side (so the front and back become the new "sides"). Mark as large a half circle as possible extending from one of the side folds (without running into any seams). (Hint: Use a large mixing bowl as a guide.) Cut along the marks.

9 Fold the circle in half again (so that it's quartered).

continued ▶

10 Measure the circumference of the bottom of the middle band (it should be the same as the circumference you took in step 1). Use the equation c = 2πr (whereby c = circumference, r = radius, and π = 3.14) to determine the radius. Subtract ½" from the radius to get y" and mark it about four times from the corner of the quartered circle, as shown.

11 Draw an arc connecting the four marks and cut through all layers. Remove the corner piece.

12 Unfold the resulting "ring" of fabric.

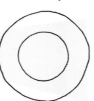

13 Pin the inside of the ring, rights sides together, around the bottom of the band. Sew around the pinned edge and remove the pins. *Note:* If you discover that the ring is too wide to fit around the bottom of the skirt without puckering, simply cut through the ring, overlap the cut ends as needed, and trim off excess fabric.

14 To make the drawstring, remove the stitching from one of the T-shirts' bottom hems, cut the loop through one side to make a strip, and pull it to make a cord. Attach a safety pin to one end and thread it through the front casing and then through the back casing.

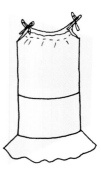

15 Pull the dress over your head and tie the drawstring over one shoulder in a bow. *Optional:* Snip through the drawstring on the opposite shoulder and tie the ends together for matching bows.

variations

- Sandwich the ruffle in with the middle band in step 6 so you have a pencil dress with a waistline ruffle.

- Use just the tube and ruffle to make a flirty skirt.

- Change it up every day with a different-color T-shirt strip as the drawstring!

96 **stuff it**
(sleeping bag stuff sack)

Toasted marshmallows, the mountain stream rushing next to your campsite, telling stories around a crackling fire. Scene change: Sleeping on the floor of your best friend's dorm room, playing "Would you rather?" till 3 A.M., polishing off a carton of chocolate chocolate-chip ice cream. Whether you're out in nature or "camping" at a friend's house, Stuff It is *the* sack to pack. Stuff your sleeping bag or a change of clothes into this cute, custom-made piece of camping gear that fairly beckons you to set out to see the world.

LEVEL 4

ingredients

- **1 T-shirt (XL)**
- **ruler**
- **scissors**
- **straight pins**
- **chalk marker**
- **seam ripper**
- **safety pin**
- **needle**
- **thread**

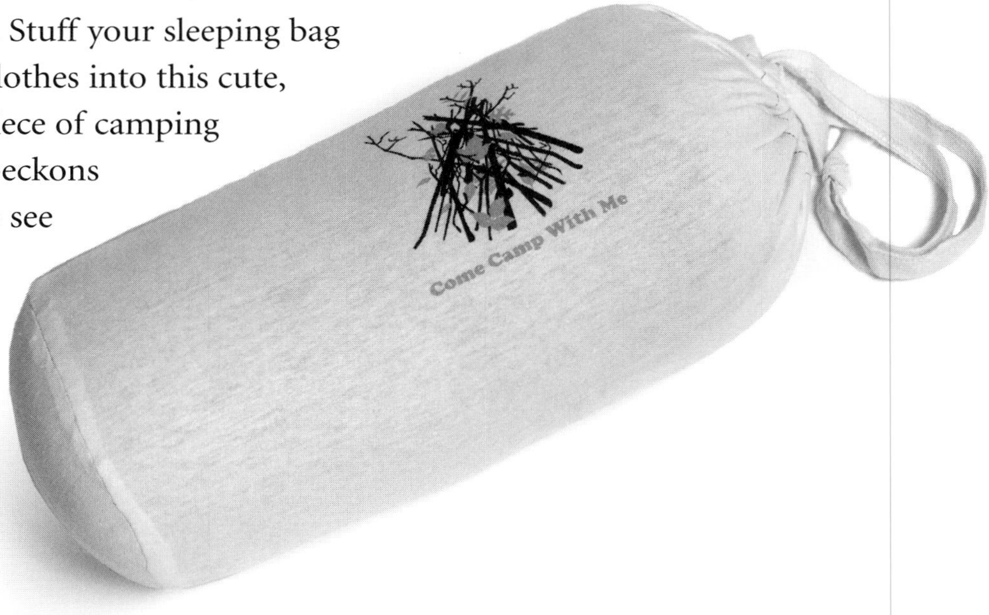

Come Camp With Me

1 Turn the T-shirt inside out and lay it flat. Cut off the hem just above the stitching. Set it aside (you'll use it for the bag's drawstring).

2 Mark a rectangle 18" by 24" on the front of the T-shirt and cut out through both layers. Set aside the back rectangle.

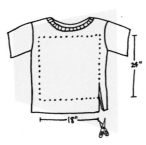

3 Fold the front rectangle in half crosswise, right side in, lining up the short edges and pinning them. Use a running stitch along the pinned section, leaving a ½" seam allowance, to create a tube (the cylindrical part of the stuff sack). Remove the pins and set aside.

4 Fold the second rectangle in half crosswise, right side in, matching up the two short edges. Mark an 8"-diameter circle. (Hint: Use the rim of a small mixing bowl as a pattern.) Cut out around the chalk lines.

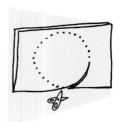
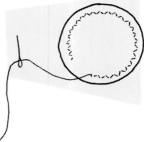

5 Around one of the circles, about ¼" from the edge, sew a zigzag stitch for reinforcement and to keep the edges from curling.

6 Pin the second circle piece, right side in, to the inside edge of the tube you made in step 3. Leaving a ½" seam allowance, use a running stitch to sew along the pinned edges around the bottom of the sack. Remove the pins.

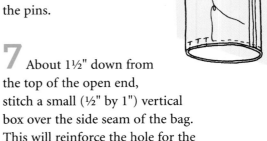

7 About 1½" down from the top of the open end, stitch a small (½" by 1") vertical box over the side seam of the bag. This will reinforce the hole for the drawstring.

8 With the bag still inside out, fold the top edge down about 1½" and pin. On the side opposite the stitched box from step 7, insert about 1" of the stitched circle (from step 5) under the fold-over (to create the top flap). Pin it in place.

9 Sew along the pinned edge, about 1" from the top, creating the casing for the drawstring and securing the circular flap. Sew a second row of stitches, parallel to and about ⅛" below the first, for decoration and reinforcement. Remove the pins.

10 Turn the sack right side out. Use a seam ripper to remove the stitches of the vertical seam inside the box sewn in step 7 to make a small hole (do *not* remove the stitches of the box but rather the stitches *inside* the box). Attach a safety pin to the hem from step 1, thread it through the hole, along the casing, and out the same hole.

11 Remove the safety pin and tie each of the ends in a knot. Stuff the sleeping bag (or other secret stash: pair of shoes, birthday gift) in the finished bag, place the flap over the top, pull the drawstring, and you're on your way.

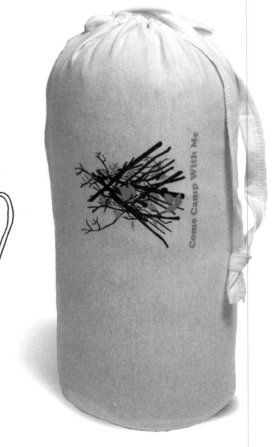

Come Camp With Me

97 **beach bum**
(beach caddy)

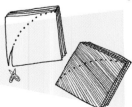

Pack your beach essentials in the pockets of this clever caddy (book, magazine, or deck of cards in one pocket, sunglasses in another, MP3 player in a third, and don't forget the sunscreen). Its colorful panels mimic that of a beach umbrella, so it'll fit right in at the beach volleyball game and along the water's edge. This caddy flattens out completely, so you can shake all the sand out before you head home.

LEVEL 5

---

ingredients

- **6 T-shirts**
- **measuring tape**
- **chalk marker**
- **scissors**
- **straight pins**
- **needle**
- **thread**

1 Lay two T-shirts flat on top of each other and mark and cut 20" squares from each T-shirt through all four layers.

2 Draw a wide arc between two opposite corners of the square, as shown. Cut along the line through all four layers.

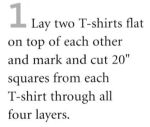

3 Separate the four wedges (quarters) and arrange them, right side down, in two large circles as shown, alternating the panels.

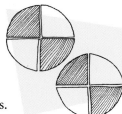

4 Pin two quarters, right sides together, along one of the straight edges to make a half-circle. Sew a running stitch or whipstitch along the pinned edge. Repeat on the other two quarter-circles. Remove all pins.

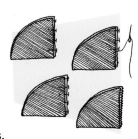

5 Pair off the half-circles, right sides together, and pin and sew along the straight edges to create a circle. Remove the pins.

6 Repeat steps 1 through 5 on two more T-shirts to create a second circle. Set aside.

7 Place the two circles together, right sides facing, and pin around the edges. Set aside.

8 Lay the fifth T-shirt flat and cut off the hem. Then cut a 7½"-high tube off the bottom of the shirt and cut through it to make a long strip.

9 Starting from one end, mark every 4" eight times along the edge of the strip. Cut straight at those points to make eight 4" by 7½" rectangles. Remove the excess fabric.

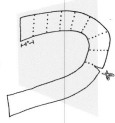

10 Take one rectangle and, wrong side up, fold the 7½" sides 1" into the center. Then fold the short ends together to make a loop. Pin at the open end, making sure to "catch" the turned-under edges. Repeat on the remaining seven rectangles.

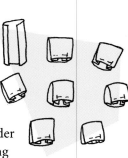

continued ▶

11 Take the pinned circles from step 7 and space the eight loops evenly around the circumference, inserting them between the layers, loop end first. Line up the open ends with the circle edges (this will ensure that the loops stick off the sides when you turn the circle right side out). Pin them in place.

12 Sew a running stitch around the perimeter of the circle, ½" from the pinned edges, securing the circles and loops together. Leave about 3" open.

13 Remove the pins, turn right side out, and fold the unsewn edges in. Pin it closed and sew a running stitch around the perimeter of the circle, ¼" from the edge.

14 Cut 12" squares through both layers of the tops of the fifth and sixth T-shirts. Follow steps 2 through 5 with the 12" squares.

15 Center the single smaller circle right side up on top of the bigger (double layer) circle. Align the cross-seams and pin.

16 Sew a running stitch along the cross-seams, connecting all layers together. Remove the pins. The four wedgelike pockets (between the large and small circles) are to hold your beach essentials.

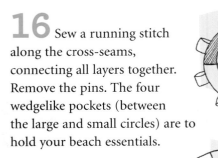

17 Cut off the hem of the sixth T-shirt from step 14 and cut horizontally across the remaining shirt to create a tube. Cut the tube in half to create two tubes. Then cut through the tubes to make two strips.

18 Lay the strips together, right sides facing, and sew a whipstitch or running stitch along one short edge. Unfold it and stretch it a little to make one long strip.

19 Run the strip through the loops on the outer edge of the circle. Bunch the opening to close the satchel and knot the ends together.

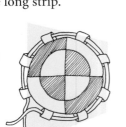

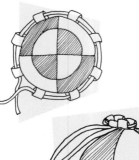

98 a fork 'n' the road
(flatware travel caddy)

Picnicking is one of my favorite extracurriculars, but some of the required accessories are less than desirable. Take plastic flatware, for instance—environmentally insidious, snaps under pressure, and so on. On the other hand, tossing metal flatware into the depths of your handbag is less than sanitary (if the bottom of your handbag looks anything like mine). A friend who makes these travel flatware sets from vintage fabric remnants inspired this jersey knit edition. *Note:* This cozy case is also perfect for a road trip, eating last night's leftovers at work, or any other time you have to eat on the run.

LEVEL 4

ingredients

- **1 T-shirt**
- **ruler**
- **chalk marker**
- **scissors**
- **straight pins**
- **needle**
- **thread**

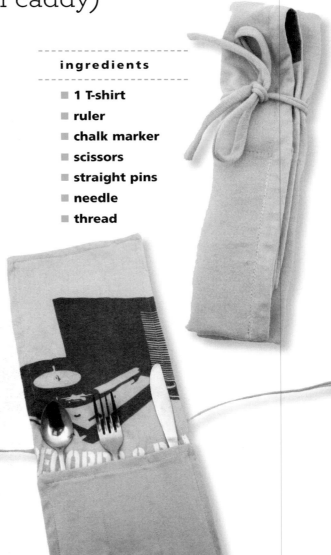

1 Measure the tallest member of your flatware set (probably the knife). Add 1" (B). Divide B by 2 and add ½" (C). Divide B by 3 and then multiply by 2 (A).

2 Turn the T-shirt inside out and lay flat. Add A, B, and C to get x and mark a 7" by x" rectangle across the front of a T-shirt. Cut out the rectangle through both layers.

3 Keeping the two rectangles together, pin around the edges and sew a running stitch with a ¼" seam allowance along the pinned area, leaving 2" to 3" open at one of the short edges.

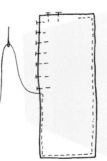

4 Turn the rectangle right side out. Tuck the open ends in and pin them. Sew a running stitch around the entire perimeter of the rectangle, through both layers, with a ¼" seam allowance.

5 Remove the pins and fold one short end (a segment equal to C minus ½") up against the panel. Pin along the side edges and sew a running stitch ¼" from the edge, over the stitches you sewed in step 4. Remove the pins.

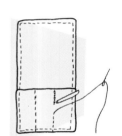

6 Measure the distance between the two side seams (should be about 6"). Divide that distance by three and mark two lines from the side seams at those intervals.

7 Sew a running stitch along those lines, making three distinct pockets.

T-shirt Mania

In 1951, with rising popularity of "underwear as outerwear," 180 million T-shirts were sold in the United States. By 1995, that figure had exploded to more than 1 billion T-shirts in one year.

8 Cut a 1"-wide strip from the bottom of the T-shirt and stretch it. Trim it to about 22" and center it along the back of the pocket, about ½" to ¾" above the lip of the pocket.

9 Pin the strip in place and sew a running stitch lined up above the center pocket and whose length is equal to that of the center pocket. Remove the pins.

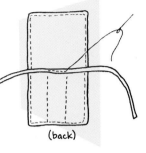

(back)

10 Flip the caddy right side up and insert a spoon, knife, and fork into each of the three pockets.

11 Fold the top flap down over the flatware and fold each side of the caddy into the center one at a time. Tie the ends of the strip into a bow at the front. Stow the set in your handbag,

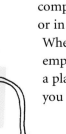

variations

■ Use the same caddy (or add a fourth pocket) for storing multiple sets of chopsticks for sushi to go.

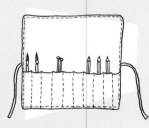

■ Make a caddy for your drawing pencils, paintbrushes, knitting needles, or crochet hooks by adding to the width of the caddy and making narrower pockets. To store this version, add ties and roll it up rather than folding it in thirds.

picnic basket, the glove compartment of your car, or in a desk drawer at work. When you unfold it, the empty caddy doubles as a place mat while you nosh.

99 soft score
(checkers/backgammon board)

Rolls out to play; ties up to go. When you're sick of playing Go Fish, and Rock Paper Scissors has lost its charm, it's time to really throw down. Stack your bottlecap kings in checkers, and then flip the board over for a round of backgammon. Like T-shirts, these games are classics that will never go out of style.

LEVEL 5

ingredients

- **2 T-shirts (XL, in different colors)**
- **ruler**
- **chalk marker**
- **scissors**
- **straight pins**
- **needle**
- **thread**

1 Lay one T-shirt flat and cut a 17" square from the top of the shirt (below the neckband) through both layers.

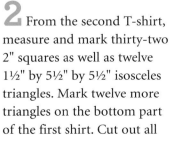

2 From the second T-shirt, measure and mark thirty-two 2" squares as well as twelve 1½" by 5½" by 5½" isosceles triangles. Mark twelve more triangles on the bottom part of the first shirt. Cut out all fifty-six shapes.

3 Take one of the large squares from step 1 and, right side up, mark a centered 16" square. Then measure and draw a grid inside that square, with all lines 2" apart. Place the 2" squares you cut in step 2 onto the alternating squares on the grid and pin in place, as shown.

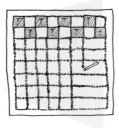

4 To secure each square, sew a running stitch across each line in the grid—both along the width and the length (that's 18 seams in all). Remove the pins.

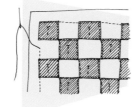

5 Take the second large square from step 1 and, right side up, draw a centered 16" square. Then draw a row of parallel lines about 1⅓" apart inside that square.

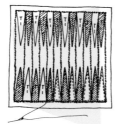

6 Gather the triangles you cut in step 2 and, alternating colors, place and pin them between the lines and against the edge of the 16" square, as shown. Sew a running or small zigzag stitch close to the edges along each triangle, adhering it to the grid. Remove all pins.

7 Place the two large squares together, right sides out, and pin. Cut a 10" by ¾" strip from the scraps and insert it 2" between the two layers at the midpoint of one side.

8 Sew a running stitch around the perimeter of the 16" square to connect the two "boards" together. Sew a second running stitch around the perimeter of the entire square, leaving a ¼" seam allowance, making sure to secure the 10" strip.

9 Roll up the mat starting at the end opposite the strip, then wrap the strip around and tuck to secure it. Ready to go!

10 For checkers or chess, orient the mat so the darker color is in the lower right corner for each contestant. For backgammon, orient the mat so that the triangle bases face each contestant. Round up two colors (12 each for checkers, 15 each for backgammon) of plastic soda tops, metal bottle caps, or buttons as game pieces. Grab a pair of dice (for backgammon) and play!

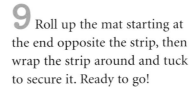

100 ants go marching
(picnic blanket)

Welcome to quilting lite. Your squares don't need to be exact (in fact, they're rectangles). You don't need to worry about batting, because this blanket's about ground cover, not warmth. And there's no binding to fuss with—so embrace those jagged edges. The result is a happy patchwork pinwheel picnic blanket. Bundle it up and it's ready to be unfurled whenever you're ready for some impromptu picnicking, wine and cheese in the grass, or lounging in the park.

LEVEL 3

---
ingredients

- **8 T-shirts (L or XL, approximately the same size)**
- scissors
- straight pins
- needle
- thread

1 Lay the smallest T-shirt flat and cut off the hem, just above the seam. Cut off the sides, through both layers, just inside the sleeves and cut off the top just below the neckband.

2 Use these layers as a pattern for the other seven T-shirts, and cut matching rectangles from each.

5 Pin and sew four more rectangle pairs into Ls like the ones you put together in step 3. Pin each L into the corner of each L in the pinwheel shape, as shown, and stitch in place, right sides together. Remove the pins.

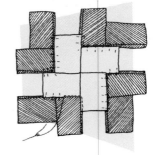

3 Separate the front and back of the T-shirts so you have sixteen panels. Arrange two panels so that one short side is matched to the end of one long side, as shown. Pin them, right sides together, along that short edge. Pin a second pair of rectangles together in the same way. Sew a running stitch or whipstitch along the pinned edges. Remove the pins.

6 Insert the last four rectangles in the gaps around the edge, as shown. Pin them in place, right sides together. Sew along the pinned edges and remove the pins.

4 Rotate one pair of the rectangles 90 degrees so that the two create a pinwheel shape next to each other. Pin along the shared edge, right sides together, and sew with a running stitch or whipstitch. Remove the pins.

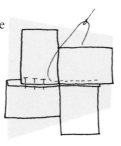

variations

■ Cut twice as many rectangles and make a matching underside so the blanket is reversible (and thicker and more durable). Or, cut a spare flat sheet to match the top shape and stitch the layers together at the edges for more thickness.

- - - - - - - - - - - - - - - - - - -

■ The bigger the picnic, the more T-shirts you'll need! Add space on your guest list by adding more rectangles to your blanket, attaching them in the same spiraling pattern.

- - - - - - - - - - - - - - - - - - -

Chapter 8

Out on the Town

Is It Hot in Here or Is It Tee?

A sassy mix of 20 fast and fabulous dare-to-bare tops, brazen boas, and garters to put flirt in your skirt and dance in your pants.

A night out may be priceless, but it's not cost-free. Hardly! Between treating your gals to a round, gifts for your bachelorette friend, or the occasional splurge on a late-night cab, your wallet can get a lot lighter as the night goes on. You still want to look good—and effortlessly fashionable—but unless you're an heiress, you probably don't want to spend a fortune on

clothing or accessories. The projects in this chapter are chic, sexy, and many of them take less time to make than it takes to wait in line at your favorite clothing megastore.

Part of the fun of going out is getting ready, tweaking the outfit and trying new things until you hit the perfect combo of clothing and accessories. Think of DIY as an earlier step in party prep, building anticipation for all the fun to come. In addition to fashioning some of the hottest tops and dresses in the book, you'll learn the tools to make your own bags, boas, and even gloves to wear when you hit the town. You'll have to get the heels yourself (until we figure out how to construct them completely out of T-shirts), but you can create more of your outfit than you realize.

And when your friends ooh and ahh over your sexy, stylin' gear, you can make a mental note of who liked what. Because it's practically a guarantee that one of them will have a birthday (sweet sixteen? the big twenty-one? thirtieths, too!) or get married before you can make a drawstring from a hem (okay, maybe not that soon)—and you'll need a gift. Design a shirt for the bride to be, or create a team of shirts for the whole bachelorette posse. I once saw a group of girls at a Coney Island Cyclones game showing solidarity with the birthday girl in their group by wearing matching T-shirts that they had proudly decorated themselves.

A few years back, my friends and I got together to make a gorgeous red top with ruffled sleeves for our friend Ellen to wear to her bachelorette party. She had the requisite veil, too, but stood out from the hordes of other engaged chicks out on the town that night, because her shirt expressed her individuality (red is her favorite color) and was made with love by her friends! And if you've already spent $40 on a platter from the gift registry, it doesn't hurt to save some cash by DIYing the bachelorette or shower present.

You can also make the party *all about* the DIY. As an alternative to the traditional toilet paper wedding gown game at the next bridal shower, use T-shirts instead of TP. Split into teams, à la *Project Runway,* to design a honeymoon outfit for the bride. Provide scissors and safety pins, assign roles of the upbeat and concerned mentor, the severe judge, the foreign supermodel. Then set a time limit, put up a makeshift runway, and start the show!

What's on Your Playlist:

"Holiday"
—*Madonna*

"Celebration"
—*Kool and the Gang*

"Girls Just Wanna Have Fun"
—*Cyndi Lauper*

"Fight for Your Right to Party"
—*Beastie Boys*

"Dancing Queen"
—*ABBA*

"Rock and Roll All Night"
—*Kiss*

"Party Hard"
—*Andrew W.K.*

"Dead Man's Party"
—*Oingo Boingo*

"Just the Best Party"
—*World/Inferno Friendship Society*

"Massive Nights"
—*Hold Steady*

"Let's Go Crazy"
—*Prince*

"I Could've Danced All Night"
—*My Fair Lady*

101 back in action (t-shirt)

Despite its complicated pattern, this "ribbed" top takes just 10 minutes to make, is no sew, and is arguably one of the hottest transformations in this collection. Layer it over a contrasting colored tank top for a flashy peek-a-boo or dare to go bare underneath for a risqué rocker look. Either way, you and your top are *guaranteed* to get noticed. And, once you've got the technique down, adapt it to any jersey knit garment—imagine the pattern snaking up the sides of your leggings or along the bottom of a stretch skirt.

LEVEL 2

ingredients

- **1 T-shirt (fitted)**
- **scissors**
- **safety pin**

1 Spread your T-shirt flat on its side so that the back and the front are the new "sides," as shown.

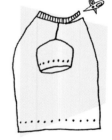

2 Cut off the hem and cut out the neckband about ½" outside the seam. Trim the sleeves about 2" in from the edge of the hem.

3 Starting at the bottom, cut horizontal slits about 6" long and ¾" apart along the fold at the back of the shirt.

4 Avoid cutting into the sleeves, and cut the last slit about 1" from the neckline.

5 Unfold the shirt and lay it flat with the back facing up. Take the bottom two strips in each hand and pull the second one behind and then around the first.

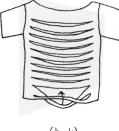

(back)

6 Release the first strip. Then pull the third strip up through the loop created by the second.

7 Pull the fourth strip up through the loop created by the third. And so on.

8 Continue to loop each strip until you reach the top. Rather than loop the last strip, use a safety pin to attach the loop made by the second-to-last strip to the center of the last strip at the neckline. *Optional:* Sew the loops in place permanently with a few stitches or attach a button instead of using a pin to make it more decorative.

(back)

9 Try it on bareback, or layer it over a tank top.

variations

■ Make two thinner columns of slits down the back of the T-shirt.

- - - - - - - - - - - - - - - - - -

■ Make thin columns down each side of the T-shirt.

- - - - - - - - - - - - - - - - - -

■ Make a thin column of slits down the center front, sides, and center back as shown, right.

- - - - - - - - - - - - - - - - - -

102 **scrap action** GREEN TEE
(necklace)

NO SEW

In a sea of beads, pearls, and fake jewels, this one hundred percent fabric necklace stands out. Use a fingerweaving technique reminiscent of middle school art projects to create a very hip and grown-up piece of jewelry. Loop it around your neck twice and wear it with a simple sheath dress, and you're bohemian elegance personified.

LEVEL 2

ingredients:

■ **5 to 7 scrap sleeves (from S or M T-shirts)**
■ **scissors**

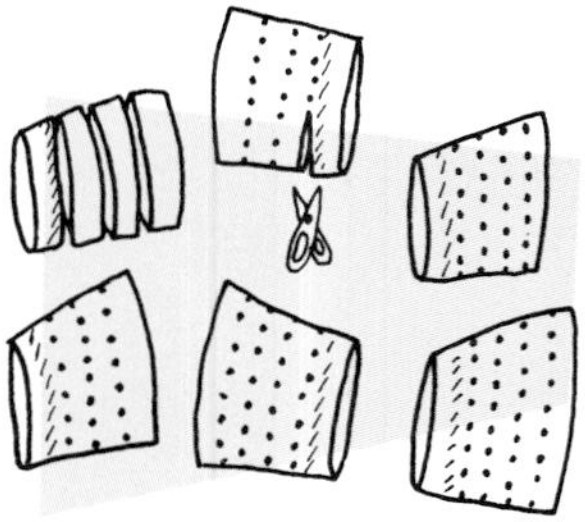

1 Cut the hem off each sleeve. Then mark and cut 1"-wide loops parallel to the first cut. (Each loop is about 1½" long on the necklace, so you'll need to cut about 32 loops to make a 48"-long necklace.) Cut through two of the 1" loops to make strips; set them aside.

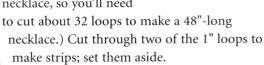

2 Take one loop and drape it around the base of the first finger of one hand, palm up. Twist it one half turn and place it around the second finger.

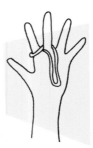

3 Continue twisting the loop once before placing it around the next finger.

4 Repeat steps 2 and 3 with a second loop. (You will have two layers of twisted loops.)

5 Pull the bottom loop on your first finger over the top loop and off your finger (from front to back).

6 Pull the bottom loop off your second finger in the same way. Repeat on the third and fourth fingers.

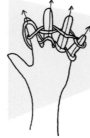

7 Repeat steps 2 and 3 with a third loop. Then pull the bottom loop over and off each top loop one at a time, as you did in steps 5 and 6.

8 Repeat the process, adding loops one at a time (don't have more than two loops on your fingers at one time). The necklace will begin to hang off the back of your hand.

9 When your necklace reaches a desired length, take one of the two strips you cut in step 1 and thread it through each of the loops still on your fingers. Carefully remove the loops from your fingers (the strip should keep the loops from unraveling), cinch, and tie the strip in a tight double knot.

10 Weave the second strip through the loops on the opposite end, cinch, and tie the ends in a double knot.

11 Wrap the necklace around your neck twice and tie the ends of the strips in a bow at the back to "clasp" it.

103 gimme some glovin'
(laced glovelets)

GREEN TEE

NO SEW

ingredients

- **2 T-shirt sleeves**
- **1 T-shirt bottom hem or 60" ribbon**
- **scissors**
- **2 safety pins**

Your name gets called over the bar microphone. The first notes of "Time After Time" crackle from the '70s speakers. You push through the raucous crowd just in time to grab the mike with your Cyndi Lauper-esque laced-up glovelets and belt out the chorus as it blinks across the karaoke screen. You *are* the Karaoke Queen. Give some extra oomph to karaoke night, your friend's '80s party, or even a slow day at the office when you transform T-shirt sleeves into these soft and simple glovelets.

LEVEL 2

1 Cut out the underarm seam from both T-shirt sleeves.

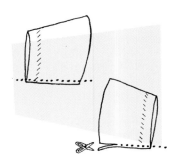

2 Lay both pieces flat. Measure a rectangle about 8" along the sleeve hem and about 5½" high on each piece. Cut out the two rectangles.

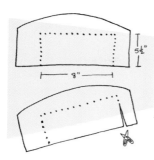

3 Wrap the fabric around your wrist (with the hem edge closest to your hand) and pinch and mark the extra fabric.

4 Trim off the extra fabric. Then trim another 1" off one edge. Trim the second rectangle to match the first.

5 Fold the rectangles in half (5½" sides together), right side out, and snip holes through both layers about ½" in from the edge and 1" apart from each other. (You should have about four or five evenly spaced holes.)

6 Cut two cords, each between 20" and 30" long, from the hem of a scrap T-shirt.

7 Attach a safety pin to each end of one cord and thread one end through the first two holes (starting at the hem). Even out the ends and then lace the cord through the holes as if you were lacing up a shoe, from inside to outside. Repeat on the second one. *Optional:* Tie the ends in bows and stop here for a pair of wrist cuffs.

8 Fold the glovelets with the lacing facing left and right. Mark a 1½" vertical line equidistant from the sides, top, and bottom edges of each glovelet. Cut along each chalk line, through just one layer, to create the thumbholes.

9 Slip them on and go about your business.

104 knot so fast
(knotted tank top)

NO SEW

Making this top involves a simple no sew technique that, once mastered, can be applied to other parts of the tee—the front, the back, *and* the sides, the tops of the sleeves, and so on, to resize and restyle. The results are addictive—you'll want to make variations of this tank top for parties, concerts, summer days in the park, and just hanging out with friends.

LEVEL 2

ingredients

- 1 T-shirt (regular fit or baggy)
- scissors
- chalk marker
- ruler

1 Lay the T-shirt flat, cut off the sleeves just inside the seams, and cut off the bottom hem. Then cut vertically up the sides of the shirt, opening them up.

2 Try on the top to see how much you need to take it in at the sides. Pinch the sides and mark with chalk or a straight pin where you'd like the side seams to be and where you'd like the top and bottom of the armhole to be.

3 Remove the shirt and draw a vertical line along each side, extending the marks you made in step 2.

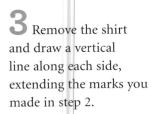

4 Starting at the bottom of one side, cut perpendicular slits about ¾" apart, stopping at the chalk lines you marked in step 3 for the armhole.

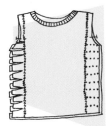

5 Repeat step 4, creating matching fringe on the opposite side.

6 Starting at the bottom of one side, tie a piece of fringe from the front to the corresponding piece on the back.

7 Repeat on the other side and trim off any excess fabric remaining at the armholes.

105 love it or weave it
(crisscross tank top)

It's a hot summer evening at the roller rink and you've just finished lacing up your retro white skates with pink wheels. "Dream Weaver" is crooning over the speakers as you push off. The wind is at your back, and the straps crisscrossing over the built-in bandeau in this tank top are the perfect '80s accent for this dance party on wheels. Warning: Your moves plus this top *might* cause a massive pileup in your wake.

LEVEL 4.5

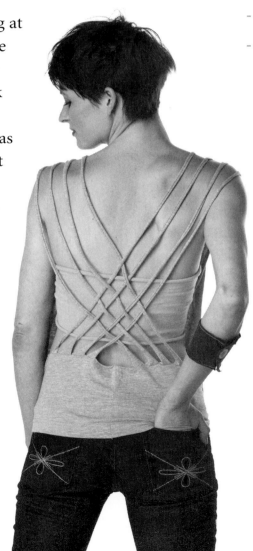

1 Lay one T-shirt flat, cut off the sleeves just inside the seams, and cut out the neckband.

2 Flip the T-shirt over. Mark and cut, through only the back layer, a horizontal slit across the full width of the T-shirt and 6" up from the hem.

3 Mark and cut vertical parallel lines beginning at either side of the neck hole down to the slit, removing a rectangle of fabric from the center.

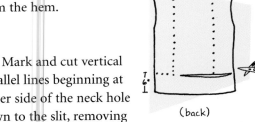

(back)

4 Cut from the left side of the horizontal slit up through the bottom of the left armhole. Cut from the right side of the horizontal slit up through the bottom of the right armhole. The strip over each shoulder should be about 4" wide (trim fabric off the sides if needed).

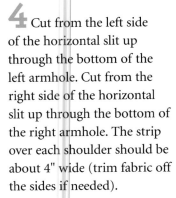

(back)

5 At the bottom of each strip and at the shoulder seam mark three evenly spaced dots (about 1" apart). Connect the dots with a ruler, making three vertical lines. Cut along the lines to create four long fringe pieces extending from each shoulder.

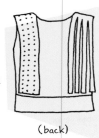

(back)

6 Pin the ends of the fringe from the left side to the right side of the bottom band.

7 Weave the fringe from the right side over and under those strips and pin the ends to the left side of the bottom band, as shown. Sew along the pinned edges.

(back)

8 Remove the pins and try it on. Pinch and pin (or mark) the excess fabric in the back of the 6" bottom band. Carefully remove the shirt, cut through the band, and trim the excess fabric. With right sides together, pin the band closed and sew a whipstitch along the pinned edge.

(back)

continued ▶

9 Turn the second T-shirt inside out and lay it flat. Cut off the hem and then cut a 9" to 12" tube from the bottom of the shirt.

10 Divide your bust measurement by 2 and mark that number (x") from one side along the top edge of the tube. Extend the mark from top to bottom in a vertical line and cut along that line through both layers to remove the excess fabric.

11 Pin and then sew a running stitch or a whipstitch along the open cut edges. Remove the pins and turn the tube right side out.

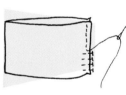

12 Try on the tube, bandeau style, and slip the tank top over it. Pin the sides of the tank top to the sides of the bandeau. Carefully remove the entire piece and sew small whipstitches to secure the bandeau to the sides of the tank top. Remove the pins and wear!

(back)

variation

■ If you already have a bandeau top in your dresser, use just one T-shirt and skip making the tube layer.

106 high tied (wrap shirt)

I f some of the other designs are a little more suited to a nighttime bachelorette party, this one's more afternoon-bridal-shower-friendly (you know, safe to wear around the bride-to-be's future mother-in-law). And it gives you options: Wrap and tie it down the side for a simpler silhouette, or gather it in the front for a funkier, bustled look. Now raise a Bellini to your casual fabulousness.

LEVEL 4

ingredients

- **2 T-shirts (1 fitted, 1 larger, preferably of the same color)**
- **scissors**
- **ruler**
- **chalk marker**
- **straight pins**
- **needle**
- **thread**

1 Lay the fitted T-shirt flat, cut off the bottom hem, and cut out the neckband. Measure about 3" down from the center of the neck hole. Draw lines connecting that point to each side of the neck hole at the shoulder. Cut along those lines, removing a triangular piece of fabric.

2 Cut a vertical line from the point of the neck hole down to the bottom of the shirt through the top layer only.

3 Measure the height of the vertical cut edge (x) and measure the horizontal distance from one of the cut edges to the side of the shirt (y).

4 Take the larger T-shirt and mark and cut, through both layers, an x" by y" rectangle from the top.

5 Separate the rectangles. Align each x" side of the rectangle with one of the x"-long edges of the V-neck shirt, and pin them, right sides together. Sew a whipstitch or a running stitch along the pinned edges. Remove the pins.

6 Unfold the panels. Mark and trim a gentle arc from the top of each seam to the outermost edge, as shown.

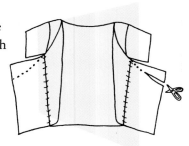

7 Cut the bottom hem off the larger T-shirt, and then cut two 2"-high tubes from the bottom of the shirt. Cut through the tubes to make strips.

8 Pin one end of each strip to the top outer corner of each panel. Sew it in place with a whipstitch and remove the pins.

9 Mark and cut a ½" vertical slit in one side of the shirt at the same level as the strips.

10 You can wrap the top in one of two ways:

a) Thread one strip across your front, through the side slit, around your back to the front. Continue as you would a typical wrap skirt, tying the ends in a knot or bow. (See photo, page 271).

b) With the shirt on, hold the left strip in your right hand and the right strip in your left hand, crossing the strips and panels across your body. Twist the fabric twice at your front (you'll need to switch hands for the second twist). Pull the strips behind you, and either tie them at the back or cross and bring them around to tie in front. Adjust the bustled fabric at your front as desired. (See photo, left.)

107 rotation station
(tank top)

Going from drinks with colleagues to dinner with friends and don't want to wear the same thing? The mood can certainly change between complaining about bosses to laughing over chocolate mousse, and your shirt can change, too. You can rotate this top for different looks—subtle twists to keep up with the shifting social circumstances.

LEVEL 3

ingredients

- 1 T-shirt (L)
- chalk marker
- scissors
- needle
- thread

1 Turn the T-shirt inside out, lay it flat, and cut off the sleeves just inside the seams. Cut off the hem, remove the stitching from the hem, and cut the loop through one layer to use later as a drawstring.

2 With the shirt still inside out, mark and cut slight diagonal lines from the top of the shoulder (about 3" to the left and right of the neckband) to the base of each armhole, through both layers, as shown. Then cut a straight line across the top, through both layers, just below the neckline.

3 Fold the top edge down about 1½" against the top layer of the shirt. Pin it in place and repeat on the back.

4 Use a running stitch or backstitch to sew along the pinned edges about 1" from each fold to create two drawstring casings. Remove the pins.

5 Turn the tank top right side out and attach a safety pin to the end of the drawstring you made in step 1. Thread it through one casing and then the other.

6 Pull on the tank top, bunch the fabric over the drawstring, and tie the ends over one shoulder. Or, rotate the shirt so that one of the armholes is centered across your chest and tie the drawstring ends behind your neck for a halter. Or . . .

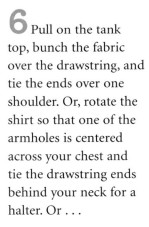

108 take the plunge
(halter top)

The silhouette of this halter looks beyond bizarre when it's off the body, more like a sack than a shirt. It's your body that gives the top structure and shape, a plunging draped halter that is movie-star sexy.

LEVEL 3

---
ingredients

- ■ **1 T-shirt (baggy)**
- ■ **measuring tape**
- ■ **chalk marker**
- ■ **ruler**
- ■ **scissors**
- ■ **needle**
- ■ **thread**

1 Measure the circumference of your waist, divide by 2, and add 1" to get x".

2 Turn the T-shirt inside out and lay it flat. Mark x" from the left of the T-shirt along the bottom hem. Use the chalk marker and ruler to mark a 24" vertical line up the right side from the end of "x".

3 Mark a diagonal line that extends from the bottom of the left sleeve to the top of the line you drew in step 2.

4 Cut through both layers along the two chalk lines. Remove excess material. Your project should still be folded on the left side and trapezoidal in shape.

5 With the hem still at the bottom, measure and mark 7" up from the bottom right corner (A). Measure and make a second mark (B) 21" up from the same corner.

6 Connect points A and B in an arc whose widest point is 4", as shown. Cut along the arc, through both layers.

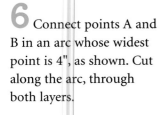

variation

■ Rather than wear it as a low-slung halter, try pulling it down around your shoulders as an off-the-shoulder sheath top.

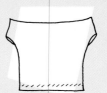

7 Leaving a ½" seam allowance, use a running stitch to sew along the two open, straight edges on the right side, excluding the arced edge.

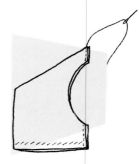

8 Turn the halter top right side out and try it on (the bottom hem remains the bottom hem to be worn at your waist, and the side hem becomes the back of the neckband).

109 x marks the spot
(halter top)

From bypassing the line out front, to finding your perch in the DJ booth, to breaking it down on the dance floor, you *are* the party—and you know it. The delicate braided piping on this flirty halter top emphasizes your silhouette as you navigate the nightlife. *Your* nightlife.

LEVEL 4

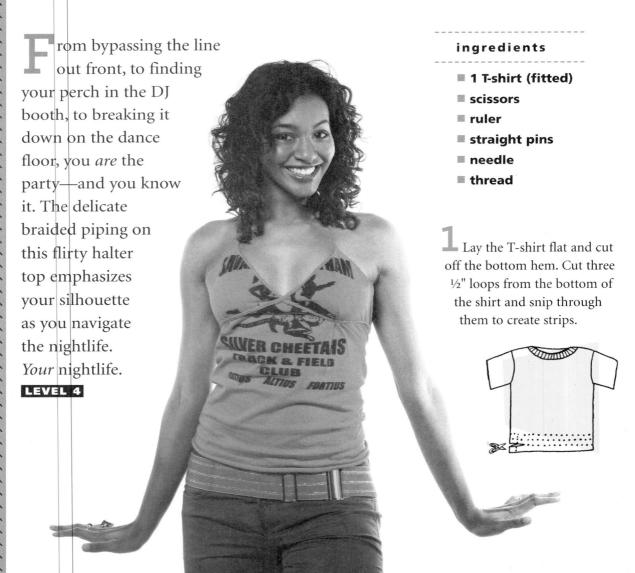

ingredients

- 1 T-shirt (fitted)
- scissors
- ruler
- straight pins
- needle
- thread

1 Lay the T-shirt flat and cut off the bottom hem. Cut three ½" loops from the bottom of the shirt and snip through them to create strips.

2 Stretch the strips out, tie them together at one end in an overhand knot, and braid them. Tie an overhand knot at the end. Set the braided cord aside.

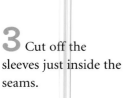

3 Cut off the sleeves just inside the seams.

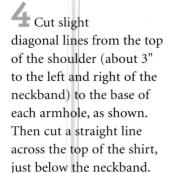

4 Cut slight diagonal lines from the top of the shoulder (about 3" to the left and right of the neckband) to the base of each armhole, as shown. Then cut a straight line across the top of the shirt, just below the neckband.

5 Flip the shirt over. On the back, mark and cut (through only the back layer) a gentle arc from the bottom of one armhole to the bottom of the other, removing a panel of fabric.

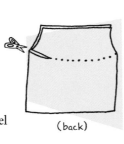

(back)

6 Try on the tube, inside out, pinching any excess fabric in the back. (Twist the tube around to the front to mark it.) Remove the tube and pin along the marked fabric.

7 Cut off the excess fabric beyond the pins, and sew a running stitch or whipstitch along the pinned edge. Remove the pins and turn right side out.

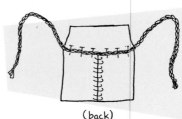

(back)

8 Lay it flat, back side up, and center the braided cord along the top back edge. Pin it along that edge.

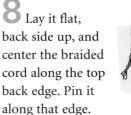

(back)

continued ▶

9 Carefully (watch the pins!) try on the top. Wrap the cords under the bust (pinning as you go), cross them, and pin them at each corner of the top front edge, as shown. (You might need help from a friend with this step!) *Note:* If needed for fit, gather the T-shirt fabric slightly along the cord below the bust at each side.

10 Carefully remove the top and sew a running stitch along the length of and through the pinned cord to attach it to the T-shirt beneath it. Remove the pins.

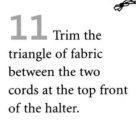

11 Trim the triangle of fabric between the two cords at the top front of the halter.

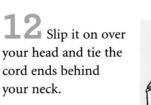

12 Slip it on over your head and tie the cord ends behind your neck.

GREEN PARTY

The Perfect T-shirt Project, started by the ethical branding consultancy Better Thinking, posits that in order for a tee to be 100 percent ethical and sustainable, it would have to be made of material that requires no chemical or harmful pesticides and is grown using a sustainable water supply; everyone involved in its creation would have to be treated fairly and in safe work conditions; its processing and coloring would be free of dangerous pathogens; and finally, its distribution would be local so its transportation would have minimal impact. Although the state of the textile industry is far from perfect, it's big ideas like these that incite serious change—Better Thinking began manufacturing and selling their dream garment in 2008.

110 **with a twist**
(halter top)

Tops that gather at the midriff classically emphasize the chest without seeming cheap or tacky—not to mention that the twist adds texture and interest to an otherwise simple shirt. Depending on the tee you choose to use, you can adapt this design for a perfect night out with friends (Poison 1989 tour T-shirt) or a chilled-out brunch in the neighborhood (Simon & Garfunkel 2003 reunion tour).

LEVEL 4

ingredients

- 1 T-shirt (L or XL)
- ruler
- chalk marker
- straight pins
- needle
- thread
- safety pin (optional)

1 Lay the T-shirt flat and cut off the bottom hem. Remove the stitching from the hem, snip the hem through one layer to make the drawstring, and set aside.

2 Make a horizontal cut across the T-shirt just below the sleeves through both layers of fabric, creating a tube at least 12" high.

3 Turn the tube inside out. Measure the circumference of your bust and divide it by 2 to get x". Mark x" along the top edge of the tube. Mark a vertical line from top to bottom at that measurement and cut along it through both layers, removing the excess fabric.

4 Pin along the edges you just cut and sew them together using a whipstitch.

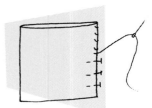

5 Remove the pins and turn the tube right side out, rotating it so that the seam is centered in the back. Mark a 2½" to 3"-high rectangle across the full width of the top front, as shown. Cut it out (through only one layer). Then cut it in half to make two small rectangles.

6 Mark and cut (through only one layer) a slit across the front, 2½" to 3" below and parallel to the cut line from step 5. Then cut through this strip of fabric, as shown.

7 Align and pin one rectangle from step 5 to one of the raw edges you created in step 6, right sides together. Repeat with the second rectangle on the opposite edge.

8 Sew a whipstitch along the pinned edges. Remove the pins.

9 Cross the two dangling strips, twist them once around each other, and pull them each to the sides they originated from. Trim the ends if needed and pin them, right sides together, to the sides of the back.

10 Pin closed the horizontal gaps on either side of the center twist, right sides together, and sew a whipstitch along all pinned edges.

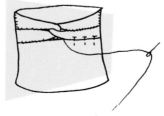

variations

■ Skip the straps and wear it as a tube top.

■ Use long strips from a different T-shirt to create the twist in the middle for a different color (this version avoids having a seam in the middle of the twist).

11 Turn the tube right side out. Snip or poke two holes, centered across the top edge, about 8" apart and 1" from the top. Thread the strip from step 1 into one of the holes, from outside to inside, and out through the other hole. Pull the strap until it is centered.

12 Put on the halter and tie the straps in a bow behind your neck.

111 clean pleat club
(tank top)

Pleats, the more studious cousin of ruffles, have the power to transform your T-shirt from unstructured and nondescript into feminine and fun with a little bit of edge. Pleats bring precise and committed texture (think the discipline of origami) to less structured jersey knit fabric. . . . So, I'll see you at the art opening?

LEVEL 4

ingredients

- **1 T-shirt (XL)**
- **scissors**
- **ruler**
- **chalk marker**
- **straight pins**
- **needle**
- **thread**

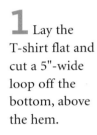

1 Lay the T-shirt flat and cut a 5"-wide loop off the bottom, above the hem.

2 Measure and mark 12" from the new bottom of the shirt. Cut horizontally across at that mark through both layers of fabric. Then snip through the side of the loop, creating a long rectangular strip.

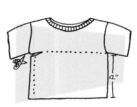

3 Lay the strip flat. Measure your bust circumference to get x", and mark that length along the long edge of the rectangle. Cut widthwise to remove the excess fabric.

4 Fold the rectangle in half crosswise, right side in. Pin along the short ends and sew a running stitch along the edge. Remove the pins and turn the tube right side out.

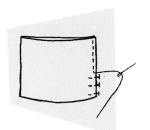

5 Take the 5" tube and make an even number of vertical chalk marks approximately ¾" apart around the entire circumference.

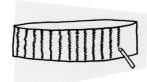

6 Pinch one chalk mark over to the one adjacent to it and pin the resulting pleat flat.

7 Moving around the tube in the same direction of the pleat fold, pinch and pin the next chalk mark to the one after it. Continue until all chalk marks are paired. Sew a running stitch along the length of each pleat fold, securing it to the fabric beneath it. Remove the pins.

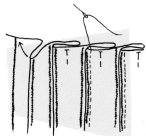

8 Lay the 12" tube flat with the seam centered in the back. Measure and mark 2½" in from each side along the top front edge of the 12" tube. Flip the tube over and mark the back in the same way. (These will be the armholes.)

9 Lay the pleated tube flat and center it above the 12" tube so that its bottom edge overlaps the 12" tube about 1". Pin the tubes together between the two marked points in the front and back and sew with a running stitch. Remove the pins.

10 Wear it with or without a halter top.

variation

■ Make a more fitted version of the pleated neckband for a wide belt.

112 **bubble play**
(tunic dress)

This dress combines the appeal of a tight miniskirt with the comfort of your favorite baggy tee. And what better pairing for a night out? The top allows you to move freely as you flit between party hot spots and hop in and out of taxis; the bottom tapers to show off your legs. Finish the look with mile-high heels and you're unstoppable.

LEVEL 4

ingredients

- **2 T-shirts (XL)**
- **seam ripper**
- **measuring tape**
- **scissors**
- **needle**
- **thread**
- **straight pins**
- **chalk marker**

1 Choose one T-shirt to be the top of the dress and remove the stitching from the bottom hem with your seam ripper (for more length).

2 Cut out the neckband and cut off the sleeve hems, just inside the seams. Then cut a 7"-long strip from each sleeve hem.

3 From the end of each sleeve, cut a straight line along the top of the sleeve.

4 Wrap a strip from step 2 through the cut you made in step 3 and through the neck hole. Tie it in a bow. Repeat with the second strip on the opposite shoulder.

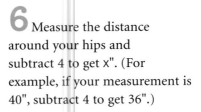

5 Sew a basting stitch around the bottom edge of the shirt (where the hem used to be) and gather the fabric over the thread.

6 Measure the distance around your hips and subtract 4 to get x". (For example, if your measurement is 40", subtract 4 to get 36".)

7 Measure, mark, and cut a tube 16½" high from the bottom of the second T-shirt. Cut through the tube to open it up into a wide rectangle.

8 Fold it in half lengthwise, right sides out, and measure and mark x" along the fold. Extend the mark perpendicular to the fold and cut along the line to remove excess fabric. Your folded fabric should measure 8¼" by x".

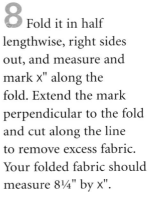

continued ▶

9 Fold the rectangle in half crosswise. Pin along the open edge opposite the new fold, and sew a running stitch along the pinned edge (through all four layers) to create a double-thick tube. Remove the pins.

10 Lay out the tube with the fold at the top and the seam centered in the back. Insert the gathered bottom edge of the T-shirt through the tube, lining up the raw edges of both. Pin the layers together (there should be three: two layers of tube and one layer of gathers). Adjust the gathers so that the width of the bottom of the shirt matches the width of the tube. Sew a zigzag stitch, whipstitch, or running stitch around the pinned edges, securing the gathers to the band.

11 Remove the pins (and basting stitches if they're visible) and fold down the band. Now slip your new tunic dress on. Pair it with leggings or go bare-legged with your favorite boots (or those mile-high heels).

T-shirt Hall of Fame

We all know T-shirts and T-shirt fashion have never been far removed from the music world. But did you know award-winning guitarist Carlos Santana crosses over in the T-shirt world with some celebrity clout? His personal T-shirt collection is the stuff of a T-shirt refashionista's dreams: He saves a T-shirt from every concert he plays. Start counting!

variation

■ Pull the skirt band up around your waist and wear it as a blousy top with a pencil skirt.

113 sashes to sashes (sash)

From Girl Scouts to beauty queens, suffragettes to bachelorettes, the sash is one accessory that announces the wearer's intention, be it to sell cookies, express a political statement, or get something off her chest. *Votes for women! I'm getting married tomorrow! Here she comes, Miss America!* And you can make it in a flash, because this sash takes *T* minus five minutes to complete.

LEVEL 1

---

ingredients

- ■ **1 T-shirt**
- ■ **ruler or straightedge**
- ■ **chalk marker**
- ■ **scissors**

1 Lay the T-shirt flat and cut off the bottom hem. Then mark a diagonal line from the bottom left corner to the top of the right sleeve seam. Mark a second diagonal that runs 4" above and parallel to the first line.

2 Cut through both layers along those lines.

3 Arrange the sash over your shoulder and you're good to go. *Optional:* Use iron-on letters to personalize for the bride-to-be, the birthday girl, or the superstar of book club! Or decorate it with your punk pin collection to show off all your pieces of "flair."

114 **atlas shrug** (shrug)

Ah, the humble yet mighty shrug—a draped swath of cozy fabric that just might be your personal savior in an overly air-conditioned room. Though shrugs are historically knit, crocheted, or constructed out of a silk or gauzy weave, this one-size-fits-all is about luxury casual—not luxury cashmere.

LEVEL 3

ingredients

- **2 T-shirts (XL)**
- **ruler**
- **chalk marker**
- **straight pins**
- **needle**
- **thread**

1 Lay both T-shirts flat and cut horizontally across them just below the sleeves to create two tubes.

2 Cut vertically through one side of each tube to create two matching rectangles.

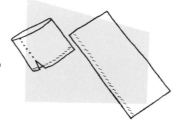

3 Place the rectangles against each other, right sides together, and pin along the long edge opposite the hems. Sew a running stitch along the pinned edge. Remove the pins.

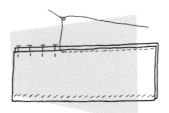

4 Measure and pin 5" in from each side along the long hemmed edges, as shown. Sew a running stitch along those 5" on each side.

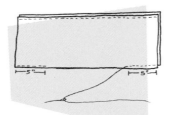

5 Remove the pins, turn the shrug right side out, and lay the shrug over your shoulders, inserting your arms through the opening and out each of the armholes at the sides.

variation

■ If the tube is wide enough to fit around your hips, you can sew halfway along the hemmed edge from one side, 5" along the hemmed edge from the other side, and slip your whole body into the tube for a slinky dress (the 5" seam rests at the back of your neck as a halter top). Va-voom!

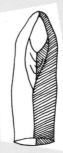

(back)

115 **tic tac boa** (boa) NO SEW

This project is reserved for T-shirts that don't necessarily hold any sentimental memories for you, but are simply very soft. The reason: You're going to chop these shirts into strips and tie them back together to create a festive boa. Toss it around your neck for a playful look that will make you feel like the belle of the ball.

LEVEL 2

----
ingredients

- **2 T-shirts (L or XL, in contrasting or complementary colors)**
- **ruler**
- **scissors**

1 Lay both T-shirts flat and cut off the hems just above the seam. Cut through the loop of one hem to make a strip and remove the stitching. Set it aside.

2 Cut into the bottom edge of one of the T-shirts on an angle and level out 1" from the bottom. Maintaining that 1" distance from the bottom edge, spiral around the bottom of the shirt until you reach the bottom of the sleeves. Repeat on the second T-shirt.

variations

■ Use scraps from other projects to make a ragtag look or speckle another color throughout for interest.

■ Attach a smaller version of the boa at the hem of a skirt or the neckline of a dress.

3 Cut 7"-long strips from the two long strips you cut in step 2.

4 Stretch out the strip from step 1 to make a long cord. Trim it to about 70" and tie an overhand knot at each end.

5 Tie one of the small strips from step 3 into a double knot around one end of the cord. Slide the knotted piece along the cord so it sits against the knot. Choose a second small strip (of either color), knot it around the cord, and slide it against the first.

6 Continue to tie on strips, choosing colors to make a pattern. You've finished when the original cord is covered—it'll look a little like a giant centipede!

116 my way or the thigh way

(leggings)

Leggings: Cute way to keep your legs warm when you're wearing a skirt or tacky substitute for pants? It all depends on how you wear them. Solve the problem by making leggings that simply cannot be a pants-substitute. Instead of being held up from the top, these leggings stay on by lacing strips of T-shirt (any colors you want!) up the sides. Think thigh-high legwarmers. You avoid all the bunching around the waist and crotch, and the leggings will stick out at the bottom of your skirt and look adorable!

LEVEL 2

ingredients

- 1 T-shirt (L or XL)
- 3 T-shirt strips (1" wide, each the full circumference of a T-shirt)
- chalk marker
- ruler
- scissors
- 2 safety pins

1 Lay the T-shirt flat, hem at the top, and mark a dot at the top center. Draw two diagonal lines from that center dot to either side of the neckband, as shown.

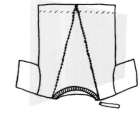

2 Cut along those lines, through both layers, and cut off the sleeves inside the seams. Cut off the shoulder seams, making the edges parallel to the hemlines.

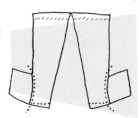

3 To fit, wrap one of the panels, hem side at the top, around your thigh. It should not wrap all the way around. Remove the panel, fold it as it was, and trim fabric off the open side if necessary.

4 Poke holes about 1" in from the edge and 1½" apart, through both layers, down the long side of each legging. Do the same on the opposite side of each legging.

5 Take one legging and one T-shirt strip. Stretch out the strip and attach a safety pin to each end. Thread one end through the drawstring casing made by the hem at the top. Even out the drawstrings and lace the ends through the holes, like shoe lacing. Tie the ends in a bow.

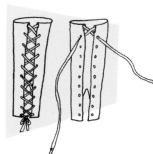

6 Repeat step 5 on the other legging with the second T-shirt strip.

7 Cut the third T-shirt lace in half and repeat step 6 with the short laces on the inside opening of each legging.

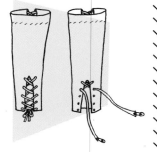

8 Remove the safety pins. Pull the leggings on over your feet and adjust them so the long lacing is on the outside of your leg. Wear them pulled up high as leggings or scrunched down as legwarmers.

117 **garter snake**
(garter)

NO SEW

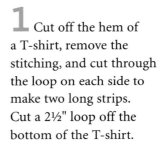

Spice up your Valentine's Day without making your hipster boyfriend think that you take the holiday too seriously. Add personality to the garter by taking words or images on a T-shirt out of context and snaking them around your thigh. *Note:* Garter Snake also makes a great DIY bachelorette party accessory.

LEVEL 2

- - - - - - - - - - - - - -
ingredients
- - - - - - - - - - - - - -

- ■ **1 T-shirt**
- ■ **scissors**
- ■ **safety pin**

1 Cut off the hem of a T-shirt, remove the stitching, and cut through the loop on each side to make two long strips. Cut a 2½" loop off the bottom of the T-shirt.

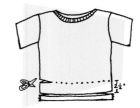

2 Mark, then poke two parallel rows of holes, each row ¾" from the edge and about 1" apart.

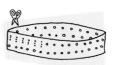

3 Attach a safety pin to the end of one strip and thread it down and up through the holes around the first row. Repeat with the second strip and the second row of holes.

4 Pull the ties to gather the loop, slip it on the leg, adjust to fit, then tie the ends in two bows.

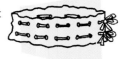

118 on the fringe
(satchel)

Nothing says casual decadence like a whimsical, fringed boho bag filled with all the essentials for a night out on the town. Don your oversize shades—who cares that it's dark out—and put on your best pout for the paparazzi.

LEVEL 4.5

ingredients

- **2 T-shirts**
- **ruler**
- **chalk marker**
- **scissors**
- **needle**
- **thread**

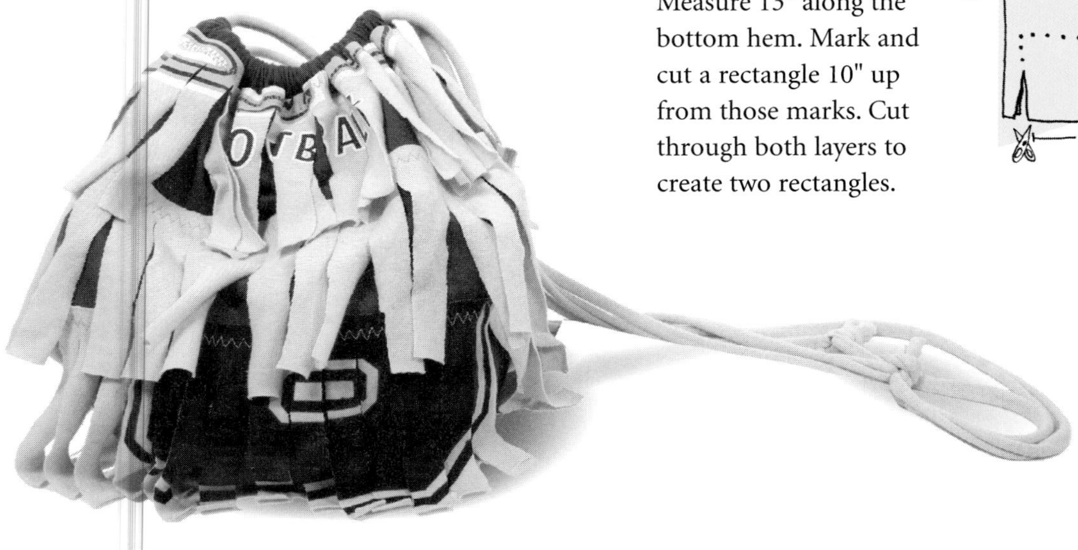

1 Turn the T-shirt inside out and lay it flat. Measure 13" along the bottom hem. Mark and cut a rectangle 10" up from those marks. Cut through both layers to create two rectangles.

continued ▶

2 Pin the two rectangles, right sides together, along one of the 10" edges. Use a running stitch to sew along the pinned edge (leaving a ½" seam allowance) and stop at the hem.

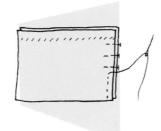

3 Spread the rectangle (now 25" by 10") right side up with the hem at the top. From the bottom, measure and mark a horizontal line at 3", 6", and 9" (the last will be even with the hem stitching).

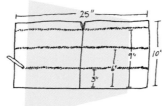

4 From the second T-shirt, cut three 4" tubes from the bottom of the T-shirt above the hem, and then cut through them to make long strips. Trim each one to 25". (Alternatively, cut strips that are at least 4" wide and piece them together to make 25"-long strips.) Cut the stitching from the hem and cut two drawstring cords from the resulting loop.

5 Starting at the bottom, lay each strip on the lines you drew on the rectangle in step 3. Pin each strip in place along the top edge. Sew, using a zigzag stitch, along the pinned edges, leaving a ½" seam allowance at the top.

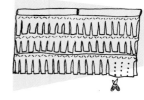

6 Make vertical 3" cuts about 1" apart in the bottom of each of the strips to make fringe. Trim a little extra fabric off the fringe on each edge of the rectangle. (This will prevent the fringe from getting caught in the seam in step 7.)

7 Remove the pins and fold the rectangle in half, right sides together, tucking all the fringe inside. Pin and then sew, using a running stitch, along the side edge (opposite the seam you made in step 2), leaving a ½" seam allowance and stopping at the hem.

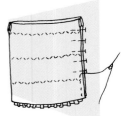

8 Mark an 8"-diameter circle on the remains of the first shirt. (Hint: Use the rim of a small mixing bowl as a pattern.) Cut out around the chalk lines.

9 Pin the circle, right side in, to the inside bottom edge of the tube, being careful to avoid the fringe. Leaving a ½" seam allowance, use a running stitch to sew along the pinned edges around the bottom. Remove the pins.

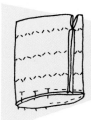

10 Attach a safety pin to the end of one of the drawstrings and thread it through one of the open holes of the hem and out the second hole on the same side. Repeat with the second drawstring, threading it through the holes in the opposite side.

11 Turn the bag right side out and pull both pairs of drawstring ends gently to make them even. Take one strand from the right side and one strand from the left and tie the ends in an overhand knot. Then tie the other two strands together. Fill 'er up and head out!

119 knicker basket
(lingerie bag)

Slip your unmentionables into something a little more comfortable.... For those few-and-far between days when you pass on wearing a T-shirt (what?!) for something more extravagant, here's to keeping a T-shirt in the mix. This jersey panty pouch protects your delicates and is also great for travel. The bag (with some sexy knickers inside, of course) makes the perfect gift at your friend's bachelorette party—especially if you personalize it.

LEVEL 4

- -

ingredients

- -

- **1 T-shirt (the softer, the better!)**
- **scissors**
- **straight pins**
- **needle**
- **thread**
- **safety pin**

1 Lay the T-shirt flat and cut off the bottom hem. Remove the stitching on the hem and stretch it to create a long loop.

2 Cut through the loop at each end to create two long drawstrings.

3 Cut one 15" by 30" rectangle from the front or back of the T-shirt.

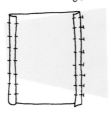

4 Lay it right side down and fold in each of the long sides ½" and pin.

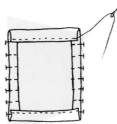

5 Fold in the top and bottom edges about 1" and pin. Use a running stitch to sew *only* the top and bottom edges to create the drawstring casings.

6 Fold the rectangle in half crosswise, right side in, so that the fold is at the bottom. Adjust your pins so that the sides are now pinned together.

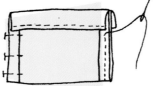

7 Use a running backstitch to sew along the side edges, stopping at the drawstring casing.

variations

■ In different sizes, this bag can be used as a jewelry stash sack, a bikini beach bag, or a catchall for an overnight change of clothes.

- - - - - - - - - - - - - - - -

■ Embellish with patches, iron-ons, or spray paint and stencils.

- - - - - - - - - - - - - - - -

8 Remove all the pins and turn the pouch right side out. Attach a safety pin to an end of one drawstring. Thread it through one of the holes around the entire perimeter of the top of the bag and out the second hole on the same side.

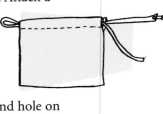

9 Repeat step 8 with the second drawstring, using the two holes on the opposite side. Pull both pairs of ends gently to make them even. Tie the ends of each pair of strings in an overhand knot to keep them from slipping through the holes.

120 **braidy character**
(braided handbag)

Your friends won't even be able to recognize your T-shirt when you hit the scene with this mod mini-handbag. The transformation from floppy old T-shirt to structured bag may be dizzying for some, but you're pulling it off just fine with your matching bold retro minidress.

LEVEL 5

ingredients

- **3 T-shirts**
- **scissors**
- **ruler**
- **needle**
- **thread**

1 Cut the bottom hems off of three T-shirts. Cut into the bottom edge of both layers of one of the T-shirts on an angle and level out the cut ½" from the bottom. Continue cutting in a spiral around the shirt until you reach the sleeves. Stretch the strip to make a cord about 210" long. Repeat on the remaining two T-shirts. Cut the three cords in half to make two bundles of three.

2 Use an overhand knot to tie one of the clusters of three strips together at one end. Start braiding the three strips together. *Note:* Wind the ends of each strip into three balls or skeins so the ends don't become as tangled when you braid.

3 Once you've finished braiding the three pieces together, pinch the end of your long braided cord in on itself about ½". Sew the two braided edges together using a whipstitch.

4 Continue spiraling the cord braid around this base, sewing it to the base braids as you go.

5 Once you've completed about eleven cycles, measure out 6" of cord, leave a 4½" space along the base edge, then resume sewing. (This begins the handle.)

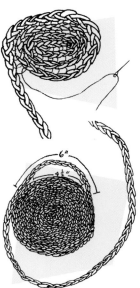

6 Make three cycles around the handle and base perimeter (the handle will be three braids thick), and sew and tie off the end of the cord at the bottom of the bag.

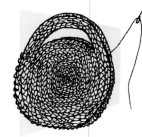

7 Repeat steps 2 through 6 with the three remaining cords to create a matching opposite side to the bag.

8 Press the two sides together, right sides facing, and stitch along the outer edges, excepting the handles.

9 Turn the bag right side out, stow the cell, wallet, and lip gloss, and let the top edges curl over to keep everything contained.

variation

■ You can stop after step 4 to make a colorful yarmulke for Rosh Hashanah or the next Bar Mitzvah.

design it yourself

Sketch your own fashions and accessories on the female and male figures provided on the next few pages. You can mix and match looks to design an entire outfit, create variations on projects in the book, decide how you'd like to add embellishments to clothes you already have, or make accessories to complete your wardrobe.

Experiment with lines, shapes, color, and texture—but most of all, be inspired, get creative, and have fun. And have your scissors at the ready, because the next step after imagining it is making it!

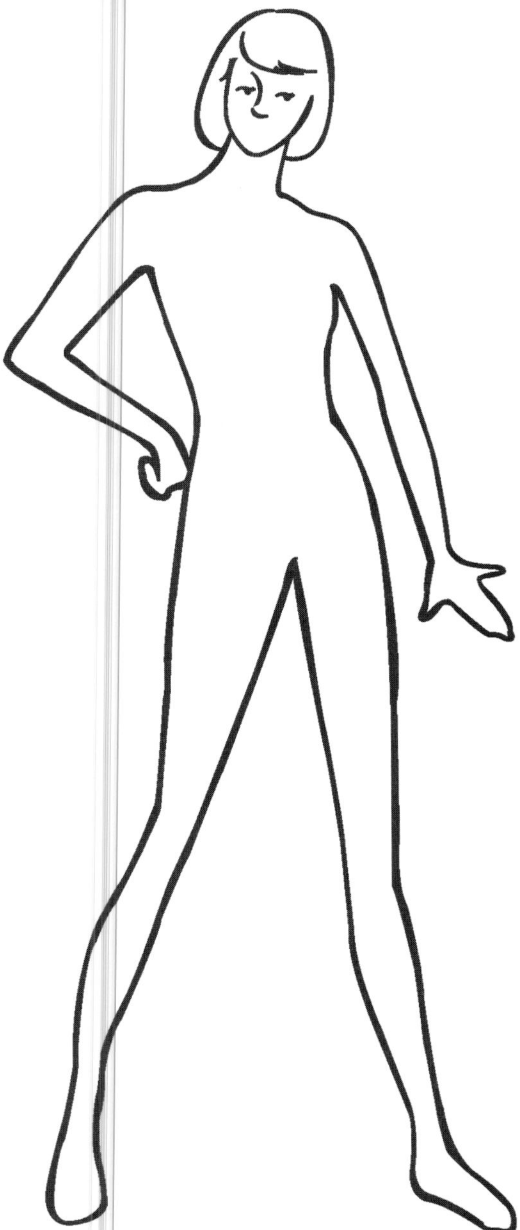

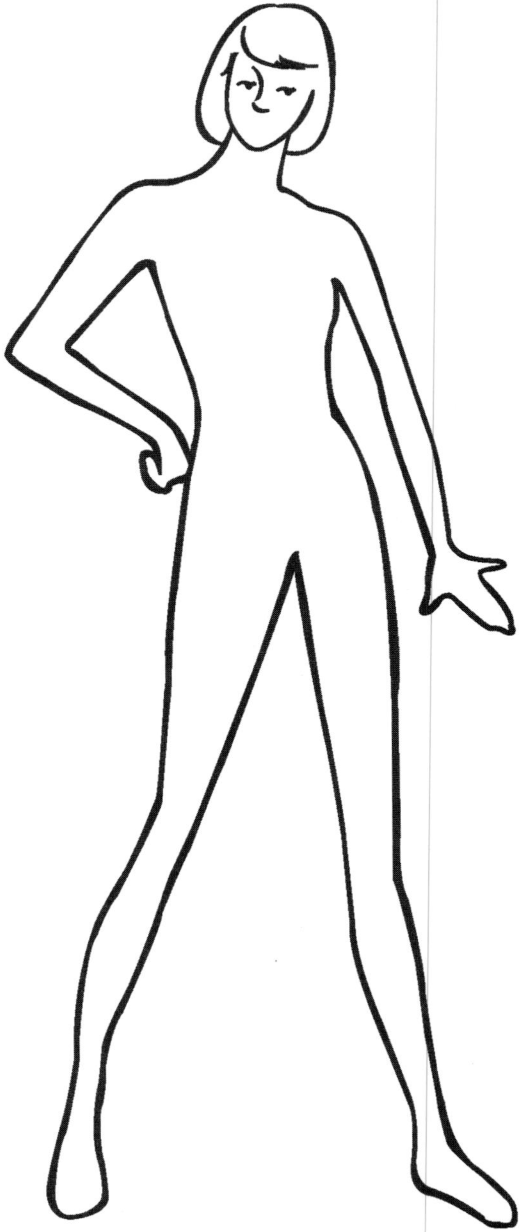

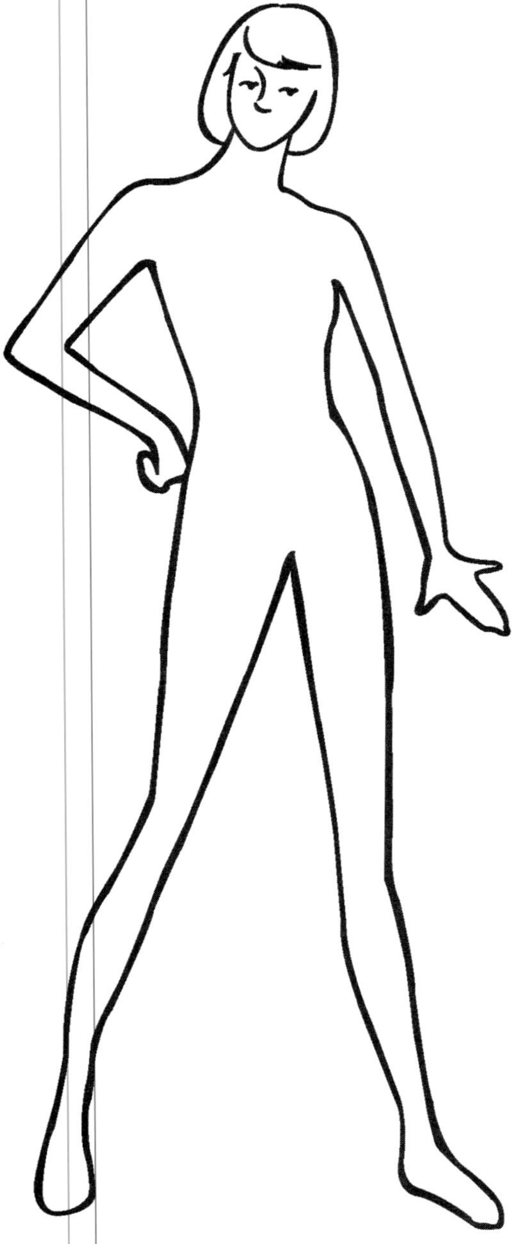

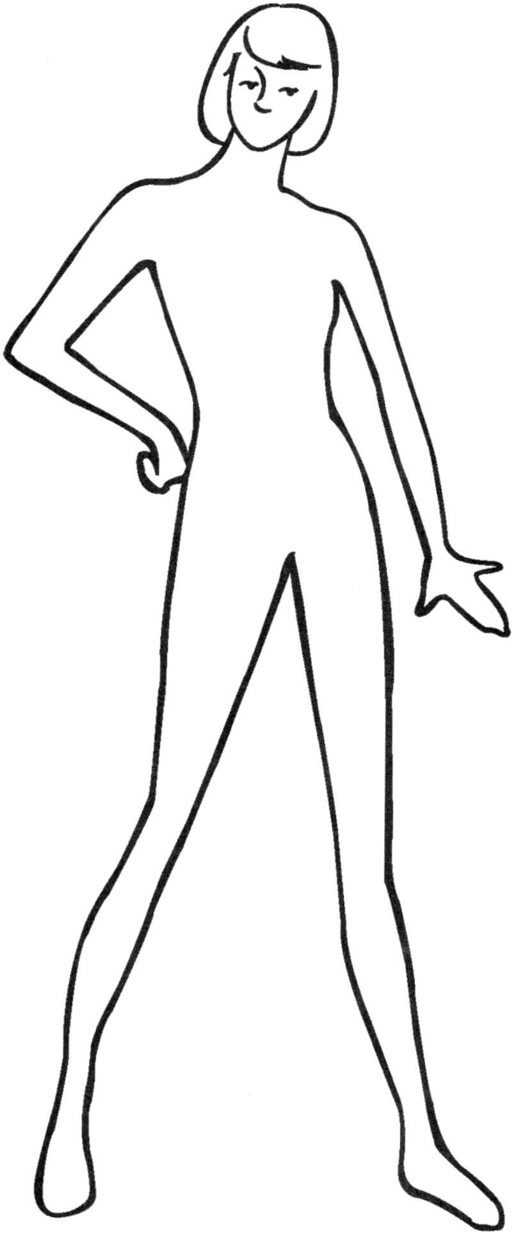

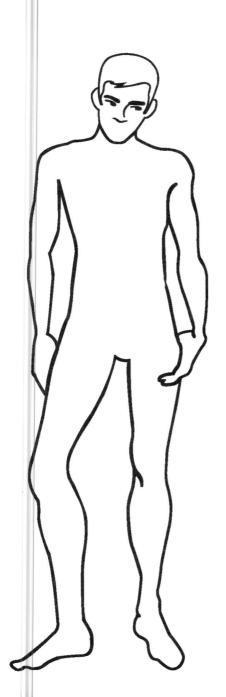
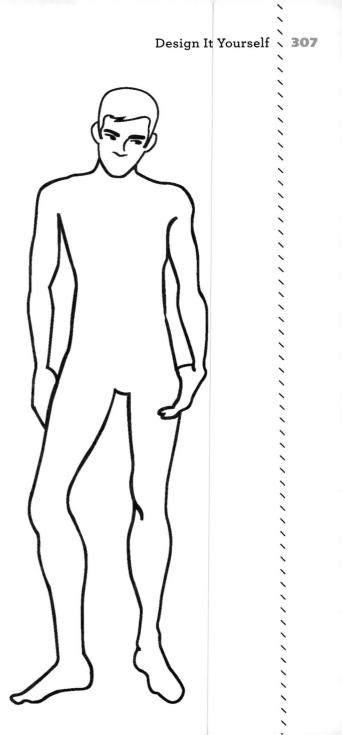

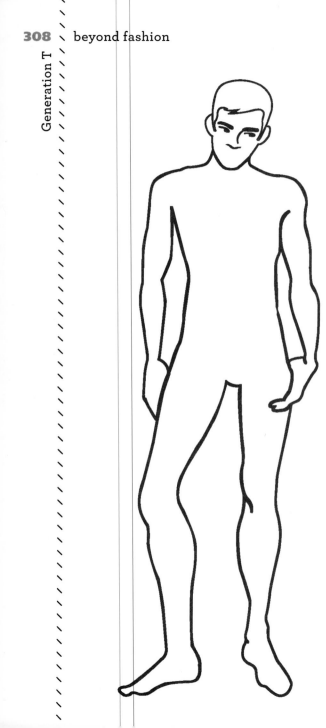
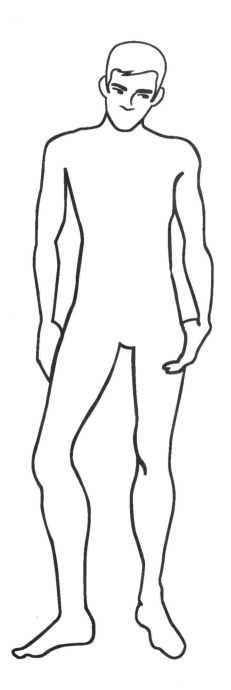